The Noise Silence Makes

Religious Cultures of African and African Diaspora People

SERIES EDITORS:

Jacob K. Olupona, Harvard University   Dianne M. Stewart, Emory University
and Terrence L. Johnson, Georgetown University

The book series examines the religious, cultural, and political expressions of African, African American, and African Caribbean traditions. Through transnational, cross-cultural, and multidisciplinary approaches to the study of religion, the series investigates the epistemic boundaries of continental and diasporic religious practices and thought and explores the diverse and distinct ways African-derived religions inform culture and politics. The series aims to establish a forum for imagining the centrality of Black religions in the formation of the "New World."

The Noise Silence Makes

*Secularity and Ghana's
Drum Wars*

MARIAM GOSHADZE

Duke University Press
Durham and London 2025

Designed by Courtney Leigh Richardson
Typeset in Garamond by Westchester Publishing Services

Library of Congress Cataloging-in-Publication Data
Names: Goshadze, Mariam, author.
Title: The noise silence makes : secularity and Ghana's drum wars /
Mariam Goshadze.
Other titles: Religious cultures of African and African diaspora people.
Description: Durham : Duke University Press, 2025. | Series: Religious
cultures of African and African diaspora people | Includes bibliographical
references and index.
Identifiers: LCCN 2024033054 (print)
LCCN 2024033055 (ebook)
ISBN 9781478031413 (paperback)
ISBN 9781478028192 (hardcover)
ISBN 9781478060406 (ebook)
ISBN 9781478094296 (ebook other)
Subjects: LCSH: Gā (African people)—Religion. | Gā (African people)
—Rites and ceremonies. | Drum—Performance—Ghana— Religious
aspects. | Noise control—Law and legislation—Ghana—Accra. |
Christianity and other religions—Ghana—Accra. | Accra
(Ghana)—Religious life and customs.
Classification: LCC DT510.43.G3 G67 2025 (print) | LCC DT510.43.G3
(ebook) | DDC 305.896/33780667—dc23/eng/20241213
LC record available at https://lccn.loc.gov/2024033054
LC ebook record available at https://lccn.loc.gov/2024033055

Cover art: Ga ritual drums, 2016. Courtesy of the author.

For Ida and David

Contents

Conclusion: Layered Epistemologies
of Contemporary Accra 153

A Note on Orthography

Ga language belongs to the Kwa branch of the Niger-Congo language group. It was first written down in the Latin alphabet in 1764 and has been revised several times since then, with the most recent revision in 1990.

The Latin-based alphabet includes twenty-six letters and three additional letter symbols: Ɛ/ɛ, Ŋ/ŋ, and Ɔ/ɔ. Longer vowels are represented by doubling or tripling the vowel symbol. Tones and nasalization are not represented. There are eleven digraphs and two trigraphs in the Ga alphabet:

gb—/gb/	ŋm—/ŋm/
gw—/gʷ/	ŋw—[ŋʷ]
hw—/hʷ/	sh—/ʃ/
jw—/dʒʷ/	ts—/ɛʃ/
kp—/kp/	shw—/ʃʷ/
kw—/kʷ/	tsw—/ɛʃʷ/
ny—/ɲ/	

A Note on Pronunciation

To assist the reader with correct pronunciation, below is a phonetic guide to the Ga words used frequently in the text:

akutso /aˈku.tsɔ/, pl. akutsɛi /aˈku.tsɛ.i/

blematsɛ /blɛˈma.tsɛ/, pl. *blematsɛmɛi* /blɛˈma.tsɛmɛi/

gbatsu /gbɑ:.tsu/, pl. *gbatsui* /gbɑ:.tsú.i/

Hɔmɔwɔ /hɔ̀.mɔ́.wɔ̀/

jamɔ /jà.mɔ́/

jemawɔŋ /dʒɛˈma.wɔŋ/, pl. /dʒɛˈma.wod͡ʒi/

maŋtsɛ /māˈtsɛ/, pl. /māˈtsɛmɛi/

ŋmaadumɔ /ŋmaˈadu:mɔ/

ŋmaakpamɔ /ŋmaˈakpamɔ/

ŋmɔ /ŋmɔ/

ŋyɔŋmɔ /ɲɔŋmɔ/

shikpɔŋ etsii /ʃikˈpɔŋ ɛtsi/

wɔŋ /wɔŋ/, pl. *wɔji* /wɔd͡ʒi/

wɔyoo /wɔjoʊ/, pl. *wɔyei* /wɔjei/

wulɔmɔ /wuˈlɔmɔ/, pl. *wulɔmɛi* /wuˈlɔmɛi/

Introduction

Altered Ontologies and Reversed Paradigms

My very first visit to Accra in 2014 marked a point of departure for my research. I was wandering around the suburb of La Paz with a friend when I was struck by the realization that the city was buzzing, humming, panting, and puffing all along our promenade. I had never encountered a city that breathed so loudly. My friend was dismissive: "This, ooooo, this is nothing. This month is quiet because of the ban." I was intrigued. "The ban? What ban?" "The Ga ban on noise for Hɔmɔwɔ, you didn't know?" he asked, clearly amused by my ignorance. While I was familiar with the Ga community of Accra and their harvest festival, Hɔmɔwɔ, I was unaware of the ban on noise. The news was riveting since it meant that the followers of the Ga religion were not only regulating the soundscape of the metropolis, but they were also doing so far from the city center, where their authority was concentrated. This reality flew in the face of the established scholarly narrative that

Pentecostal/Charismatic Christianity had swallowed up Accra's religious market, prevailing over traditional religions and permeating almost every dimension of urban life via "a centrifugal dispersion of audiovisual signs" (Meyer 2006a, 299).

I was first introduced to traditional religions as a subject of scholarly interest in a course taught by my MA advisor, Robert M. Baum, at the University of Missouri–Columbia. In fact, my enchantment with Paul Stoller's *In Sorcery's Shadow* (1987) served as my portal to the religious life of Africa. As uncomfortable as it is to admit this today, enchantment is the word that most accurately describes my frame of mind at the time. Having reflected extensively on my own positionality since then, I realize that my background played a decisive role in my scholarly journey (Madison 2005; Reinharz 2011). I grew up in post-Soviet Georgia, where the institutionalized religiosity of the Orthodox Church of Georgia dictated the patterns of the new national identity, and my public-school education was heavily flavored with the Christian ethos. My religious horizons gradually expanded as my studies took me to various parts of Europe, yet I remained profoundly unprepared for the allure of the mysterious world that Paul Stoller chronicled. The reality of traditional religions did not dawn on me until my visit to Accra in the first year of my doctoral studies. I had come to explore the notorious witch camps in the northern part of the country, a topic I had been working on for several years. Much to my surprise, I was ready to sweep all previous plans under the rug the moment I learned of the ritual noise restriction that affected Accra. It was the ordinary omnipresence and unassuming mundane flavor of traditional religions that attracted me most. The urbanity of the Ga religious presence also proved decisive in rectifying some of my own misconceptions about traditional religions. Far from the remote, isolated rural backdrop that prevailed in the early anthropological imagination, traditional religions flourished in the heart of Ghana's administrative, financial, and entertainment center. Thus began my long journey of learning about the history, culture, and language of the Ga community, attending services of Pentecostal/Charismatic churches throughout the city, and talking with government officials about noise-abatement politics in Ghana. The research adventure would span fourteen months of fieldwork and several visits in 2014–2018, during which I would learn that the Ga religion shows no signs of waning in the face of the Pentecostal/Charismatic presence. With time, I also began to experience a sense of familiarity with the postcolonial struggles of Ghanaians that echoed my own feelings of inferiority and discomfort derived from the perpetual sense of flux so familiar to the citizens of postsocialist countries. Perhaps the most difficult part of my research was breaking down the distance between the sense of affinity I felt for my interlocutors on a sociopolitical level and the Euroamerican identity immediately ascribed to me because of the color of my skin. Nonetheless, I like to think that the combination of the shared struggle to come to terms with the neoliberal order and disenchantment with the state as caretaker—attributes postcolonial and postsocialist countries share—paved my path to better appreciating the complexities of Ghanaian modernity.

As Ga elders will tell you, the tradition of the ban on drumming—the official name of the ritual noise restriction—dates far back in time, before Ga people settled the territory of present-day Accra and brought with them their customs structured around the Hɔmɔwɔ festival. Since then, the Ga have remained faithful to the tradition, annually inaugurating their sonic fast in preparation for their sacred holiday. Even as Ghana transitioned into a modern nation-state, the Ga community continued to be granted the privilege of extending the ritual restriction on noise to the entire city, including commercial and religious institutions, because they are the official guardians of Accra's lands under customary law.

At least that was the case until the late 1990s, when the Ga community's right to shape Accra's soundscape was challenged by Pentecostal/Charismatic churches. Against the backdrop of a rapid influx of labor migrants and media liberalization, the newly popular churches refused to reduce their sonic footprint to honor the ritual silence.[1] This act of defiance should be seen in light of the salience of sound in Pentecostal/Charismatic services and its central role in establishing the monopoly of this strand of Christianity over Accra's public spaces. In the late 1990s, the long-standing antagonism between the Ga traditional community and the Pentecostal/Charismatic congregations in Accra reached a critical point. Vexed by discriminatory comments and disdainful treatment from popular born-again pastors as well as numerous socioeconomic issues plaguing the community, the Ga community retaliated with physical attacks on wayward congregations. The state responded by resurrecting a 1995 noise abatement bylaw and mobilizing a Nuisance Control Task Force, a special interinstitutional body whose mandate was to enforce the bylaw about noise abatement in the city. The newly enforced sonic control was publicized as a remedy for the problem of noise pollution, yet the issue was settled in favor of the Ga community, as the regulations were enforced only during the ban on drumming.

In West Africa, writes Mamadou Diouf (1999), "the city has long been thought of exclusively in terms of the colonial ethnology of detribalization, rural exodus, and the loss of authentically African traits and values" (44). In what follows, one of my main objectives is to rewrite the prominent account of traditional religions as being out of place in contemporary urban Ghana or as the evil twin of Pentecostal/Charismatic Christianity, sustained only for their function as the undeniable Other. In recent literature, African religions in urban contexts have received some attention, but mostly through their entanglement with Pentecostal/Charismatic Christianity or Christianity more broadly. With respect to Ghana, the works of Birgit Meyer (2015), Marleen de Witte (2008a, 2008b), Kwabena Asamoah-Gyadu (2005a, 2015), and Paul Gifford (2004) are particularly noteworthy. While I appreciate the visibility that their perspectives accord to traditional religions, I think that it is also crucial to produce counternarratives that present these religions as authorities that dictate the terms of engagement with Christianity. Despite significant shifts in the study of religion, there is a persistent tendency to push traditional religions to the margins, to the domain of the local, suspended outside the common trajectory of history. Achille Mbembe (2001) argues that even as we are increasingly trained to discern the traces of missionary and colonial prejudices, "the corpse obstinately persists in getting up again every time it is buried" (3), tenaciously finding its way into new approaches and theories. Recentering traditional religions demonstrates their engagement with modern urbanity and, more important, counters the implicit hierarchization of religions still evident in the study of religion.

This book places the Ga community and Ga religious life at the center of the discussion via a close reading of the ban on drumming as a historical, religious, and above all, political phenomenon that has provoked its share of turmoil in contemporary Accra. The confrontations surrounding the ban serve as the nucleus of the book, from which I branch out into the past and the future to tell a story about colonial techniques of power and the role of religion in modern secular Ghana through the lens of the transformation of noise-control procedures. The narrative begins with the rise of official noise-abatement initiatives in Europe and North America in the late nineteenth century and their spread to colonial urban centers with the goal of managing specific sociocultural groups. Monitoring the sonic profile of traditional communities exploited epistemic differences between the colonizer and the colonized in order to produce docile religious subjects. As I unfold this history, I juxtapose these top-down ventures with the bottom-up ritual techniques of silence embedded in the Ga custom. I chronicle how noise-control strategies transformed from an instrument of Christocentric colonial hegemony in the British Gold Coast into a quasi-religious structure jointly supervised by the Ga community and the independent Ghanaian state. While the colonial tactic of noise control was deployed to oppress and control the local population, contemporary measures to regulate noise represent a blend of customary and secular notions of order that the Ga used to counter Pentecostal/Charismatic Christianity and reassert their guardianship over the city. I suggest that the state-assisted imposition of the ban on drumming on the territory of Accra cannot be disengaged from its discursive designation as part of the custom or culture that exists in tandem with the Christocentric rhetoric of the Ghanaian public sphere. The arrangement, I argue, typifies Ghanaian secularity, a layered epistemic and sensory order that blends the customary, community-centered orientation that favors shared religious space and shared custodianship of land, and secularism, a Christocentric institutional and ideological regime that pushes traditional lifeworlds either to the bottom of the religious hierarchy or outside it altogether as nonreligion or culture.[2]

Unlearning the Classical Paradigms

A remarkable feature of the Drum Wars—as the media astutely dubbed the noise-related conflict of the late 1990s—was the new noise-abatement patterns they spawned. As extensive literature on noise ordinances suggests, similar initiatives elsewhere have been mostly instituted by the state in the name of communal well-being and peaceful cohabitation (Bijsterveld 2001; Cardoso 2017; Sykes 2015). Ideologically, they echo the post-Enlightenment hierarchy of senses, and structurally, they tend to be biased against the poor and vulnerable factions of society. In line with the established paradigm, a religion with the most power and recognition is accorded the privilege of expressing its sonic identity and imposing restrictions on other religious communities. Consider, for instance, the opposition to the Muslim *adhan* in various European countries because of the alleged noise it generates, even though church bells are seldom perceived as a nuisance (Tamimi Arab 2017). Adopting a *longue durée* perspective has led me to argue that the legislation and monitoring instruments the Ghanaian state instituted in the aftermath of the Drum Wars replicate the noise-abatement strategies of the colonial administration, but with one major difference. The colonial tactic was deployed to repress and control a range of human and nonhuman personhoods perceived as rowdy, barbaric, and demonic. Over time, the technologies came to be indigenized, mutating into a mechanism that the Ga community, which had been the targets of noise control in the colonial context, have deployed against the most dominant religious movement in Ghana. In the aftermath of the Drum Wars, the state allowed adherents of the Ga traditional religion to control and regulate the most popular expression of Christianity for one month each year, signaling a paradigmatic shift in the classical model of nuisance control. My treatment of the subject was inspired by Brian Larkin's (2008) account of the use of radio technologies in Nigeria and his conclusion that technologies imposed by colonial power structures transcend their designers' imagination, often mutating into unruliness. Although Larkin is specifically concerned with the media infrastructure the British introduced, I reconceptualize the notion of technologies as sound-control techniques the colonial authorities used to manage, discriminate against, and ostracize the Gold Coast population.

The mobilization of formerly top-down noise control techniques to challenge the power of the most popular religious movement in Ghana represents a significant shift in the previously recognized patterns of sonic authority, especially in reference to religious entities. At first glance, it is also a counterintuitive development, given the status, authority, and state support that Pentecostal/Charismatic Christianity enjoys in contemporary Africa. Public discourse in postcolonial, Christian-majority African countries is structured around an implicit hierarchy of religions that presents Christianity as a civilized and advanced rendering of religious belief. Traditional religions, on the other hand, are relegated to the lowest rung of the religious ladder or are even pushed out from the taxonomy to become trapped in the category of culture.

To translate these hierarchies into the classical model of sonic authority, the closer a religion is to the top of the given evolutionary taxonomy, the more control it is granted to express its sonic identity and to impose restrictions on other religious communities (see Bailey 1996; Payer 2007; Thompson 2002; Yablon 2007; and Weiner 2014). Through the lens of history, the hierarchization of sounds on the spectrum between quiet and loud has often coincided with how proper or improper these sounds were deemed, with louder sounds classified as noise when they were emitted by social, religious, or cultural Others. "Noise does not exist in itself," writes Jacques Attali (1985), "but only in relation to the system within which it is inscribed" (26). Alterations between noise and silence allow groups to communicate their identity and erect boundaries (Oosterbaan 2009). In fact, noise-abatement regulations were essentially born out of the desire of the upper class to safeguard its mental "refinement" from the sonic manifestation of socially, culturally, religiously, ethnically, and racially defined spaces (Bijsterveld 2008; Scales 2016; Sykes 2015). The most recent expression of this tendency is the association of disadvantaged, low-income neighborhoods with unbearable noise in the imagination of the secular middle class and the subsequent noise-abatement campaigns in urban areas (Chandola 2012).

In light of the missionary and colonial legacy and of the religious hierarchies inherent in secularism as an ideological and institutional regime (de Roover 2011), Christianity is publicly recognized as the epicenter of modern religiosity in contemporary Ghana. Thus, within the auditory hierarchy, it should be licensed to dominate the soundscape and dictate the sonic terms. What we see instead is that traditional religions and Christianity occupy opposite ends of what Isaac Weiner (2014, 57) calls the "auditory evolutionary matrix," but this time the prevailing archetype is reversed. With the encouragement of the state, the Ga community acts as the guardian of silence, conventionally a sign of "mature faith," and Pentecostal/Charismatic Christianity insists on producing excessive noise, the historically recognized trait of the barbarous Other. Sound thus emerges as a historically contingent category, expanding and retracting, shifting and transforming in shape and form in relation to the tangled power dance between those who produce it and those who monitor it.

Isaac Weiner (2014, 20) writes that the production of sound is not a matter of actual capacity to make a loud noise but rather the implicit or explicit right to do so. Against all odds, the champions of "progressive" sensibilities in Accra—Pentecostal/Charismatic denominations—became a sensory nuisance while representatives of traditional religions, a category that in the conventional paradigm would be designated as noisy, emerged as the principal advocates of a tempered urban soundscape. In this new framework, members of the Ga community, despite their lower socioeconomic status, find themselves side by side with the middle- to upper-class groups who insist that religious activities should not disturb others in a "civilized" society.[3] In light of a global recognition of Pentecostal/Charismatic Christianity as the most formidable presence in the religious market of Africa, I suggest that state authorization of a traditional religion to control the aural template of a megapolis like Accra is an unmistakable indicator of the weight of that religion in Ghana's sociopolitical affairs. In this framework, silence is political since its production requires taking command of noise, an inherently subjective category contingent on the distribution of power between the involved parties (Ballinger 1998). Along the same lines, the fact that Pentecostal/Charismatic noise remains the subject of complaint intimates that the actual authority of those congregations is by no means absolute.

In the course of my research, I became aware of the fact that the strong sensory dimension of my inquiry meant that conversations with my interlocutors and my attendance at various events could produce only a fragmentary picture of what was really happening. "As part of our listening positionality," writes Dylan Robinson (2020), "we each carry listening privilege, listening biases, and listening ability" (7). A full engagement with the situation called for reflexivity about my own listening positionality—a recognition of the varieties of acoustic perceptions and their rootedness in cultural and historical landscapes (Howes 1991, 2005; Classen 1993, 1997).

This involved comprehending not only cross-cultural acoustemologies—Steven Feld's prominent notion of sound as a "habit of knowing" (2012, xxvii)—but also a mindfulness of cross-world sonic exchanges understood in terms of a "ritualized cohabitation and relationship between humans and nonhumans" (Etikpah 2015, 344). Shifting sensory gears proved to be decisive in taking seriously the sonically determined relationship between human groups and between human and nonhuman actors, both of which were at stake in managing the conflict. Settling in Adabraka, a Ga neighborhood in the central part of Accra, for the longest stretch of my fieldwork was also invaluable for fathoming both the existential and political meanings behind the city's sonic happenings. Adabraka is composed of an eclectic mix of Ga and non-Ga residents with equally eclectic aural tracks. At specific points each day, I heard the sound of the *adhan* from a nearby mosque, and in the early morning, the racket of the neighboring Pentecostal/Charismatic churches repeatedly reminded me of the rationale behind the Drum Wars. On weekends, I shared the soundscape of my neighbors' weddings and child christenings, celebrated with vigor in makeshift tents on the streets, and I jubilated with soccer fans as their team scored a goal at the Sahara soccer field next to my street. The proximity of Adabraka to the nucleus of Ga traditional authority was especially beneficial during the ban on drumming as I could capture the gravity of noise restrictions in the daily life of Accra's residents. To put it in the words of Alex Waterman (2017, 118–19), I "listened to how I listen" more frequently and this alertness enveloped my other sensory experiences as well.

ANOTHER KEY IMPETUS for my project is a close examination of the nature of secularity in Ghana. In 1999, as an amendment to his earlier position, Peter Berger (1999), one of the early proponents of the secularization thesis, declared that the world was "as furiously religious as it ever was, and in some ways more so than ever" (2). Recognizing that religion was far from the brink of extinction, scholars in the late twentieth century set out to reconceptualize its role and status in the contemporary world (Casanova 1994; Cox 1984; Stark and Rainbridge 1987). The critical dissection of the secular as a category and secularization as a historical process has meant scouting out new pathways for interpreting the multiple secularities that thrive in non-Western contexts. Although the complex relationship between religious institutions and the state around the world has been substantially theorized, the configurations of power on the ground are rarely addressed. Furthermore, the subject of the secular remains grossly underexamined in Africa. In the few existing accounts, authors usually focus on the relationship of Christianity and Islam with the state, while little attention is paid to understanding the role of traditional religions in the public sphere.[4] This is partially because of the discursive culturalization of the latter, a process rarely recognized in studies of the secular in Africa (see Meinema 2021).

In what follows, I aim to remedy these shortcomings by shedding light on Ghanaian secularity. I should clarify that I distinguish between secularism and secularity. In this book secularism refers to an archetypal epistemic and institutional framework derived from the European model and secularity denotes the reality on the ground in a given geographical context, including institutional, discursive, and epistemological dimensions. I engage with these concepts through a close reading of the ban on drumming, which I believe represents a convenient entry point for the study of secularity in Ghana. Ghanaian secularity is a blend of secularism, imported without much refinement or adaptation to the existing ideological and power structures, and customary understandings of the role and place of Ghana's three religions, along with the associated human and nonhuman actors. Taking inspiration from Shmuel N. Eisenstadt's multiple modernities (2000) and Monika Wohlrab-Sahr and Marian Burchardt's multiple secularities (2012), I treat the secular reality of Ghana as an alternative, viable version of being secular. Going beyond the narrative of deficiency and incompleteness that presents non-Western secularities as flawed copies of the Western original allows us to appreciate the cultural specificity of the current setup and to unsettle the vision of secularism as the engine behind the "civilizing" mission of the West (Cady and Hurd 2010; Göle 2010).

The response of government agencies to the Drum Wars illuminates Ghanaian secularity: the state collaborates with traditional authorities in the administration of the Accra metropolitan area yet publicly grants Islam and (especially) Christianity a superior status. In violation of the country's constitutionally mandated right to religion, the Ga traditional religion is endowed with significant authority to co-manage the city's soundscape. Collaboration between the state and customary religious authorities is made possible by the amended public status of traditional religions as a common culture that all citizens can claim. The arrangement is further facilitated by Ghana's parallel system of justice that marries modern constitutional law and the plurality of customary laws. While Christianity and Islam are managed as religions, traditional religions are commonly regulated by customary law, a practice rooted in Ghana's colonial and missionary past. As missionaries undertook to invalidate the indigenous world view, they reframed it as culture, demarcating it as a religiously neutral and therefore less threatening context (Meyer 1999). In the postindependence era of cultural revival, neutralized culture was a building block of the new national identity (Coe 2005). The culturalization of traditional practices, a process that historically aimed to marginalize those practices, now endows traditional authorities with the sociopolitical leverage to function as prominent actors in the Ghanaian public sphere.

The ban has received some scholarly attention following the hype surrounding the attacks on Pentecostal/Charismatic churches in the late 1990s. The perspectives offered by Justice A. Arthur (2017), Marleen de Witte (2008a), and

Rijk van Dijk (2001) were particularly valuable in the course of my research. While none of these studies address the two central concerns of this book, they have helped expand my understanding of the purview of the ban on drumming and its impact on Ghanaian society. Van Dijk's (2001) elaboration of the Christian use of music to oppose the traditional mandate was instructive for my conceptualization of the struggle against all expressions of backward culture in light of the globally oriented Pentecostal discourse. My discussion of Ga and Pentecostal/Charismatic theologies of sound benefited greatly from Marleen de Witte's (2008a) nuanced claim that beyond the political role of sound in the conflict as a tool for gaining symbolic control over Accra, it is construed similarly by the conflicting parties as a fundamental force that can both thwart and foster spiritual advancement. By far the most informative source—given the rich ethnographic data and multifaceted analysis of the conflict—is the only monograph on the subject written by Justice A. Arthur. Published in 2017, Arthur's work served as an important resource for fact-checking some of the information I collected and for finetuning my findings. As with the other authors mentioned here, Arthur's primary concern is the interfaith confrontation, which he analyzes through sociological theories of boundary making and social conflict. Despite our distinct interests, Arthur and I agree on the indispensable import of the Drum Wars in uncovering the pertinence of traditional religions in contemporary Ghana.[5]

Religion, Culture, Custom

Before moving forward, I would like first to elaborate on the terms "culture," "custom," and "religion" as I use them in the course of the book, and second to emphasize the ultimate inadequacy of these terms in wholly capturing the lived reality of intercommunal relations. While religion as a universal category tends to be taken for granted in popular discourse, it has been rigorously questioned in the academic study of religion. A range of scholars including Timothy Fitzgerald (2000), Jonathan Z. Smith (2004), Tomoko Masuzawa (2005), and Russell T. McCutcheon (1997) have repeatedly challenged religion as a universally disguised rendering of Euroamerican theological notions of religiosity. In Ghana, missionaries were the first to introduce the term, but it did not gain traction until the colonial period. Even so, as the tension between the categories of culture and religion in the context of the Drum Wars reveals, the term continues to be only haphazardly applied to traditional lifeworlds. Since the declaration of independence in 1957, the state has officially recognized three religions that are central to the country's history—Christianity, Islam, and traditional religions. Yet it is rare to find a common word for these three religions in local languages, which often distinguish between traditional practices, on the one hand, and Christianity and Islam, on the other. The Ga community, for instance, uses the word *jamɔ*, roughly translated as "to worship," to delineate practices associated with Christianity and Islam, and they speak of *kusum*, interpreted as "custom," when referring to their own practices. The etymology of the word *kusum* is debatable. Although the Ga-English dictionary suggests that it derives from the Portuguese "costume," meaning "custom," my Ga interlocutors argue that it is a combination of two Ga nouns—*ku*, which officially stands for "heap, pile" but is understood as "group," and *su*, which means "nature, character, color, appearance" (Kropp-Dakubu 2009). In the latter interpretation, then, *kusum* is the overall character or nature of a community that permeates all aspects of life. In order to properly convey these semantic and ideological intricacies, I use the term "traditional religions" only when speaking of indigenous lifeworlds in the post-1957 context, when the label was officially recognized in public and state discourse, and I talk about "traditional practices" or "traditional lifeworlds" when referring to the colonial era.

Even then, however, I am aware of the challenges that the term "traditional religions" poses for scholars of African religions. On a fundamental level, the adjective "traditional" has been criticized for intimating obsoleteness, immutability, and geographical boundedness as opposed to the novelty, progress, and outreach of world religions.[6] Since formerly used terms such as "primal religions" or "primitive religions" are widely recognized as not only derogatory but also grossly inaccurate, some scholars have turned to the label "indigenous religions" instead. I find this choice counterproductive since "indigenous" evokes very similar associations as "traditional" with an even more pronounced sense of locality. Moreover, the use of the term is often quite general and derives from the world religions model, in which indigenous religions are simply a leftover, "residual category" (Shaw 1990, 341). As Bjørn Ola Tafjord (2013, 226) has noted, the problem is that the majority of the so-called indigenous religions are not similar at all; they ended up in one category because Europeans perceived them as the generic Other.

The term "traditional religions" comes up against similar obstacles but has a richer, more complex history in the context of Africa. To start with, it derives from "African Traditional Religion," a term Geoffrey Parrinder introduced in 1954 that African scholars of religion popularized in the 1960s and 1970s in an attempt to give due recognition to African religiosity as a single, pan-African belief system framed in terms of the world religions paradigm (Mbiti 1970; Idowu 1973; Opoku 1978). This meant emphasizing, or even ascribing, attributes that are central to the Judeo-Christian cosmology to African religions, including the supreme God, prayer, and the prominence of belief over practice (Horton

1984). Since these authors were leading members of the postindependence intellectual elite who played a key role in the construction of African identity in the context of nationalist and pan-Africanist movements, their use of the adjective "traditional" had rather positive implications. The incentive, after all, was to devise a positive and respectful label that would suggest that African Traditional Religion "consists of that which is handed down from generation to generation as an integral part of life" (Shaw 1990, 342). A return to traditional lifestyle for inspiration in the nation-building process was considered as the only viable way to extricate Africa from colonial epistemologies. The inadvertent by-product of the concept of African Traditional Religion, however, was not only the Christianization of African religions but also purist readings of them as part of an ancient, unchanging wisdom.

In contemporary Ghana, "traditional religion(s)" is the term most commonly used in reference to African forms of religiosity in state and popular discourse as well as within Ghana's numerous traditional communities. For lack of a better alternative and to avoid neglecting contemporary usage of the term by the Ga people themselves, I refer to Ga religiosity throughout the text as traditional religion. However, when speaking of the multiplicity of these religions across the country or the continent, I use the term in the plural because a wide variety of religious expressions are accommodated under this umbrella. At times, as I look into the Ga insights on religion and culture, I also resort to emic categories, fully recognizing that a complete reliance on emic terms does not resolve the challenges mentioned.

The concept I routinely use in conjunction with religion, especially when speaking of the legal dimension of the conflict, is culture. Much like religion, culture is a widely debated construct that does not stand for a coherent system of meanings. It is rather a constant effort to form, negotiate, mobilize, contest, and challenge these meanings, which in turn are solidified in institutionalized, materialized, and bodily forms (Lentz 2017). While acknowledging its shortcomings, I stand with authors who see value in working with the term (Brumann 1999), if only to observe how the meanings behind it are appropriated, contested, shaped, and delineated in the relevant discourses in this book. In state discourse in particular, culture refers to a set of practices, habits, beliefs, values, and life forms that are collectively recognized as constitutive of the traditions and knowledge of past generations that must be preserved and perpetuated for the sake of reinforcing national identity. Tradition, an analogous construct, is the building block of culture; it, too, is invented or imagined as a timeless, static product (Hobsbawm and Ranger 1983; Ranger 1993). Cultural programming has been central to the construction of Ghanaian national identity since the declaration of independence, as evidenced by the establishment of the Institute of African Studies and the

Arts Council of Ghana (renamed the National Commission on Culture in the 1980s) during the presidency of Kwame Nkrumah. The legal dimension of this particular understanding of culture is customary law, which seeks to safeguard the traditional lifestyle of various communities in Ghana. Culture as a national heritage, as Michael Bomes and Patrick Wright (1982) propound, is an over-simplified articulation of the past since it insists on historical timelessness and "projects a unity which tends to override social and political contradiction" (264). While the general sentiment within this national discourse is to celebrate and preserve culture, its treatment is also bogged down by the imperial understanding that culture belongs to the domain of the primitive and backward. This leads to attempts to refine and neutralize the historically bounded culture via acts of reimagination in order to make it fully compatible with modernity.

Scholars recognize that there is a profound connection between religion and culture, but the exact nature of the relationship is debated. While some suggest that religion and culture are fundamentally opposed to one another (Niebuhr 1951), a position that is articulated in Pentecostal/Charismatic rhetoric, others argue that religion can transcend culture, as it encompasses the mundane and per-ceptible as well as the extraordinary and the imperceptible (Albanese 1999). More commonly, however, religion is seen as a subset of culture and religious studies as the study of religious cultures (Hulsether 2005). Indeed, culture is also the cat-egory to which traditional religions are often assigned in the public discourse. Practically speaking, this can be explained by the conceptual overlap between the two terms because traditional practices fail to neatly correspond to the academic definitions of religion, which are modeled after the Judeo-Christian template (see Fitzgerald 2000; Masuzawa 2005; and Smith 2004). Moreover, culturalization of traditional religions dates back to the hierarchy of religions and its associated discourse on civility and barbarity (Fitzgerald 2007). Since religion in this frame-work was associated with Christian truth, traditional lifeworlds were viewed through the prism of falsity. The lack of a pronounced religious value, however, did not mean that local practices had to be disregarded; instead, they were re-framed in terms of culture. In the current context, while the state officially rec-ognizes traditional religions, there is a tendency to refer to their public expres-sion as cultural. Such culturalization not only downplays the religious fervor of the practices in question but also removes them from real time as displays of premodernity (Guss 2000, 14). In this discourse, culture and custom are usually used interchangeably. While culture is a more established yet also more ambig-uous term in the official state, international, and nongovernmental discourse, custom is commonly used in a positive context by the traditional communities or is more narrowly associated with customary law.

Contemporary discourses of culture date back to the missionary enterprise on the Gold Coast. Cati Coe (2005) divides the missionary treatment of culture into two forms—the romantic notion of history and traditions and the efforts to preserve them and the notion that traditions, which ultimately constitute the totality of culture, are an obstacle to being modern. While both of these approaches can be recognized in state discourse, it is the second one that we find in the Christian reading of culture as the realm of the devil and a domain that is in complete opposition to the progressive and civilizing impulse of Christianity (Steegstra 2005). The polarization of culture and modernity intensified with the rise of Pentecostal/Charismatic Christianity and its clearly pronounced hostility to anything traditional. Within this discourse, traditional religions are false belief systems that are part of culture and must therefore be eliminated if Ghanaians are to move forward.

Finally, as I demonstrate in this book, the meaning behind these concepts is always situational and thus merits close work with the discourses prominent in the research context. The Ga community is incredibly versatile in its use of the categories of religion, culture, tradition, and custom in relation to its practices, changing the designations depending on the context and purpose of its engagement. The Drum Wars are an example of how the realization that practices attributed to culture have more freedom to navigate the public sphere than practices attributed to religion, which led to the framing of the ban on drumming as a cultural rather than a religious operation. As elsewhere, the traditional leaders of the Ga community are aware of the political power nested in these terms, so their semantic choices often correspond to the specific goals they have set for the community.[7] In the process of interaction and negotiation, the categories merge, overlap, and borrow from each other. By highlighting the inaccuracies and imperfections of these terms in capturing lived experiences, I hope to encourage readers to be critical of them when considering intercommunal relations in a modern state.

Who Let the Noise Out?

The analysis that follows centers on three players who were involved in the Drum Wars and the subsequent negotiations. My research strategies with these actors alternated between participant observation, semi-structured interviews, and informal conversations. The majority of these interactions took place in English, the official language of Ghana and the preferred mode of communication for many Pentecostal/Charismatic congregations. My interactions with the Ga community transpired in a blend of English and Ga, and I often relied on the kind assistance of my friends and companions for discussions that were exclusively in Ga. By virtue of my modest reading skills in the language, I was able to transcribe the interviews I recorded with the help of my Ga language teacher, Adokwei Sacker. To corroborate the collected data and validate my conclusions, I also consulted with prominent Ghanaian scholars and Ga public figures.[8] I was also invited to attend numerous rites associated with the Hɔmɔwɔ festival, opportunities that I always welcomed with great pleasure and curiosity.

Since I will be referring to the three key actors in the Drum Wars in general terms in the course of the book—the Ga traditionalists or the Ga community, the Pentecostal/Charismatic churches, and the state—I should delineate these categories for the reader. The Ga traditional community consists of *wulɔmɛi* (priests), *maŋtsɛmɛi* (chiefs), *wɔyei* (priestess mediums), musicians, and devotees of the Ga religion as well as members of the Ga Traditional Council (GTC) and all individuals from the six Ga townships who endorse the position of the Ga traditional authorities. The GTC is composed of priests and chiefs from selected royal houses and is the proxy for the Ga community in the public domain. Following the Drum Wars of the late 1990s, the GTC has been coordinating Ga participation in the regulation of the ban on drumming. It provides storage space for confiscated instruments, publishes statements about the impending ban, and is the main liaison with the state and Christian representatives.

The reader will notice that when speaking of the Ga, I use the term "traditionalists" interchangeably with "Ga community." Both the public and Ga individuals ubiquitously use the label "traditionalist" to refer to those who subscribe to the traditional community as defined above. In a general sense, a traditional community is a group of people who occupy one of Ghana's traditional areas, territories under the authority of traditional councils established under the Chieftaincy Act of 1970 (Act 370) (Atiemo 2015, 158). My use of the term "traditional community" is not intended to suggest that there is a separate analytical category with fixed content that represents this group. Instead, I see this designation as a discursive tool that is useful for referring to people who claim the Ga identity via associated enactments, productions, and contestations of the Ga culture.[9]

The term "traditional community" does not fully capture "the reality of physical mobility, overlapping networks and multiple group membership" (Lentz and Nugent 2000, 9). Individuals who represent the Ga traditional community can and do often regroup based on other identity markers. This is evidenced by the fact that the Ga community was not unanimous in its interpretation of the Drum Wars. In particular, individuals who identified as Pentecostal/Charismatic Christians felt that the Ga backlash in the late 1990s was excessive. Nonetheless, I continue to refer to the community as a unit because by and large, the communal consensus that Ga traditional authority in Accra was being unfairly singled out for disrespect, especially compared to other regions of Ghana, repeatedly outweighed the dissenting voices. Although traditional communities are frequently conceptualized as ethnic groups in public discourse, I prefer to avoid references to ethnicity due to the associated conceptual challenges. Cultural primordialists trace the concepts of ethnic groups or tribes to Africa's precolonial past, but constructivists such as Eric Hobsbawm and Terence Ranger (1983), John Iliffe (1979), and John Lonsdale (1994) maintain that the parameters of the category are historically defined—in this case, in the course of the colonial enterprise—and that we should be wary of its implications in the contemporary context.

On the other side of the conflict is the collective category of Pentecostal/Charismatic churches in Accra. This group encompasses pastors, ministers, and congregants of this particular brand of Christianity, with a focus on the churches that were attacked during the tensions.[10] When speaking of the historical role and self-positioning of the broader Christian community with respect to the conflict, I also have in mind representatives and members of mainline churches[11] and ecumenical bodies directly involved in the interfaith dialogue, such as the Christian Council of Ghana and the Ghana Pentecostal and Charismatic Council.

The term "Pentecostal/Charismatic" was coined by David Barrett (1988) in reference to the third-wave Pentecostal renewal, which includes both Pentecostal and Charismatic denominations. Barrett divides Pentecostalism into three waves: the first wave originated in 1741 and is known as Pentecostalism, the second wave dates to the 1906 Azusa Street Revival in Los Angeles and is generally recognized as the Charismatic movement, and the last wave emerged around 1970 (119). As the fastest-growing Christian denomination, Pentecostal/Charismatic Christianity has received ample scholarly attention in the context of Ghana, Africa, and the world at large.[12] Scholars of African Christianity celebrate the movement because of its bottom-up, localized, and Africanized nature, which, in their view, determines its capacity to cleanse the continent of the legacy of the Western missionary enterprise and inaugurate Africa as an important actor in global Christianity (Kalu 2008; Omenyo 2005). The rapid proliferation of the Pentecostal/Charismatic movement has been chalked up to a lengthy list of variables, including the alleged inability of Western Christianity to meet the needs of Africans (Idowu 1965), economic hardship and deteriorating health care systems (Gifford 2004; Sackey 2001), the movement's strong inclination toward a global presence (Meyer 2004a), sanctified consumerism derived from the prosperity gospel (Kirby 2019; Yong 2010), high compatibility with liberal capitalism (Berger 2010; Comaroff and Comaroff 2000; Comaroff 2012), and the movement's focus on entertainment (Asamoah-Gyadu 2005b). Unlike mainline Christian churches, born-again denominations do not have one supervisory body to guide their interfaith relations and public statements. However, one feature that unites these churches is their ambiguous relationship to traditional religions. On the one hand, they share many attributes with these forms of religiosity, such as a belief in evil forces, a concern for material welfare and healing, and an emphasis on the urgent need for deliverance. On the other hand, Pentecostal/Charismatic churches are almost ubiquitously hostile toward all expressions of traditional religions, including cultural expressions.[13]

Because the Ghanaian state interceded in the wake of the Drum Wars to mend crumbling interfaith relations, it is the third principal actor in the analysis. Within this broader category, I bring together several state bodies involved in negotiating the conflict at various stages, including Ghana's Environmental Protection Agency, the National Commission on Culture, the National Commission for Civic Education, and the National Peace Council. The primary institution of significance, however, is the Accra Metropolitan Assembly, the political and administrative authority of Accra that is part of Ghana's decentralized system of local government and administration. The actions of the Accra Metropolitan Assembly are always coordinated with state policies, and hence when I refer to the Ghanaian state in the book, I usually have this particular institution in mind. At the local level, it is responsible for, among other things, "the overall development of the district," "the maintenance of security and public safety in the district," and "the preservation and promotion of cultural heritage within the district" (Section 12.3, Local Governance Act 936). Most important for the Drum Wars, the assembly inaugurated and managed the Nuisance Control Task Force, a multisectoral group officially charged with ensuring compliance with state-mandated noise-abatement guidelines.

It would be an oversight not to address the shortage of Islamic aurality in the study, since Islam is a key player in Ghana's religious landscape. Much like mainline Christians, Accra's Muslims pride themselves on maintaining cordial relations with Ga traditional authorities, which includes accommodating their traditional religion (Odotei 2002, 27; Owusu 1996, 322). The only attribute of the Muslim sonic profile that figured in the discourse surrounding the ban on drumming was the call to prayer. Even then, it did not enter the picture until tensions escalated, and then always alongside other types of urban noise (de Witte 2008a, 705). My Ga interlocutors often pointed out that their Muslim brethren never contested or disrespected their customary authority and that there was therefore no need to impose constraints on their call to prayer. This situation changed somewhat in the 2010s when Pentecostal/Charismatic Christians began to earmark the early morning *adhan* as a sonic disturbance and their subsequent demands to the GTC that Muslims be subject to the same supervision as Christians. In response to this pressure, the GTC decided to prohibit the use of loudspeakers for announcing Muslim prayer times during the ban on drumming.[14] However, my conversations with council representatives suggest that the restriction was mostly formal. Given these factors, coupled with the fact that there were no reported conflicts over the ban with Accra's Muslim community, the latter are not included in my analysis of the Drum Wars.

The Guardians of Accra

Before concluding, I should properly introduce the guardians of modern Accra, the Ga, by offering a concise historical profile of the group. Oral tradition suggests that the Ga have occupied the territory of present-day Accra since the fifteenth century. In this respect, they are the quintessential urbanites, a community at the center of Accra's transformation into a cosmopolitan commercial center. There is no consensus on the place where Ga people originated, but scholars generally agree that they came from the east, likely the region of present-day Nigeria, Benin, Togo, and Chad (see Field 1937, 142; Henderson-Quartey 2002, 54; Reindorf [1895] 1966, 5; and Ward 1967, 57).[15] Recently, Ga intellectuals have been particularly fond of the hypothesis that the Ga people originated in Israel or Egypt, a theory that has the merit of inscribing the community into Judeo-Christian history (see Abbey 1967; Omaetu 2006; Amartey 1991; Ammah 2016; and Laryea 2011). The claim is based on the presumed similarities between Ga people and biblical Jews, including the practice of out-dooring children, puberty rites, priestly leadership, male circumcision, and resemblances between Hɔmɔwɔ and Passover.

From the time they arrived in Accra, the productive activities of Ga people focused on agriculture, fishing, salt production, and livestock. Gradually, however, the combination of their strategic location and the arid climate of Accra encouraged them to transition to fishing and trade. Soon enough, the Ga people made a name for themselves as skillful intermediaries between Europeans and inland traders. They mastered the Portuguese trade jargon and later taught themselves Dutch and English. Sensing an opportunity to expand their authority, they established a monopoly on trade with Europeans. According to Georg Norregard, "the Accra [Ga people] did not allow the traders coming from the interior to enter into direct trade with the foreign ships, thus they were assured of a substantial profit, often 100 percent or more" (1966, 44–45). In 1677, the monopolistic policy of the Ga Kingdom culminated in a military conflict with the Akwamus and the subsequent loss of command over their lands (Anquandah 2006, 5). In the aftermath, the majority moved inland, while those who were

FIGURE INTRO.1. The Nungua traditional community performing *gbɛje* (path clearing).
Photo by author. 2016.

engaged in trade formed *akutsɛi* (quarters) around the coastal forts and capitalized on their role as middlemen. By the end of the seventeenth century, there
were three forts in Ga territory: the Crèvecœur (Dutch), the Christiansborg
(Danish), and the James Fort (English) (Odotei 1995). In 1742, Accra was incorporated into the Ashanti Empire, where it remained until the mid-1820s, when
Ga joined forces with the British to defeat the Ashanti (Wellington 2011, 31;
Parker 2000, 29). In the period 1874 to 1880, the city was transformed from the
three largely autonomous Ga townships that flourished around the forts into
the colonial capital of the British Gold Coast.

Owing to their active engagement with Europeans, foreigners have often
viewed Ga people as tainted by the world views and lifestyles of others (Parker
2000). This view has left its mark on scholarship. Despite, or perhaps because
of, their conspicuous location, Ga people continue to be the underdogs of academic inquiry, which has favored groups believed to be unaffected by European
influence. Consequently, only a handful of in-depth ethnographic studies of the
Ga community exists, most notably by Margaret J. Field (1937), Marion Kilson
(1974), and E. A. Ammah (2016).

The groups that established the six Ga townships—Ga-Mashie, Osu, La, Teshie, Nungua, and Tema—allegedly migrated via distinct routes at various times
and maintained relative authority despite various political alliances (Omaboe

2011). British colonial policies, including the Town Councils Ordinance (1894), the Public Lands Ordinance (1876), the Native Jurisdiction Ordinance (1910), the Municipal Corporations Ordinance (1924), and the Native Administration Ordinance (1927), sabotaged Ga chiefly authority (Quayson 2014, 43). To smooth the way for uninterrupted governance, the colonial administration also attempted to elevate the Ga-Mashie *maŋtsɛ* to the position of the paramount chief. The Ga-Mashie community found it hard to disassociate itself from the superior reputation accorded to them by virtue of their chief, even after other Ga chiefs were reinstituted in the postcolonial period.

Although the Ga community maintains four cults of worship, one of them— *Kpele*—is the primary mode of religious expression.[16] The Ga word *kpele* means "all-encompassing" and could be understood to refer to the pervasive nature of the cult as an ideology that encompasses all aspects of the Ga world view. In contrast to the other three modes of worship, Kpele is "national" in character, meaning that it is practiced by all six Ga townships and is tightly interwoven with the Ga social structure (Nketia 1964). When I talk about the Ga religion in the book, I opt for an open-ended definition that includes various amalgamations of the four modes of worship combined with whatever additional practices the Ga choose to incorporate into the categories of religion or custom. I concur with Marijke Steegstra's (2005) argument that traditional religions can only be studied in tandem with Christianity since the latter is largely accountable for the categorization of traditional religion as culture or custom. I therefore keep Christianity in mind as I analyze the ban on drumming in the context of Accra.

The primary actors in the Ga cosmology are the *jemawɔji* (deities) and Ataa Naa Nyɔŋmɔ (Father Grandmother God). Ga people also recognize the existence of lesser powers called *wɔji*, but these have no names and are not usually handled by ritual specialists (Laryea 2011, 48; Field 1937, 111). Because my work is concerned with institutional forms of the Ga religion, I deal exclusively with the *jemawɔji*. Even Nyɔŋmɔ, who is often described as the creator and governor of all things, is not physically involved with humans and is normally represented by the *jemawɔji* (Laryea 2011, 63). The highly involved nature of the *jemawɔji* is consistent with the theory that the term derives from a combination of two Ga words: *jɛmɛi* (here) and *wɔŋ* (deity), designating deities who are worldly and are engaged in daily affairs (Kilson 1971, 68; Kudadjie 1975, 32).[17] While Kpele *jemawɔji* are associated with topographical features, other deities are not tied to specific locations because they were borrowed or purchased from various groups the Ga interacted with over the centuries. Unlike the *wɔji*, which humans instrumentalize for their own benefit, the *jemawɔji* cannot be subjected to human whims. Each Ga township has its own pantheon of *jemawɔji* who

FIGURE INTRO.2. The Ga-Mashie community performs *nshɔ bulomo* (sea purification). Photo by author. 2016.

oversee the land. However, their position is by no means permanent. If the deities cease to benefit the community, they are gradually forgotten.

Ritual specialists play a pivotal role in the daily life of the Ga. In fact, the *wulɔmɛi* rather than the *maŋtsɛmɛi* bore the burden of leadership for centuries until the taboos attached to their position—above all, the prohibition against venturing outside their respective traditional areas—rendered them incapable of participating in political affairs. To negotiate treaties with partners and enemies, the Ga appointed *maŋtsɛmɛi* as representatives of the *wulɔmɛi* (Reindorf [1895] 1966, 113–14; Robertson 1984, 1). The power delegated to the *maŋtsɛmɛi* gradually blossomed into full-fledged leadership and was legally endorsed by the British system of indirect rule (Akrong 2007, 142). Philip Laryea (2011) notes that the primary function of the *wulɔmɛi* today is that "the *jemawɔji* narrate to them their goals and desires to be translated to the townspeople so that they pray for the town" (113). To ensure a pure state for channeling the *jemawɔji*, the *wulɔmɛi* must desist from all forms of conflict and follow ritually prescribed directives. They are not allowed to see a corpse, eat salt or fermented food, talk to anyone while eating, or have sexual intercourse on certain days of the week (Omaetu 2006, 25–26; Laryea 2011, 113; Manoukian 1950, 96). Messages that the *wulɔmɛi* receive from the *jemawɔji* and translate to their people are channeled through the *wɔyei*, the female priestesses (Field 1937, 8).

Accra is located in an arid region where periodic droughts lead to shortages of staple food crops (Parker 2000). One could argue that the Hɔmɔwɔ festival, which is performed in commemoration of a great famine in the past, celebrates another year of survival in these adverse conditions and defines the essence of being Ga.[18] Socially speaking, the festival binds the community together since it is the only time of the year when individuals living outside Accra are compelled to return to their ancestral homes to bolster kinship ties with living and deceased family members and to give thanks to the *jemawɔji*.[19] Hɔmɔwɔ is the main Ga celebration that is common to all six Ga townships and the only harvest ceremony that belongs to all Ga people (Kilson 2013, 92–93).

Road Map

Chapter 1 and chapter 2 complement each other because they both provide the historical backdrop for the ban on drumming in contemporary Accra. The first chapter explores the previously overlooked history of noise control in the British Gold Coast, with a particular focus on the racial politics that propelled the evolutionary sonic taxonomy used to subordinate the local population. Looking closely at the legal and practical dimensions of nuisance control in the Gold Coast, I illustrate the conflation of colonial and Christian sensory registers and the mobilization of these registers in opposition to African religions. I suggest that the earmarking of the drum as the vilest form of noise production derives from its "sensational quality"—that is, its capacity to mediate between the human and transcendent worlds. An analysis of noise-abatement initiatives from other parts of the world corroborates the arguments presented.

Chapter 2 spans the period from 1957, when Ghana declared its independence, to the mid-1990s, before the escalation of tensions between Pentecostal/Charismatic churches and the Ga community in Accra. I detail the gradual transformation of the ban from a routine custom to a scandalous affair of public concern through a close reading of the most prominent state-owned newspaper, the *Daily Graphic*. In addition to analyzing the public discourse on urban noise pollution and its impact on the changing attitudes toward the ban on drumming, I demonstrate how the Ga community instrumentalized the growing public concern about the repercussions of noise on citizens' health to engineer a defense of the ban on drumming as a custom in the service of the public.

In chapter 3, I break down the sonic theologies and practices of the Ga religion and Pentecostal/Charismatic Christianity by drawing on ethnographic material and secondary sources. I pay particular attention to the centrality of quiet in the Ga ritual practice and the Pentecostal/Charismatic reconceptualization of noise as a positive experience. I argue that despite the overt hostility between the two parties, their apprehension of sound is surprisingly analogous. Here, I focus especially on the shared understanding of sound—or the lack thereof—as a force that can both thwart and foster spiritual advancement. Based on these conclusions, I argue that the conflict over the ban on drumming signifies not only a desire to establish political control over Accra but also an attempt to sacralize the urban space and offer respect to the nonhuman actors involved.

I elaborate on the centrality of the case study for conceptualizing the relationship between the state and the two respective communities in chapter 4. I introduce the sonic tensions that unfolded in 1998 to 2001 and examine the legal frameworks the conflicting sides adopted as they defended their positions. My approach diverges from previous works in its explicit interest in the secular discourses employed in the negotiations—the Ga defense of the ritual ban via customary law and the Pentecostal/Charismatic insistence on the constitutional right to practice religion. The distinct legal discourses of these two communities illuminate the culturalization of traditional religions and the religionization of Christianity, a configuration informed by the Christocentric orientation of secularism as an ideological and political regime and the discursive culturalization of traditional lifeworlds in missionary, colonial, and nation-building contexts.

The book's argument about secularity in Ghana is presented in chapter 5, which can serve as an entry point for discussing secularity throughout Christian Africa. The star of the narrative is the state-governed Nuisance Control Task Force, which was established in the aftermath of the conflict. The state presented the task force as a secular enterprise designed to alleviate urban noise pollution and raise awareness about its perils. In practice, however, the Nuisance Control Task Force came together during the period of the ban and continues to function in collaboration with the Ga community. I argue that this arrangement sheds light on Ghanaian secularity, a synergy of the customary understanding of shared religious space and the authority of the custodians of the land and secularism as a regime that despite ostensible religious neutrality grants institutional and ideological advantages to Christianity.

The final chapter introduces two initiatives that engage with the Hɔmɔwɔ festival from different angles. First, I discuss the Hɔmɔwɔ Thanksgiving service that the Christian Council of Ghana launched in 2015. This initiative was designed to contribute to intercommunal peace via Hɔmɔwɔ-themed lectures and services organized in selected mainline churches in Ga neighborhoods. Second, I look at Homofest, a national celebration that the Ministry of Tourism, Arts & Culture inaugurated in 2014. Homofest combines the Hɔmɔwɔ celebrations in the six Ga townships into a carnival-like festival open to tourists and citizens of all cultural or ethnic backgrounds. The core similarity between these two initiatives is the omission of religious elements in favor of an explicitly cultural interpretation of the festival, an approach consistent with the understanding of traditional festivals as spaces of cohabitation. While acknowledging the intercommunal benefits of these two projects, I also argue that they build on the idea that traditional religions need to be neutralized into cultural expressions in order to become serviceable in the contemporary secular state.

1. Jumping on the Anti-Noise Bandwagon

Drumming Permits for Accra's Residents

On August 1, 1903, a Cape Coast–based newspaper, *The Gold Coast Leader*, published an article that defiantly denounced the actions of a British district commissioner. With prudent yet caustic language, the author deplored the frequent interference of district commissioners in native funeral customs under the pretext of eliminating nuisance.[1] Public denunciation of high-ranking British officials was not a common practice in the Gold Coast and the fact that this contributor voiced community grievances suggested that the commissioner had overstepped the boundaries of cultural propriety. The author accused the transgressor both of violating the 1892 Criminal Code on Public Nuisance and of sacrilege because he had interrupted the singers who were guarding the deceased. The author elaborated on the gravity of the offense: "Death is always and everywhere a solemn thing, and the presence of death in any household carries with it such a solemnity, and forcibly brings to mind the touch which should make the whole world akin: any one therefore who should so far forget himself to let his racial prejudice or enjoyment of his officialism overpower him in matters connected with this impartial Visitor, will be well nigh laying himself open to be characterized as being inhuman."[2]

The contributor recalled another occasion when a district commissioner had tampered with the burial ceremony of a prominent community figure, spotlighting the discrimination and racism the population of the Gold Coast endured at the hands of British officials. He wrote that as soon as they are surrounded by "their colour, and some mischievous blacks who would make them believe, that being D.C's [district commissioners] [sic] they can [of] course do as they like, and treat people as they fancy," they "[throw] all gentlemanliness and consideration to the wind, and if the worse comes to the worst, they have an Ordinance to 'protect' them."[3]

I chose this notice from *The Gold Coast Leader* to illustrate the complex array of issues associated with nuisance control in the colony. Even before the official establishment of the British Gold Coast in 1867, the sonic "outlandishness" of Ga funerals, which to British ears featured "a concert of tomtoms and drums ... dances and other fantastic evolutions," was a quality of early Accra that threw the British off balance (Daniell 1856, 18). British residents of Ghana relentlessly derided the propensity of Accras and other coastal peoples to memorialize their life occasions with sound as a conclusive sign of primitiveness that served to elevate the alleged moral and cultural superiority of the British.[4] William F. Daniell (1856), a member of the British Ethnological Society and the author of a detailed description of Ga quotidian life in the 1850s, did not hide his disgust toward "the vociferous chanting, boisterous mirth, and clamorous bickerings" of the indigenes, which he took as a clear sign of moral degradation that persisted despite the centuries-long presence of the "more enlightened Europeans" (32).

To provide historical context for the sonic battles of present-day Accra, this chapter travels back in time to examine the nuisance control discourse and techniques of the colonial Gold Coast with a particular focus on Accra, which became the capital of the Gold Coast in 1877. I suggest that ventures aimed at curbing the aural tracks of particular communities have a long history in the city and communicate techniques of claiming, contesting, and building authority. In accordance with a Eurocentric ranking of societies, the most conspicuous feature of the late nineteenth-century sonic discourse was the juxtaposition of Accra's buoyant sonic profile with the more solemn aural tastes of Europeans. The discourse was accompanied by specific regulatory measures that confined, managed, and restricted Accra's indigenous inhabitants and is critical for understanding the current noise-abatement negotiations in Accra.

The Birth of the "Refined Ear": Early Noise-Abatement Campaigns and the Hierarchy of the Senses

Before scrutinizing the top-down substructures that monitored the urban sound waves in the late nineteenth century, let us take a closer look at the preconceptions that underlay the inauguration of these policies. Most Westerners believed that vision was the superior sense, followed by hearing, smell, taste, and touch. This had been the case ever since Aristotle introduced the classical hierarchy of the senses (Schmidt 2000, 16–17). The belief in the nobility of sight reached its zenith during the Enlightenment. Robert Jütte maintains that for Westerners, the dominance of vision was reinforced by the advent of typography (see Bailey 1996, 55; Jouili and Moors 2014) and became permanent during industrialization (Jütte 2005, 186), a period that Martin Jay (1998) aptly dubbed the "scopic regime" due to the ascendancy of sight over the other senses in both theory and practice.

The hierarchization of the senses was but one fragment of the evolutionary schema that was supposed to mark human progress from oral to literate societies. Although the modernist narrative of the ascendance of sight has since been condemned for its complicity in the colonial enterprise, the paradigm survived well into the second half of the twentieth century in the comparative perspective of communication scholars Walter J. Ong (1982), Marshall McLuhan (1962), and Harold Innis ([1972] 2007). These authors opted for sensory differentiation rather than hierarchization by presenting print as a crucial marker of "visual cultures" as opposed to the heightened auditive capacities of "oral cultures." As a case in point, Walter Ong (1982) argued that "print replaced the lingering hearing-dominance in the world of thought and expression with the sight-dominance which had its beginnings with writing but could not flourish with the support of writing alone" (121). In his 1982 book *Orality and Literacy*, Ong attempted to avoid linking orality with "primitivism" but ended up walking into the trap when he ranked sight as the more advanced form of reality because it enabled human consciousness to reach its fuller potential. He imagined "oral peoples," in contrast, as bound to tradition and to the present, devoid of the capacity for abstract and creative thought.

Both earlier and later models split the world into sensory communities that, depending on one's perspective, occupied different ends of the spectrum of good and evil, cultured and savage, moral and immoral. The categories assigned to cultural Others were virtually empty, ready to be filled with "whatever was beyond the pale of one's own social imagination" (Rath 2013, 150). By breathing life into these signifiers, those with power delineated and reinforced their distinctness from the rest, whether the latter meant the colonized peoples of the Gold Coast, Native Americans in the antebellum South, or immigrant communities in London. Various forms of otherness, whether ethnic (Boutin 2015), racial (Smith 2013), or class based (Radovac 2011), were ascribed their individual sonic qualifiers. The lower classes were scolded for being obnoxiously loud, indigenous populations were said to emit barbaric and outlandish sounds, and women were expected to be soundless.

A vital attribute of postindustrial ocularcentrism was the refined ear that needed to be protected from "the din and hiss of steam engines, the nerve-racking clatter of mechanical looms, the monotonous whirring of automatic spinning machines and the hellish noise of riveting hammers and pneumatic drills" (Jütte 2005, 203). Restrictive sonic procedures imposed in late nineteenth-century Euroamerica and subsequently in African colonies echoed the disdain of the middle and upper classes for illiterate factory workers and immigrant communities at home and for colonial "oral peoples" of insufficient finesse abroad. The discourse of sonic superiority thrived on the conviction that loudness and tolerance of high sonic frequencies were signs of hampered mental progress. The German philosopher Arthur Schopenhauer ([1819] 1969) strongly believed that "the amount of noise that anyone can bear undisturbed stands in inverse proportion to his mental capacity and may therefore be regarded as a pretty fair measure of it" (199). "All people of much intellect, are without exception absolutely incapable of enduring any noise," he wrote, while those insensitive to noise are "coarse and dull-minded" (Schopenhauer ([1819] 1969, 197, 199). In the same vein, Viennese ethnologist Michael Haberlandt argued in 1900 that the more noise a community could tolerate, the more "barbaric" it could be considered. Since noise was also believed to interfere with the efficient functioning of the mind, individuals whose professional activity required intense mental concentration were especially concerned to protect themselves from it.

In the colonies, the same logic led colonial administrators to argue that vulgar soundscapes were partly accountable for the sluggish idleness of their subordinates. In the colonial context, noise came to be defined in spatial terms as a sound that was difficult to contain and organize and thus impossible to control. Music, on the other hand, in its organized and formally symmetrical rendering, came to embody not only order but also the "iconic civility" that was so central to "the self-fashioning of Enlightenment thought" (Radano and Olaniyan

2006, 8). Nick Yablon (2007) explains that while freely circulating sounds were perceived not only as threatening but also as crude and garish, music was safe as long as it was contained within "the enclosed spaces of the auditorium, concert hall, or parlor" (630).

The propensity of culturally and cognitively "sophisticated" social circles to shield their refined aural senses from the exposure to unwholesome sounds metamorphosed into organized noise-abatement campaigns at the turn of the twentieth century that were specifically tailored to guard the finesse and sanity of the intelligentsia. In their dissection of imperial listening, Radano and Olaniyan (2006) also connect "the command to silence" to "an effort to contain the din—the noise of the 'Negro,' 'Chinaman,' and 'lazy native' . . . together with those interior, domestic forms of irrationality and difference within emerging empires: the hysteria of women; the clatter of the rabble" (8). Theodor Lessing, the founder of the Antinoise Society in Vienna, famously pronounced noise as a sign of urban depravation and a menace for "brainworkers" (Payer 2007, 783). Anchored in the ocularcentric taxonomy of the senses described above, these campaigns were introduced not only in the colonies but also domestically, where they served to reinforce class divisions. In Britain, for instance, noise-abatement efforts translated into an ongoing struggle to contain the unrefined sounds produced by the lower classes (Bailey 1996; Sharpe and Wallock 1987; Winter 1993). In the British colonies, sonic regulation drew sharp distinctions between the colonizers and the colonized.

Attempts to control noise in the Gold Coast should be seen as an extension of similar ordinances in Europe and North America. Historians have investigated the changing tolerance for certain types of noise across social, religious, and cultural lines in the first half of the twentieth century and the power dynamics that informed these transformations (Bijsterveld 2001; Bijsterveld 2008; Thompson 2002; Weiner 2014; Payer 2007). Systematic anti-noise campaigns started in New York and quickly spread to the rest of the United States and to major European cities (Payer 2007, 781). Emily Thompson (2002) reports that in Baltimore in the early twentieth century, "anti-noise policemen" patrolled the city to eradicate any unwanted sounds. She lists the bizarre assemblage of sounds that one anti-noise officer reportedly quashed in the course of a week: "the noises of streetcar bell-ringers, and squeaky-wheeled trolleys, a baker noisily unloading bread from his wagon, a shouting fishmonger, raucous school children, three roosters, six cats, another noisy baker, twenty-four more cats, news-boys, a scissor grinder, and several rag-and-bone collectors" (126). The wide range of items on this list demonstrates the scale of the anti-noise frenzy that was set in motion by a combination of the postindustrial amplification of urban din and the discourse that presented sound as menace. Karin Bijsterveld's (2008) study of noise management efforts in European and American public spaces in the period 1875 to 1975 suggests that American initiatives were more successful than their European counterparts. In addition to condemning noise as an indication of primitiveness, American campaigns stressed its adverse impact on the workers' productive power: "noise in industry and business offices was widely believed to threaten employees' powers of concentration, and city noise in general was understood to undermine public health" (103).

According to Bijsterveld (2003), the growing concern over noise led to two major waves of noise abatement in Western Europe and North America: first in 1906–1914, and again in 1929–1938. The second wave was characterized by increased reliance on scientific noise measurement following the introduction of the decibel as a unit of loudness in 1925 (Bijsterveld 2003; Vaillant 2003). Even when using science to measure noise, however, noise ordinances have never been implemented in a comprehensive manner, in large measure because noise regulation is inherently about maintaining and redistributing power via cultural signs and discourses that mark "good" and "bad" sounds. In his work on noise in contemporary São Paulo, Leonardo Cardoso (2017) suggests that as a combination of "culturally localised practices and universalistic assumptions about public life and the human body," noise-related debates are ultimately a manifestation of unequal rights to the city (920). The precolonial and postcolonial patterns of noise regulation in Accra discussed in this book attest to the highly political nature of noise regulation.

"The law is such a ticklish thing": Racialized Noise Politics in Colonial Accra

In colonial Accra, the British administration introduced and enforced racial noise politics. The othering of certain sounds and the bodies that produced them was conspicuous to varying degrees. White colonizers, the educated upper classes, and foreign visitors often combined charges against the city's sonic profile with complaints about the allegedly improper lifestyle of the Ga people. Their living conditions were a common topic of criticism. It is in these descriptions of early Accra that the parallels between noise, dirt, and disorderliness as conceptual categories of otherness become most apparent (Douglas [1966] 2002). Even before the British claimed the Gold Coast as a colony, the writings of many European travelers placed African peoples at the bottom of the hierarchy of human societies, deprecating them as idle, superstitious, and unkempt. Accounts of their lifestyle and environs echo these prejudices. Mid-nineteenth-century travel accounts depicted ordinary dwellings in Accra as uninhabitable by European standards. William F. Daniell (1856) claimed that the town lacked "any definite plan or system of arrangement," describing compactly grouped buildings in "narrow, tortuous, and intricate" streets that were akin to "some mysterious labyrinth" (26). In their account of the British expedition to Niger of 1841, William Allen and T. R. H. Thomson described the towns they saw as featureless and dirty, intersected by deep water courses that formed an "unwholesome marsh" if they were not cleaned regularly. These authors repeatedly emphasized that the filth and stench could be easily managed if not for the "constitutional indolency or love of ease" typical of the locals (Daniell 1856, 26). Simply put, European writers interpreted the dismal living conditions Accra's inhabitants endured as an indication of moral failure.

Although my work focuses on aurality, it is crucial to remember that what Europeans perceived as the visual, olfactory, and aural inadequacies of the indigenes coalesced to create the profile of a racialized Other. In addition to complaining that the densely packed settlements of Accra were hard on the eyes, they criticized them for failing to contain the sounds and smells of their inhabitants, largely due to the porosity of building materials such as mud, palm leaves, reeds, and straw (Daniell 1856, 27). British visitors and administrators frequently complained about the unruly soundscape of the Gold Coast, which they perceived as an extension of the inhabitants' obstreperous nature and general barbarity. In her historical study of how sound has been racialized in American culture, Jennifer Stoever (2016) maintains that listening functions "as an organ of racial discernment, categorization, and resistance in the shadow of vision's alleged cultural dominance" (4). In the British colonial context, race was sonified along a spectrum that ran from "primitive" to "evolved," producing an aural taxonomy that paved the way for various forms of control. In this aural genealogy, the sound of the colonizer was an invisible or neutral category that despite its racial specificity enjoyed a universalized status, while anything that deviated from this norm was judged as aberrant (12).

British efforts to curb what they considered the corrupting racket of the local population intensified as the Gold Coast became fully established as a colony. A Public Nuisance Ordinance was incorporated in the Criminal Code of the Gold Coast Colony in 1892 under the category of "offenses against public order, health and morality." Section 119 of Ordinance 12 included three subsections that outlined the aural allowances for the citizens:

1 Every occupier of any house, building, yard or other place situated in any town, who, without a license in writing from the Governor or a

District Commissioner, permits any persons to assemble and beat or play or dance therein to any drum, gong, tomtom, or similar instrument of music, shall be liable to a fine of two pounds.

2 It shall be lawful for any constable to enter such house, building, yard, or other place where any persons may be so assembled, and to warn them to depart and to seize and carry away all such drums, gongs, tomtoms, or other instruments, and the same shall be forfeited.

3 Whoever, after being so warned, shall not depart forthwith (except the persons actually dwelling in such house or building), may be apprehended, without warrant by any constable or person acting in his aid, and shall be liable to a fine of ten shillings. (Griffith 1903, 729)

We know that noise-abatement initiatives outside the colonies were designed to subject immigrant or working-class communities to strategic policing. Such initiatives are evidence of the resistance of elites to the sociospatial shifts that followed urbanization (Bailey 1996; Yablon 2007; Bijsterveld 2008; Payer 2007). These efforts to regulate noise were packaged as public health measures aimed at reducing the general level of urban noise from a variety of sources, such as traffic, factories, small-scale industry, and street music. In legal terms, all types of sounds could be prohibited as long as they were pronounced to be constitutive of noise. By contrast, the sonic restrictions outlined in the Gold Coast specifically targeted the sounds of humans or human-operated musical instruments.[5] While in the Euroamerican context the officially cited rationale for acoustic control was a combination of human-produced and machine-generated sounds, the Gold Coast Ordinance targeted "the natives" and their tonal language, singling out instruments like drums, gongs, and tomtoms that were almost exclusively used by locals in communal celebrations that activated cross-world pathways with nonhuman actors.[6]

In public discourse, assaults on the freedom of the local populations to lead uninhibited communal lives echoed some of the health-oriented arguments of Euroamerican laws and policies. The negative impact of noise on the ability of brainworkers to concentrate, for instance, was one of the main complaints voiced at the April 20, 1914, meeting of the Board of Education in Kumasi, the largest settlement in the Ashanti region. Ashanti became a colony of the British Crown in 1901, much later than the Gold Coast, and did not have the same kinds of nuisance control mechanisms as those in the Gold Coast's Ordinance 12. At the meeting, Rev. Arthur Jehle, a missionary and educator from Basel who was stationed in the Eastern Region, raised concern that school work was "frequently rendered impossible by the unnecessary noise made by townspeople. Brass bands have increased in numbers and parade the towns not for single days but for weeks at a stretch. Drumming is sometimes continuous."[7] To protect those who were determined and willing to work, Rev. Jehle offered to introduce stricter legal measures that would establish systematic and consistent noise directives for all residents of the colony. The proposal included a recommendation to limit all forms of gatherings to at least "300 yards from the nearest habitation." While the board members agreed that such directives would save them a lot of headaches, the proposed amendments were not passed due to the legal hurdles involved.

Given the centrality of musical performance in the Ga lifeworld, the Gold Coast's noise directives would certainly have discouraged individuals from assembling not just in public spaces but also in private homes or yards. Although the colonial administration said that the nuisance control measures of the Gold Coast were universally applicable, the stringency with which the regulations were enforced hinged on the whims of the administrators, who were clearly prejudiced against the uneducated locals. Obtaining a permit from a district commissioner would have been nearly impossible for the average citizen, as applications had to be submitted in writing, a luxury not readily available to the majority of Gold Coast residents at the time. Since music was an essential prerequisite for entertainment and basic social functions, the obligation to apply for a permit must have significantly inhibited the citizens' communal life, freedom of expression, and power to congregate. Last but not least, the fine of two pounds for assembling or playing instruments without a permit was a large sum of money in the late nineteenth century; it was the equivalent of six days' wages for a craftsman in England and would have been worth considerably more for a Gold Coast native.

Subsection 2 of the Public Nuisance Ordinance gave any constable—a-rank-and-file police officer with limited policing authority and decision-making power—the right to enter the private property of citizens and arrest those assembled there. According to the Nuisance Ordinance, drumming was illegal in houses within the perimeter of major towns. Since the level of noise produced was neither measured nor standardized, the application of this law would have depended on the diligence of police, who sources suggest often abused their authority. In 1899, the colonial secretary issued a circular notice interdicting late-night drumming permits for "uneducated natives." The same notice emphasized that applications from "educated natives" and "Europeans" seeking music for entertainment would be considered on a case-by-case basis. "His Excellency is of opinion that as a general rule, there is no reason why such applications should not be granted in full," read the statement.[8] Bias in enforcement was, of course, commonplace in the late nineteenth-century noise-abatement movement, which was as much an instrument of racial politics as it was a stage for managing class struggle and civilian resistance. It is no coincidence that a sizeable number of educated locals who professed modern sensibilities gladly participated in racialized noise politics to secure a better standing in the British-governed socioeconomic ladder. The discriminatory nature of drumming permits in Accra went far beyond British colonialists' alleged concern for the health of citizens and revealed a strategy for sabotaging any seeds of social unrest by keeping the "uneducated" in a state of fear and paralysis. The fact that the musical utterances of locals became the target of surveillance underscores the political nature of communal sound as a weapon of resistance (Scott 1985; Kelley 1993) and "a tool for the creation or consolidation of a community, of a totality" (Attali 1985, 6).

Still, the pressure was not unidirectional. The few sources available suggest that ordinary citizens actively challenged the unequal application of the law. Newspapers of the period served as a platform for criticism of administrators, and noise restrictions were often the entry point for raising broader questions about racial segregation. The author of the article discussed in the beginning of this chapter passionately denounced the Public Nuisance Ordinance, insisting that it had never prevented "his white cousin [from making] as much noise, as he can, up to any hour without any molestation from the D.C." He maintained that the officials presiding over such matters must have been "taught to believe that the Laws in the land are meant for the blacks and blacks alone."[9] "The law is such a ticklish thing," wrote another contributor that same year, "that any quixotic magistrate may easily read anything into any of the [ordinance] sections, at all events the *shouting* may be conventionally construed to include *singing* which modern Commissioners are seeking to put down so far as it is done by natives with a high head."[10]

Another piece criticized the lack of respect and cultural ignorance prevalent among the officials charged with enforcing noise restrictions, often to the detriment of people's customs. The author clarified that Ordinance 137.9 on nuisance and obstruction explicitly stated that the colonial administration would fine anyone who "willfully or wantonly" shouted, blew a horn or shell, played a musical instrument, sang, or made any other loud or unseemly noise.[11] It could not be said, he went on, that funeral customs were "willfully and wantonly" annoying anyone when they represented an age-old tradition of mourning: "we sit up with our dead till day-break, spending the time in weeping in singing—singing to comfort ourselves as well as to keep us awake. This is repeated on the eighth day, when mostly singing is done, during greater part of the night, crying beginning at the dawn of the day." The ruthless interruption of funerals was especially outrageous when "other people"—possibly referring to the British—"ma[d]e as much noise as their lungs and fists [could] allow them in pursuit of pleasure and enjoyment."[12] Bearing in mind the significance of properly conducted funerals to the grieving family and to Ghana's indigenous communities as a whole, it is not an exaggeration to interpret the obstruction of funeral customs as a grossly offensive act. Besides, any unwarranted interference with the ceremony violated the right of the indigenes to practice their custom, as enshrined in Ordinance 137.15, which imposed a fine on those who behaved "irreverently or indecently or insultingly" at or near a funeral (Griffith 1903, 319–20). The author of the piece attributed such blatant disregard for the laws of the land to district commissioners who flaunted their power and sought to please their own kind, especially if they "happened to be a Boss of some sort." The article culminated in the bitter conclusion that despite the pronounced universality and supremacy of the law, the interpretation and application of the Gold Coast's ordinances testified to rampant "racial prejudice and distinction" in the legal sphere.[13]

An incident reported in the same newspaper a week earlier speaks to the pervasiveness of the double standards of the Gold Coast justice system. In Axim, the westernmost coastal town of the colony, the district commissioner was allegedly attending a "dinner given by one of his friends where comic songs of all, and no description, were lustily and loudly sung," when he was informed of a funeral taking place nearby. The commissioner is said to have rushed to the household where the deceased lay to harass those who were present. Much like the residents of Cape Coast, the people of Axim were aggrieved by the discriminatory application of the law and outraged that British officials would object to their sacred funeral songs while they themselves freely indulged in loud celebrations and indecency.[14]

By far the most comprehensive assault on all forms of discrimination in the early twentieth-century print media comes from an impassioned opinion piece published in *The Sierra Leone Weekly News* in 1915. Judging by the fact that *The Gold Coast Nation* promptly reprinted the story, it must have had a wide appeal. The piece decried segregation as a symbol of inhumanity, "a cold shoulder word . . . a trespassers-will-be-prosecuted sort of word so unkind in its significance, as to chill one to the bone." With a satirical twist, the author chronicled the travels of segregation, a disagreeable character of sorts, from England to the colonies. Hopping on an express liner, segregation reached new pastures for its wicked dream of bringing into the world segregated congregations, shops, offices, and trains "where no black face, whether by night, or by day, whether man or woman, [would] dare to show itself." In fashioning his safe haven in the new land, segregation chose the best locations, surrounded himself with white neighbors, and above all, sheltered himself from sonic distractions—the "noise of the tom tom, and the harsh, unmusical unmelodic native sing song on a moon light [*sic*] night." The author's placement of aural tranquility in the same category as owning a luxurious home underscored the urgent need of the average foreigner in the West African colonies to manage sound.[15]

The Obscene Sound of Heathenism

Christian missionaries added cosmological fervor to the racialized sonic taxonomy of the colonial state. The sonic tastes of state and church often converged, most obviously in the area of tribal dance. Historian Mhoze Chikowero (2015) argues that tribal dance emerged as "a performative instrument for articulating a self-justifying discourse of conquest and domination in a process that produced the African 'Other' as a lesser, 'tribal' being with no claim to 'modern' rights" (132). Christian sensibilities were pivotal in pronouncing the aural tracks of indigenous lifeworlds among the terrible sounds of Africa that had to be restrained if indigenes were to be disciplined and subjugated. Due to its versatile nature, sound figured prominently in the protracted colonial endeavor to substitute local epistemological registers with the Western sensory regime. The Christianizing mission served as the flesh to the bones of the colonial administrative skeleton, permeating all aspects of existence and carrying the potential for self-dissemination as converts internalized the cultural prejudices inherent in Christianity. As early as 1602, the Dutch trader and explorer Pieter de Marees reported that Gold Coast inhabitants in regular contact with the Portuguese refrained from discussing their beliefs and practices with foreigners and even pretended to be Christians, no doubt as a result of the visitors' discriminatory treatment of their practices (De Marees [1602] 1987, 72).

Peter van der Veer's (2001) work on India brings to light the fundamentally Christian nature of Western imperialism. The reordered hierarchy of the senses that followed the Enlightenment also encompassed ideas about what advanced religions should sound like. "Ritualism" was placed at the bottom of what Isaac Weiner calls the "auditory evolutionary matrix" (Weiner 2014, 57) and was recast as a primitive form of religious expression compared to the solemn and mature musical exposition of Christian churches. The conflation of notions of progress, development, and evolution with Christianity in official discourse meant that sensory predilections gravitated toward smells, sounds, and tastes that conformed to Christian morality. In his work on tonality as a colonizing force in Africa, Kofi Agawu (2006) suggests that by speaking European tonal languages, the colonized could triumph on two levels: they could gain access to "some precious accouterments of modernity" in the physical world and they could secure a place in heaven (338). By the same token, Christians regarded sounds produced in the context of indigenous ceremonies as not only primitive but also soul-polluting and thus deeply threatening to the colonial moral order (Chikowero 2015).

A favored topic of debate among foreigners, missionaries, local elites, and Christian converts was the performance of customs. Their overarching concern was whether such practices were permissible for Christians or in public spaces. This issue was examined in dialogue with scripture and vague notions of Christian-influenced public morals. These early critics of African sonic expression were especially troubled by fears of adulteration, both tonal and spiritual, by the drumming and blowing of horns, the essential attributes of virtually all ceremonies performed in the Gold Coast.[16] Although the performance of songs at festivals such as Hɔmɔwɔ or Kundum was unwelcome but tolerated, the "blending together" of Christian music with the non-Christian tunes was viewed as utterly abominable. In 1898, an opinion piece in *Gold Coast Aborigines* bewailed the corrupted sanctity of Christmas by "hideous noise" and "all sorts of vulgar and obscene songs" that competed with "the sacred songs" of Europeans.[17] Nearly fifteen years later, a contributor to *The Gold Coast Leader* harbored the same animosity toward the concurrent celebration of Hɔmɔwɔ and the annual Harvest Festival of the Wesleyan Church, insinuating that the two simply could not be held on the same day because that would damage the sacredness of the church event.[18] Such attacks on the acoustic contours of traditional lifeworlds betray Christians' deep-rooted abhorrence of syncretism and their ingrained fear of cross-world contamination of Christian spaces by nonhuman presences invoked through music. For Christians, the polluting potential of indigenous songs was particularly menacing when it coincided with the "sanctity" of Christian songs because the conflation of the two sensory registers threatened the symbolic system Christian beliefs hinged upon (Douglas [1966] 2002).

Conversion to Christianity usually meant adopting the prejudiced outlook that "tribal" soundworlds were incompatible with the "civilized" colonial state of being. That discriminatory sensory epistemology was especially prevalent among progressive indigenous elites. An example that illustrates that tendency is a 1903 article by a local journalist who was scandalized by the fact that ritual specialists were allowed to perform "backward" expressions of local culture in broad daylight—and in the capital of the colony at that:

> Public demonstrations of Fetish dances is so much encouraged in Accra the Head Quarters of the Gold Coast Colony than the other places.
>
> Fetish Priests and Priestesses can be seen now and again disturbing the Peace of the Town with their drums and noise and no Constable goes to put a stop to them.

On Sundays at the Horse Road from 4 P.M. to 6 P.M. all sorts of dances take place regularly. Dances which ought not to be entertained by any Civilized and Christian Government. The Police allow all this to go on, sometimes they are seen enjoying them as spectators—we ventured to ask if this indulgence (if so we are to call it) forms a part of the means by which we are to be enlightened, if not is it not high time enough that this sort of Sabbath breaking be dealt with as committing of nuisance.[19]

Not surprisingly, analogous sentiments were most commonly voiced in reference to "traditional" festivals, particularly Hɔmɔwɔ—the epitome of the Ga religion and the most extravagant celebration held in Accra, complete with provocative inversions of social order and sexually revealing dances. In his social history of the city, John Parker (2000) describes the Hɔmɔwɔ festival as "a time of controlled chaos, when normal codes of conduct were suspended and outrageous behavior was sanctioned" (133). In a Turnerian sense (Turner [1966] 1995), the pandemonium that transpired in Accra during Hɔmɔwɔ is a crucial building block of ritual transition—it represents a liminal state of undifferentiation that ensures a realignment of hierarchies at the cusp of the new year. In the eyes of the British, however, Hɔmɔwɔ and other indigenous festivals were the embodiment of African religiosity and its diabolical essence and had to be kept in check until they would naturally disappear with the spread of Christianity.

Although British residents of Ghana celebrated Christian holidays with great pomp and show, traditional festivities required the approval of the colonial administration, which could be obtained only by written application. In accordance with the 1892 Native Customs Ordinance 11.3, "the celebration of the native customs known as 'Yam Custom,' 'Black Christmas' or 'Kuntum' without the permission in writing of the district Commissioner" was prohibited in the major towns of the colony, including Accra. The records of the secretary for native affairs at the National Archives of Ghana house an impressive collection of permit applications from chiefs and ritual authorities. The applications invariably specify the purpose, the exact date, the duration, and the location of the event. In 1895, for instance, the district commissioner of Accra granted the chiefs of Christiansborg permission to drum for two days from 6 a.m. to 6 p.m. in celebration of their annual custom dedicated to a deity that presided over the lagoon and fishing areas.[20] On another occasion in 1909, Mantsɛ Tackie Obile petitioned Secretary of Native Affairs W. C. Robertson to lift the prohibition on performing Sibi Saba and Ashiko dances, which had been banned on the pretext that they encouraged immorality and debauchery.[21] The punishment for violating the directives and celebrating without a permit was imprisonment "for a term not exceeding three months or to a fine not exceeding twenty-five pounds" (Griffith 1903, 658–59). This was an enormous sum at the time, roughly the value of two cows in England. The penalty is all the more absurd when one considers that the raucous commemoration of Christian holidays and British national celebrations was a common practice.

Mhoze Chikowero has developed a credible argument regarding the regulated yet continuous presence of traditional festivities in colonial Africa. He suggests that by staging and (re-)creating the dances, the colonial government reproduced and reinforced the distance between the colonizer and the colonized while deepening domestic divisions (Chikowero 2015, 132). Each year, the *mantsɛmɛi* (chiefs) from across the Ga traditional area were obligated to appeal to the Accra district commissioner for the right to perform dances in connection with Hɔmɔwɔ or other major customs, a requirement that reinforced their subordinate status and drew attention to the allegedly questionable nature of traditional celebrations that required the permission of the colonial state. This was in addition to the damage the restrictions did to the integrity of Ga communities and their lifeworlds. An outline of the role of Hɔmɔwɔ in Ga cosmology illustrates the gravity of the matter. Hɔmɔwɔ is the principal Ga celebration that not only provides merriment and entertainment but also cleanses the community of evil and sin, regenerates familial bonds, and reinforces sociopolitical hierarchies (Field 1937; Kilson 2013; Odotei 2002). It is the time when the deceased ancestors (*blematsɛmɛi*) and the *jemawɔji* are remembered and invited to partake in the festival meal of *kpoikpoi* (Gyimah 1985, 120).[22] Since Hɔmɔwɔ "is the quintessential celebration of Ga ethnic identity" and a ceremony common to all six Ga townships, its successful implementation—with the timely and unabridged performance of each of its components—is absolutely critical (Kilson 2013, 92). Both "punitive legal measures" and "widely shared social norms" used to manage various religious sounds, writes Isaac Weiner (2014, 3), serve the purpose of constraining the communities that produce them. Given the weight of Christianity as the ideological foundation of the colonial enterprise, it would be an oversight not to interpret the sonic restrictions imposed on Ga practices as an official affirmation of Christianity's acoustic dominance.

The discriminatory circulation of drumming permits in favor of the British and a select few educated natives not only bolstered a hierarchy of acoustic communities based on their religious affiliation (Weiner 2014, 23) but were also an assault on Ga cosmology. In a 1907 appeal to the colonial administration, Mantsɛ Tackie Obile explained that "without the performance of the [Lakum] custom the Homowo season [would] never be considered as over."[23] The execution of certain dances and rituals has a metaphysical significance, as it brings the previous year to a close and welcomes a fresh beginning for the community. Permissions that were granted in response to such appeals rarely fulfilled the ritual requirements, often jeopardizing the spiritual harmony of the Ga community. For instance, in 1886, the governor of Christiansborg did not allow the chiefs of Osu to celebrate their annual custom on a Sunday, as was customary, and instead moved the occasion to a Tuesday in order to accommodate the visit of an important political figure.[24] Although the source does not chronicle the consequences of this adjustment, we know that certain days of the week have special significance in the Ga ritual calendar, as they are associated with individual deities or major events of the lunar year.

The list of restrictions on the Ga community in response to Tackie Obile's application for a Hɔmɔwɔ celebration permit in 1891 included the following:

1 No drumming except one large tomtom;
2 No exhibition in public streets of indecent symbols;
3 No passing from Usher Town to James Town;
4 No firing;
5 No procession.[25]

Meticulous adherence to the ritual directives—the use of a specific number of drums, elaborate outfits for the participating priestesses, processions, and carefully planned routes—are decisive for maintaining a rewarding reciprocal relationship with the *jemawɔji* and the ancestors. Thus, the seemingly insignificant changes the British administration introduced would have had unfavorable reverberations for the Ga community that affected the crop yield, health, and fertility.

Even at this time, one can find instances where the colonial state or local communities deliberately reframed traditional rituals as either cultural or pseudo-Christian events in order to smooth the way for their public presence. Newspapers also report occasions when Christmas was celebrated with "native dances perambulating the streets," an intimation that expressions of traditional culture were still condoned in certain contexts.[26] As we will see later, the independent Ghanaian state continued this culturalist approach by propelling the decorative and entertaining dimensions of traditional festivities outside the category of religion and into the realm of culture. But as in the colonial context, the culturalization of traditional lifeworlds proved to be a powerful tool in the hands of individual communities for negotiating the public presence and continued relevance of their practices.

There Is Something about the Drum:
An Implement of Peace and Chaos

As we saw above, Ordinance 12 on public nuisances prohibited drums, gongs, and tomtoms—the most common local instruments used in the production of traditional music. In the public nuisance ordinances enacted a decade later, however, there was a curious focus on drums as the primary source of nuisance: "Whoever beats a drum with intent to challenge or provoke any other person to commit a breach of the peace or with intent to insult or annoy any other person, shall be liable to a fine of twenty-five pounds or to imprisonment for three months" (Ordinance 12, Section 121, Griffith 1903, 729–30). If all traditional instruments played an equally important role in the production of sound, why did Ordinance 15 single out the drum as a source of communal provocation? I argue that culturally specific attributes of the drum were instrumental in its designation as the most menacing source of aurality and as a powerful political agent in the colonial period. I focus on two qualities of the instrument: its status as what Birgit Meyer (2006b, 29) calls the "sensational form" of mediation between Ga worshippers and transcendent reality and its demonization as a pagan symbol that was antithetical to the Christian doctrine, a treatment that stems from its potential as a sensational form of mediation. It follows that contemporary clashes over the violation of ritual restrictions on drumming reflect a long-standing consensus among Christians that this particular form of sound production is inherently controversial.

It is no coincidence that drumming always accompanies festivals in Ghana, the primary platforms for dispute resolution, forgiveness, communal revival, and cultural innovation. The drum is conspicuous at all major social events, except for those occasions when the *jemawɔji* specifically demand a seasonal halt to mundane life. Although various other sounds were incorporated in the sonic prohibitions imposed on Accra prior to Hɔmɔwɔ, drumming was the only constant in such laws, possibly because it carries the most weight as a powerful emblem of communal solidarity and an instrument of mediation with the *jemawɔji*. Most notably, the special drums used in the ritual context possess a worldmaking potential (Meyer 2013) greater than any other religious media because they mediate between human and nonhuman worlds (Rattray 1923; Blacking 1973; Nketia 1974). When the drums announce the ban on drumming, they call the *jemawɔji* down to the human realm to work on the gestation of the planted millet. A chief drummer of Nungua, a Ga community outside Accra, explained the special relationship between the *jemawɔji* and drumming by emphasizing that drums invoke the spirits and condition them to enter (*bote*) human beings by pulling them down (*gbala*).[27] Each deity typically has its own set of songs and a preferred genre of music that incites it to mount the priest medium who is dedicated to its shrine (Manoukian 1950, 95; Nketia 1964, 266). Moses Nii Dortey, an ethnomusicologist specializing in Ga music, postulates that it is due to the drum's distinct capacity to transmit messages to and from the *jemawɔji* that Ga ritual music does not accommodate change. If a drummer diverges from the classical pattern, the respective *jemawɔŋ* will immediately alert him through its devoted medium. I have witnessed this control mechanism in action at various ritual dances I attended across Ga townships: sensing when the music was off target, the relevant priest medium would adroitly approach the drummers and correct them with either standardized dance moves or rhythmic cues.

As a mediator between the human and nonhuman worlds, an instrument that speaks the language of the gods, the drum holds a special place in the Ga pantheon. I have been told on several occasions that individual drums represent various *jemawɔji*. For instance, *oboade*, the largest of the three drums engaged in the production of Ga ritual music (Kpele music in local terms) epitomizes the voice of the supreme god, Ataa Naa Nyɔŋmɔ (Nii-Dortey 2012, 94). The deferential treatment of the drum is further evidence of its superior status. Ritual drums are kept out of sight in special spaces where they are safe from contamination. Before they are brought out for annual customs, they are bathed in a mixture of protective substances and are dressed in medicinal leaves. In addition, only ritually certified individuals who have been purified for the purpose are allowed to handle the sacred instrument (149–50). Consequently, unsanctioned seizure of the drum or its suppression by outside authorities, especially secular administrators, could pollute the sacred ceremonies or even sever the link between the visible and invisible worlds.

Besides their central function in ritual occasions, drums were also a key implement in the enstoolment and destoolment of various community figures within the traditional system of authority. The police commonly confiscated drums during the process of enstoolment, which ultimately meant that the appointment was not finalized.[28] In parallel with their world-making potential, drums thus served as a crucial source of social organization and a means of consolidating communal boundaries (Oosterbaan 2009). This quality of music and musical instruments is widely recognized in other religious contexts. The Sufi bandir drum, for example, became an emblem of the schism between the Tijani and Qadiri orders in Kano, Nigeria, beginning in the mid-twentieth century. The Qadiri community of Kano capitalized on bandir-led recitation of prayers and sacred verses, *dhikr,* to announce its presence in the city and attract young followers, an innovation that the Tijanis harshly condemned (Loimeier 1997, 59–61). In a more contemporary context, Martijn Oosterbaan's (2009) work

FIGURE I.I. The Ga ritual drums prepared for a ceremony. Photo by author. 2016.

focuses on the synergy of music and urbanity in the favelas of Rio de Janeiro and its role in the production of aurally delineated spaces. In all of these scenarios, music functions as an attribute of power in the production of a new communal profile or the consolidation of an old one in the face of competition.

In accordance with Ordinance 15, the drum had the potential to not only breach the public peace but also to challenge, provoke, insult, or annoy another person (Griffith 1903). The application of the instrument in customary enstoolment ceremonies is an obvious example of how it could challenge the authority of a newly appointed chief or provoke members of an opposing social faction. But how could drumming insult anyone? In his critical exploration of musical practices in Canadian First Nations communities, Dylan Robinson (2020, 10) captures the invisibility of colonial "listening positionalities," meaning the listening biases and abilities we possess, by articulating them as "unmarked structures" rather than singular events that enact epistemic violence through their displacement of indigenous modes of being. The racialized sensory regime discussed earlier is one of these unmarked structures that not only pronounces that drumming is displeasing to the ear but also identifies it as a menace to the soul. The frequent debates about the permissibility of native music in churches and the data British colonial ethnographers collected lead me to believe that colonial administrators were aware of the role of drums in indigenous epistemology.[29] Indeed, drums were the first to be listed among the "tribal emblems" of the

1892 Native Customs Ordinance, along with "bell[s], head-dress[es], stool[s], figure[s], badge[s], fetish charm[s], or other thing[s] having a symbolic meaning" (Griffith 1903, 658). In view of this, the interdiction of drumming was part of a deliberate strategy to undermine the Ga lifeworld.

In epistemological terms, the prohibition of drumming echoes the tensions between material and immaterial economies of representation central to the formation of Western modernity against which the colonies were assessed. Let us not forget that the mentalistic approach of Protestantism privileged the immaterial side of religion—beliefs, ideas, and so forth—over its material and ritualistic expressions, which Protestants considered superfluous and crude (Meyer 2012; Orsi 2016). The British colonial enterprise promoted a Protestant-flavored knowledge and sensory regime in which the drum could not serve as a legitimate form of mediation (Meyer 2011; Eisenlohr 2011; Engelke 2010). When an individual is entrenched in a sensory regime and its corresponding ideologies, they are conditioned to receive and acknowledge sonic signals that are meaningful within the given cultural context. Jennifer Stoever (2016) refers to such a bodily orientation to sonality as the "embodied ear," or how "individuals' listening practices are shaped by the totality of their experiences, historical context, and physicality, as well as intersecting subject positions and particular interactions with power" (14). By this logic, the rejection of the drum as a physical form of mediation may have translated into the inability of Europeans, and to some extent of Christian converts, to perceive and appreciate the value of drumming in cross-world exchange. Inaudition, J. Martin Daughtry (2015) argues, is "an intentional decision or unconscious ability to not recognize or acknowledge a sound that is physically audible" (322). It would seem, then, that colonial restrictions on drumming did not simply stem from a desire to curb the sociopolitical capacity of Ga ceremonies or to deliberately assault their cosmology. While these factors were clearly present, sensory analysis would also suggest that those who had adopted the "British ear" were unable to comprehend the sacred function of the drum since they were operating within their own normalized system of sonic production in which the drum and other indigenous instruments could not establish a connection to the transcendent. To avoid falling into the structuralist approach that ascribes a sight-oriented sensory metamorphosis to post-Enlightenment Europe and enchanted musicality to Africa (Schmidt 2000), we should maintain a nuanced outlook and emphasize that the world of aurality and other senses depends on culturally distinct epistemological meanings that are seldom universal (Gautier 2014). Simply put, while culturally attuned bodies may invest certain sounds with power, these associations are situational and negotiable rather than comprehensive. What we have, then, is what David Howes would call a multiplicity of sensory intelligences that are pliable and responsive to the sociocultural circumstances in which they operate (Howes 1991). When we consider the unrest engendered by the tremendous musicality of Pentecostal/Charismatic congregations in subsequent chapters, we will also explore how discord over animate sounds can develop between parties of not only contrasting but also analogous sensory intelligences.

State-driven acoustic control was first introduced in Accra with the establishment of the Gold Coast colony. Much like its counterparts in other parts of the world, the Gold Coast's noise-control initiative was disguised as a public-oriented intervention designed to enhance the well-being of citizens. In practice, it targeted lower-class Gold Coast residents and constricted their lifestyles and beliefs. Today's ban on drumming and noise making represents a curious inversion of the long-established power dynamics inherent in noise-abatement technologies. Whereas in the early colonial discourse, secular and Christian registers were fused to form the "progressive" sensory order that was juxtaposed against the "backward" sound of "heathenism," in the present context the secular register is blended with Ga sensibilities that are then mobilized against the noise of the most modern Christian movement. Indeed, as I demonstrate later in the book, by the end of the twentieth century, the Ga community had effectively domesticated noise-control strategies in the context of the Hɔmɔwɔ festival, exerting authority over Accra, particularly against the encroachment of Pentecostal/Charismatic churches. We will see how the policing of religious noise acquired new protagonists across multiple historical eras, culminating in the unexpected sonic triumph of the Ga in the modern secular state of Ghana.

2. Winds of Change

The Ban on Drumming Enters the Public Sphere

Postindependence Ghana was far less preoccupied with managing the aural affairs of its urban enclaves than the colonial state had been. Understandably, the ruling Convention People's Party and its successors poured all their efforts into establishing political and economic institutions that would function autonomously. At the same time, reinforcing a national self-awareness that would serve as the scaffolding for the newly born institutions was the ideological priority. Keeping up with this trend, the public media also shifted its gaze to more pressing issues. These circumstances ensured that until the 1980s, the ban on drumming was rarely the focus of public discourse. But in the 1990s, it reappeared with a vengeance. By the end of that decade, the restriction on sound introduced as part of the Hɔmɔwɔ festival had emerged as the source of a disagreement that spread like wildfire in Accra between Ga traditionalists and churches that subscribed to born-again theology. In this chapter, I offer a brief look at the postindependence evolution of the ban on drumming from a custom performed in the Ga community that was rarely challenged to a matter of national concern that the media publicized as the Drum Wars.

My conclusions regarding the historical depth of the ritual transformation in question are drawn from the most widely read daily newspaper in Ghana, the state-owned *Daily Graphic*. During my fieldwork in Accra, I rented a small apartment in Adabraka near the Public Records and Archives Administration Department of Ghana. On days when I did not have interviews, I spent long hours poring over every issue of the *Daily Graphic* available in the archival records, hoping to discover patterns in the changing public disposition toward the ritual prohibition on noise making. I was particularly interested in the frequency and scope of media coverage and in the terminology used to discuss the prohibition. True to my expectations, I discovered that both the ban on drumming and the Hɔmɔwɔ festival developed into matters of public concern at a measured, subtle pace in the 1980s. But in the late 1990s, they rapidly escalated as Accra diversified in terms of culture and religion.

In our conversations, ritual specialists who are responsible for the orchestration of Hɔmɔwɔ maintained that the Ga people had adhered to the ban on drumming for centuries, since the day they migrated to the present-day area of Accra or even before, when they still inhabited the distant lands of ancient Israel or Egypt. Reports of the ban are scarce in colonial and precolonial sources. On the rare occasions when they do appear, they are presented in the form of succinct and sober newspaper announcements from the turn of the twentieth century. One example is an 1899 statement in the general news section of the *Gold Coast Chronicle* alerting the public to certain sonic restrictions imposed "in pursuance of the usual Custom": "There will be no drumming or blowing of horns in the town of Accra for about 6 weeks from today until the guinea corn planted for the yam custom is fully grown."[1]

This announcement does not reference the name of the sonic restriction that came to be known as the ban on drumming and it does not elaborate on the specifics of the prohibition. The ban on drumming was also not conspicuous in defining interfaith relations in the early twentieth-century Accra. We know of only two occasions prior to Ghana's declaration of independence when the ritual provision caused tension between Christians and the Ga community members. Kwabena J. Amanor recounts an incident in 1948 when young Ga men interrupted a worship session at an Apostolic church located in the La neighborhood of Accra. The intruders allegedly seized drums, tambourines, and a bass guitar used in the service. Only after the pastor identified himself as a native of La, and thus a person of Ga origin, did the chief of the area agree to release the confiscated items, but he did so with a stern warning that the ban on drumming would have to be respected in the future. A few years later, in 1953, a newly established Apostolic church in Teshie was damaged by Ga youth following a breach of the ban. Once again, the attackers impounded instruments and communion paraphernalia and destroyed some of the church's religious pamphlets (Amanor 2009, 132). These two episodes were mild compared to the intensity and number of collisions between the two groups beginning in the late 1990s. The scarcity of such encounters until the last decade of the twentieth century suggests that either the ban on drumming carried significantly less disciplinary weight in its early days or it was normally observed and thus required little intervention on the part of the Ga. This chapter examines the pull of various interrelated factors in the increased observance and popularization of Hɔmɔwɔ toward the end of the twentieth century by focusing on the transformation of associated discourses in the *Daily Graphic* between the announcement of Ghana's independence in 1957 and the first instances of the Drum Wars in 1998.

Drumming Will Greet Us Home: Drums as a Symbol of Culture

The early media discourse on drumming can be classified into two broad frameworks.[2] On the one hand, as discussed in chapter 1, because of its intimate association with traditional religion, drumming was one of the controversial practices that the media reevaluated in the light of the proliferating Christian world view. On the other hand, it came to be celebrated as part of the national heritage in the course of anticolonial and national independence movements, a heritage that had to be cherished and preserved for the sake of fashioning a genuinely African identity. Both of these approaches grappled with the cultural and spiritual weight of the drum in postindependence Ghana, yet neither paid particular heed to drumming as a means of sound production, an attribute that would come to the fore in the era of the Drum Wars.

The incorporation of the drum in the "tribal emblems" outlined in the Native Customs section of the 1892 Gold Coast Ordinance illustrates the extent to which the instrument was imagined as a constituent of a traditional lifestyle and in particular of traditional religiosity, which colonizers saw as the enemy of Christianity (Griffith 1903). The drum's status as a key implement in traditional ritual practice largely determined its elimination from the Christian musical repertoire throughout the nineteenth century. Kwabena Nketia (1974) notes that "the Church's evangelists preached against African cultural practices while promoting Western cultural values and usages. [The Church] adopted a hostile attitude to African music, especially to drumming, because this was associated with what seemed to Christian evangelists 'pagan' practices" (14–15). Whether drums should be permitted in Christian worship became a matter of contestation as the number of mission-trained Africans proliferated in the Gold Coast at the turn of the twentieth century. The debate was part of a broader discussion about the place of African cultural forms in Christianity, including libation pouring, festivals, dress, and music (Atiemo 2006b). Educated African Christians such as Rev. Samuel Attoh Ahumah and John Mensah Sarbah took issue with the idea that African identity was at odds with an individual's ability to be a good Christian (Ahumah 1911, 40; Sarbah 1906, 256).

The determination to encourage and celebrate African pronouncements of Christian devotion found its expression in the so-called African Initiated Churches,[3] popularly known in Ghana as *sunsum sorè* (spiritual churches). These churches celebrated African custom and world view, reconciling Christian and African identities. The strong puritanical ethics and shunning of traditional ritual praxis associated with witchcraft that was typical of the African Initiated Churches was countervailed by an embrace of African music and dress that the mission churches dismissed. Even with the active promotion of African lifestyles by these increasingly popular churches, however, controversies over the admissibility of certain expressions of African identity among Christian converts persisted well into the second half of the twentieth century as proponents of Africanized Christianity confronted those who advocated for precise replication of a Western style of worship. Christians who favored a "classical" liturgy, which simply meant a Western Christian liturgy, denounced the drum for its capacity to distort their moral habitus by exciting the spirit and prompting emotional behavior.[4]

The adjustments introduced by the Second Vatican Council and the establishment of the All Africa Conference of Churches in 1963 accelerated the process of indigenization in mainline churches, especially since they actively promoted the continental particularities of Christianity. Ghanaian clergy from traditional denominations began to push back against the demonization of cultural practices. In 1973, Rev. Peter Kwasi Sarpong, the Catholic bishop of Ashanti and Brong-Ahafo, called for a reexamination of "aspects of Ghanaian culture" in order to incorporate them into Christian worship.[5] A few years later, in 1977, a Catholic priest from St. Peter's Cathedral in Kumasi was reported to have denounced the early missionaries' downgrading of expressions of "the culture of the people" such as libation pouring, drumming, and festivals, arguing that branding these practices as satanic and ungodly was tantamount to denying the birthrights of

Ghanaians.[6] These shifts in attitude led to the incorporation of drumming into the services of some mainline churches. Finding that the drum was closer to "the African spirit," proponents of drumming saw it as a source of elation in the otherwise dull musical repertoire of conventional Christian worship. Others deemed drumming, dancing, and clapping as lesser evils compared to the pouring of libations and polygamy, which were associated with "the enemies of the cause of Christ" and regarded as the worship of "familiar spirits," an abomination in biblical terms.[7] Amid the burgeoning discourse of decolonization and self-determination that prevailed among the elites in the second half of the twentieth century, drum-heavy services also became more widely associated with political resistance to the psychological dimension of colonialism that dehumanized African culture.

Apart from Christian institutions, questions regarding the merits of drumming and libation pouring were salient in the postindependence discourse on heritage and culture that emerged in tandem with the decreased focus on Christianity at the level of national consciousness during the period when Kwame Nkrumah promoted scientific socialism (Assimeng 1995, 5). Much like other African politicians of the time, Nkrumah articulated a vision of an African society that thrived on a dynamic unity of traditional ways of life, Islamic traditions, and Euro-Christian traditions (Botwe-Asamoah 2005, 42). He called this new philosophy Consciencism, arguing that it would ensure the "harmonious growth and development" of society (Nkrumah 1970, 70). By incorporating precolonial cultural and historical achievements in the contemporary lives of Africans, Ghana's first president sought to re-historicize the continent. In practice, this meant promoting and restoring African indigenous forms of cultural expression at the national level, but because Nkrumah feared transferring too much political and social power to traditional chiefs who might vie for local influence, his cultural policies remained largely inchoate and selective (Coe 2005, 61). In an attempt to create a uniquely Ghanaian set of national symbols in order to disentangle the country from its British past, his administration conceptualized national culture as an essentially homogeneous amalgam of ethnic elements, an approach that led to the increased showcasing of traditional attire and artistic performances taken out of their symbolic context (Hess 2001; Yankah 1985). "The valuable aspects of the diverse cultures of Ghana were to be identified, recovered, and re-presented in the frame of a national heritage style," suggest de Witte and Meyer (2012), which "entailed a strong preponderance of Akan culture" (47). Nkrumah was particularly fond of incorporating drumming and dancing into important political events for a uniquely Ghanaian festive flavor.[8] He also adopted royal insignias representative of Akan chieftaincy and priesthood; he is known to have appeared in public with a white cloth, carrying a horsetail and a linguist's staff. He would also pour a libation and offer prayers at memorial services or state functions (Botwe-Asamoah 2005, 120–21). A captivating black-and-white photograph from a 1963 issue of the *Daily Graphic* depicts him holding a bottle of gin and pouring the liquid on the ground with a face of utter concentration. The caption reads "To the Gods . . . ," referring to the invocation of blessings from the gods for the speedy completion of the Akosombo Dam.[9] By contrast, the saturation of public spaces with Christian symbolic markers in the contemporary context has made it unthinkable for political leaders to be seen with a bottle of a libation drink lest they be associated with idol worship.

Cultural gems like drumming and libation maintained their luster during the era of the National Liberation Council (1966–1969) through their incorporation into national celebrations. News reports from the 1960s are rife with stories of ritual specialists pouring libations either to cleanse areas associated with misfortune or to thank deities for effective realization of various construction projects. Upon the completion of the headquarters of the Indigenous Diamond Mining Company in 1968, for instance, Sakumɔ Wulɔmɔ Numo Komme Otsiata II poured a libation to secure the success of the venture.[10] Since most large-scale initiatives were located in Accra, special occasions warranted the presence of ritual specialists from the Ga community, the official guardians of the Accra lands, as mandated by custom.

A rapid succession of governments in the following years significantly stalled the nation-building project and the promotion of national culture. Throughout the 1970s, military and civilian regimes showed a preference for Western liberal capitalist models (Shipley 2015; Schauert 2015). However, another shift in the country's equilibrium occurred in the early 1980s when Jerry John Rawlings returned to power. Rawlings's rigorous cultural programming aimed at rebuilding national pride signaled a renaissance of the traditional belief system. He resuscitated Nkrumah's policy of cultural nationalism, Sankofa, which would be further developed in the 1990s under the auspices of the National Commission on Culture (NCC). Advocating a return to traditional roots, Sankofa recognized traditional religions, customs, and structures of authority as the fountainhead of authentic African identity (Coe 2005; Meyer 1999; Meyer 2015; de Witte 2004). In 1988, a *Daily Graphic* contributor described Sankofa as an attempt to "dig into" the past to expose "ideas, practices, and innovations" that would "give meaning to the African Identity and provide a momentum for socio-economic development."[11] The Afrikania Mission, a neo-traditional movement that advanced traditional beliefs by polishing and modernizing their content, was an embodiment of the new cultural turn (de Witte 2004, 2005).[12] Although Kwame Nkrumah was the initial mastermind behind the cultural revival project that flourished in the hands of the NCC in the 1990s, it could be argued that it was Jerry Rawlings's political party, the National Democratic Congress, that gave a prominent national presence to traditional festivals and to drumming and dancing. Rawlings met regularly with chiefs and tasked the NCC and allied agencies with conducting consultations to determine the right "content, orientation and direction of the nation's culture."[13] As part of the endeavor to instill African pride in the younger generation, cultural studies were incorporated in the school curriculum in the framework of the Cultural Enrichment Program (Coe 2005). So strong was the spirit of cultural affirmation in the 1980s that the Ghana Education Services announced a plan to use drums instead of bells to announce recess in schools. Commenting on the initiative, the Greater Accra regional director of education, Mr. Yegbe, argued that because the country's cultural values were embodied in songs, drumming, and dancing, it was particularly important to promote them.[14]

State-level championing of national festivals and traditional religions went hand in hand with the altered status of chiefs, who promoted their own cultural agendas. The 1992 Constitution endorsed the cultural import of chiefs but attempted to push them out of the domain of political decision-making by framing their role as nonpartisan and apolitical. This shift in the legislative status of chieftaincy coincided with a period of economic adversity in Ghana that demanded a different response from traditional leaders. Increasingly, local communities expected their chiefs to demonstrate business acumen and an entrepreneurial spirit to garner the material resources that NGOs and international organizations, which had become increasingly active in the public sphere, were eager to provide. As a consequence, throughout the 1990s, traditional governance systems gradually reshaped themselves to complement the emphasis on "development" that the state encouraged and that was bolstered by international funding. This ensuing breed of *nkɔsuohene*, or "development/progress chiefs" and queen mothers, as George B. Bob-Milliar (2009) aptly categorizes them, made significant contributions to community development.

The projects that were implemented had a strong cultural component and complemented the state's efforts to elevate festivals into tourist events designed for consumption by both Ghanaian residents and members of the diaspora. As in previous decades, these initiatives maintained a narrow focus on drumming and dancing as the core dimensions of cultural identity. While the majority relished the entertainment-centered interpretation of culture, a significant portion of the population argued that culture was greater than the watered-down rendering that had taken root in the public domain and instead proposed a more holistic vision that encompassed the "people's view of life."[15]

Opinion pieces from the *Daily Graphic* articulated this indignation over the shallowness of cultural display programs:

> The very noticeable, yet rather superficial aspects of Ghanaian culture, nowadays often amateurishly displayed at so-called cultural events, are not culture.
>
> Culture is in our heads, our hands and feet. It is thought and habit. We carry it with us wherever we go. It is not the artifact, the carving, the painting or weaving as such, but what makes us produce it that is culture.[16]

The key point of contention was that "culture on display" represented a disembodied rendering of individual elements of communal self-expression rather than an interconnected web of ever-changing practices and ways of thinking that determined how a group inhabited the world. It would be fair to say that the late twentieth-century cultural policies largely continued the colonial project of inventing tradition, producing an objectified model of indigenous belief and practice that was frozen in time (Ranger 1983). Nonetheless, it is also fitting to suppose that these same policies contributed to the projection of Hɔmɔwɔ and a set of associated customs beyond the plane of Ga communal memory and onto the national scene. How this projection continued to embed traditional religions in the realm of tradition and Christianity in the domain of modernity is a key question that will be discussed in more detail in the following chapters.

"Those days it was really, really observed": Memories from the Past

One bright morning in September 2017, I was sitting in the office of Daniel Lankai Lawson, the newly appointed second minister at the Ebenezer Presbyterian Church. Located in the heart of the Osu Traditional Area, Osu Presby, as the locals call it, was formerly known as the Basel Mission Church of Christiansborg. Founded in 1847 by the Basel Evangelical Missionary Society, it is one of the oldest mainline churches in the area. It has an active community outreach and numerous followers from the ranks of Ga traditionalists. Born and raised in Osu, Daniel Lankai Lawson has vivid memories of observing the ban on drumming when he was growing up in the 1970s: "When I was growing up, in my family when there was a ban on noise and drumming, they would tell me you can't even whistle. We were young, it was like there is absolutely no noise. You can't play music loud, you can't talk loud, you can't clap, you can't play any music in church. Those days, they even were not using drums much. When it started, 'today the corn has been sown,' we say in Ga, 'adu ŋmaa'; once it is done, it is absolutely noiseless. Those days it was really, really observed."[17]

This narrative confirms my conclusion that prior to the wave of Pentecostalization (Gifford 2004; Asamoah-Gyadu 2005a), pre-Hɔmɔwɔ ritual prohibitions of various kinds were obeyed in Accra without much resistance.[18] In addition to the sociopolitical transformations of the Fourth Republic, the weakened deference to Ga ritual prescriptions is evidence of a tug-of-war between multiple epistemologies that was accelerated by the secularization and Pentecostalization of the public sphere. Rev. Lawson told me that there was little need to plaster the neighborhood with noise-abatement warnings when he was a child because every member of the community had an almost instinctive bodily awareness of the city's sonic seasons. This brings us back to the sensory positionalities discussed in chapter 1 and the idea that our "sensory responsiveness," to use Charles Hirschkind's (2006, 112) term, is an ability that is often cultivated in a communal context. The heightened controversies associated with the proliferation of Charismatic churches were provoked not only by individual acts of transgression but also, and more importantly, by a systematic assault on the Ga sensory ontology carried out by Pentecostal/Charismatic Christians. "You know," Rev. Lawson told me in a calm and cautious manner, "the charismatic churches make a lot of noise. Let me not use 'noise' . . . they use a lot of sound, and the sound sometimes is very loud. So when the charismatic churches started, that's when it became an issue."[19]

Lawson's designation of the emergence of Pentecostal/Charismatic churches in Accra's religious marketplace as a watershed event in the city's interfaith relations could be attributable to his Ga background. But it is also evidence of covert interdenominational tensions within Christianity. In fact, representatives of mainline churches I spoke with typically had no qualms about expressing their distaste for the sound of Pentecostal/Charismatic denominations. To a degree, their sensory disposition revealed their precarity and distress in the face of the unprecedented popularity of the newer denominations. More importantly, however, it revealed their alignment with middle-class concepts of moral discipline and self-control, symbolized by visual order and sonic temperance in public spaces (Payer 2007, 774). If anything, the Ga advocacy of quiet in the pre-festival period was more in line with the sober sensory predilections of mainline churches than with the loud sonic outpouring of Pentecostal/Charismatic congregations.

Although Hɔmɔwɔ-induced friction reached its peak in the late 1990s, my conversations with older Accra natives disclosed earlier signs of the forthcoming muddying of intercommunal waters. Shortly before concluding my fieldwork in the spring of 2018, I made an unanticipated discovery. I had heard from some of my friends in Jamestown that Faith Evangelical Mission in Osu was one of the congregations involved in the notorious Drum Wars. I also knew from word of mouth that the church was led by Bishop Rex Noi, who had eventually succeeded in smoothing out relations with the traditionalists and had become close friends with Sakumɔ Wulɔmɔ Numo Ogbamey III, one of the traditional priests who had made a name for himself by inciting attacks on Pentecostal/Charismatic churches. Determined to find out more from Bishop Noi but unable to get hold of him, I located Faith Evangelical Mission on Google Maps and paid them a visit. Bishop Noi, as I would find out, had recently passed away, but Pastor Prince Bochway, whom I met at the church, was kind enough to speak to me about the ban on drumming incident. It turns out that the friction developed in the late 1970s rather than in the 1990s, when the majority of similar conflicts took place. This meant that I was hearing a firsthand account of one of the earliest acoustic clashes in Osu. Pastor Bochway told me that the traditionalists had paid them more than one visit during that fateful Hɔmɔwɔ season. Once, they were having a service and he admitted that the music was quite loud. The second time, however, the service had not yet even started:

> A group of people invaded our premises, including the Sakumɔ wulɔmɔ. They collected our musical instruments. We wrote a memorandum to then president of this country, Acheampong, and they did not pay attention to us. Then we took the matter to the police station. They did not pay attention to us either. So our late chief, Bishop Rex Noi, asked us to leave everything and commit everything to God. In fact, people wanted to get us new instruments but Rex said no, we should commit everything to God. And we started praying. Low and behold, the then Ga mantsɛ sent for us.[20]

Pastor Bochway told me that it was God's intervention that brought the matter to the attention of the Ga mantsɛ, who ordered his subordinates to return the confiscated instruments. Following Bishop Noi's instructions, the congregation prayed three times a day until the matter was finally settled. Since then, the church has adhered to the pre-Hɔmɔwɔ sonic regulations and, in return, has had no further issues with the Ga community.

This scenario follows the same pattern, albeit with a more favorable resolution, as numerous other encounters between the traditionalists and representatives of Charismatic Christian churches that occurred at the end of the twentieth century. The story of Faith Evangelical Mission deserves special mention, however, since at the time of the tensions in the late 1970s, representatives of Ga religion were not yet routinely wrangling with Pentecostal/Charismatic leaders over social status and authority. Apostle Samuel Yaw Antwi, the former general secretary of the Ghana Pentecostal and Charismatic Council, remembers growing up in the 1960s and 1970s, when people had just started to convert to Charismatic Christianity en masse. "The Pentecostal churches would attack traditional religion in those times—the falseness of tradition," he admitted with regret. "It got to the point that they got government somehow interested in that."[21] Apostle Antwi is convinced that Jerry John Rawlings's policy aimed at the advancement of traditional religions in the 1980s, especially the popularization of the neo-traditional Afrikania Mission, was a reaction to the unfair treatment of indigenous beliefs by newer Christian denominations. While it is hard to know whether Rawlings's cultural project of Sankofa was specifically designed to protect traditional religions, its revolutionary anti-imperialist spirit prioritized the promotion of African authenticity over imported forms of evangelical Christianity.

Another record of early opposition to the ban on drumming can be found in the work of Cynthia Gyimah, whose PhD dissertation focused on the Ga Hɔmɔwɔ festival. Gyimah recounts witnessing the Church of Pentecost file a lawsuit in the High Court against the Ga *mantsɛ* and the Ga Traditional Council for organizing a group that allegedly vandalized the church because of their use of drums. She writes in a footnote, however, that according to rumors, church members had provoked the traditionalists by "organizing a procession, drumming and dancing around certain 'sacred places'" (Gyimah 1985, 96–97). This account is consistent with the assertions of many of my interlocutors that Pentecostal/Charismatic churches, unlike mainline churches, deliberately harassed and offended traditional communities with their insensitive and accusatory comments or by consciously transgressing sacrosanct ritual regulations. The transgression recorded here also deserves special attention because of its embodied and acoustic scope, which, in contrast to discursive denigration, targeted not only human representatives of the Ga community but also its nonhuman members who inhabited the desecrated spaces.

These developments cannot be divorced from the socioeconomic shifts that transformed Accra from the 1980s onward. Two controversial economic recovery programs that Rawlings launched did little to alleviate the plight of average Ghanaians and heightened the allure of Pentecostal/Charismatic churches that had recently been reinvigorated by the American evangelical movement (Gocking 2005, 201). The years of curfew (1982–1984) and heavy taxes on the entertainment industry under Rawlings pared down the leisure scene in Accra (Gifford 2004, 35). With drinking spots and discos no longer an option, young people flocked to gospel revivals and crusades. "You got a generation of people who would come to church to dance and be happy because you could not get it outside of the church," explains Kwabena Opuni-Frimpong, the former general secretary of the Christian Council of Ghana.[22] Pentecostal/Charismatic ranks swelled rapidly throughout the 1980s as migrants from around the country settled in the capital in search of work opportunities. Born-again churches founded by Ghanaian pastors trained by the internationally renowned Nigerian preacher Benson Idahosa catered to these newcomers by offering a sense of community built on hope for a better future. The promise of upward mobility and material success delivered with a large serving of entertainment proved to be irresistible (Atiemo 2006a). Once the media were liberalized after the 1992 elections, there was no stopping the movement. Against the backdrop of the declining cultural momentum of Sankofa, Accra's public spaces and popular discourse experienced a rapid wave of Pentecostalization.

The Ga community found itself in an ambiguous position. On the one hand, as the caretakers of Accra's lands, its members felt emboldened to assert their authority. On the other hand, in the midst of the rapidly changing religious marketplace, they were being squeezed out of networks of material and symbolic capital in the country's spiritual economy. The relationship of the Ga community with the newcomers was exacerbated further as Accra's new Christians began looking for more land to expand their congregations. By custom, traditional chiefs are the rightful caretakers of the land; they are responsible for ensuring that it is equitably distributed among the community. Because of the economic and social capital held by Pentecostal/Charismatic churches, Ga community members accused some of them of bypassing customary negotiations with responsible individuals so they could acquire land without proper authorization (Asante 2011, 99–100). These tensions, along with the disrespectful attitude of some Pentecostal/Charismatic Christians toward Ga traditional authorities and ritual practices, and their propensity for loud worship, culminated in confrontations over the Pentecostal/Charismatic violation of the Ga ritual regulations. Father Ernest Tackie Yarboi, an assistant priest at St. Barnabas Anglican Church in Osu, recalls how Pentecostal/Charismatic churches were targeted for special acoustic control in the 1990s: "Of course, since I was growing up, there has always been confusion between the churches and traditional authorities. Because what happens is that the churches, they don't mind [the ban on drumming] and the traditional people go in there to seize their equipment, and sometimes there is confrontation, there is fight."[23]

There is no question that Pentecostal/Charismatic churches seized Accra's soundscape in the 1990s. A combination of factors—easier access to powerful sound systems and their status as a symbol of affluence, the liberalization of the airwaves, and the theologically legitimized power of sound—was instrumental in the disproportionate aural amplification of Pentecostal/Charismatic worship. Bidding to keep up with the wave of charismatization sweeping over Christianity in Ghana, mainline churches also diversified their musical repertoire, upgraded their sound systems, and introduced instruments that had traditionally been absent from their worship, adding to the overwhelming sense of amplified Christian piety in the city.[24] Prior to this shift, the sonic profile of mainline churches was limited to organs, hymn singing, and occasional drumming, which did not generate enough noise to cause concern in the Ga community. Even today, Anglican, Presbyterian, and Methodist services are considerably tamer than Pentecostal/Charismatic worship. When I asked Father Tackie Yarboi about the role of music in the Anglican Church, he explained that worshippers usually use organs and avoid clapping and drumming as a compromise during the period of the ban. "We understand that if you don't play drums, you can't stop worshipping our God," he told me. "The charismatics, the way of their worship, they can't do without the drums. When they don't do drums, they don't feel comfortable. The understanding is that you don't bow to any fetish god."[25] Father Tackie Yarboi and my other interlocutors from the mainline churches believe that the willingness to compromise stems from their long-established presence in Ga neighborhoods and from the large number of Ga adherents in their membership ranks.

Interpreted through the lens of sonic theologies, the willingness to compromise is also tied to the fact that mainline churches have no prescribed sounds they need to perform in order to uncover or, in Guy L. Beck's terminology, to "un-sound" their ultimate reality (Beck 1993, 215). In contrast, Pentecostal/Charismatic Christians apprehend sound, both Christian and "pagan," as central to the experience of the divine. The ubiquity of Pentecostal/Charismatic soundscapes in Accra and the pairing of particular sounds and embodied practices of making sound with religious experience undoubtedly fostered the development of a moralized sensory orientation among Pentecostal/Charismatic adherents that significantly inhibited their ability to recognize and condone the Ga sensory order.

Homɔwɔ Preparations: The Festival Spirit Permeates Public Media

By the time Accra's religious imagination was becoming suffused with the aural markers of Pentecostal/Charismatic congregations, the Homɔwɔ festival was slowly entering the collective urban civic consciousness. With it, the ban on drumming was on its way to being the most rigorously and unapologetically enforced policy in the history of Ghana's ritual sonic restrictions, first by Ga traditionalists and then by the state of Ghana. How did the Hɔmɔwɔ festival and the practices associated with it take charge of Accra's public discourse? What was the initial reaction of various public segments to the ban? To answer these questions, I tracked the evolution of two types of announcements in the *Daily Graphic*: articles dedicated to festive ceremonies that concluded the Hɔmɔwɔ season and notices that alerted the public to the month-long sonic abstinence in the city.

Hɔmɔwɔ, like other major traditional festivals in the country, received little media coverage immediately after Ghana's declaration of independence on March 6, 1957. In all likelihood, this was because the fledgling state was struggling to establish its presence on international and domestic terrains, a process that left scant room for routine customs of little political consequence. The situation changed, however, during Kwame Nkrumah's project of cultural nationalism, which advocated a renewed focus on African culture and tradition as decolonizing ways of marching into modernity (Botwe-Asamoah 2005). In practice, this meant a selective revival of cultural elements such as festivals, traditional dance, and music. Given this tendency, it is not surprising that the Hɔmɔwɔ announcements of the 1960s were visually prominent and focused on the ceremonial dimensions of the celebration. They were consistently accompanied by photographs depicting the most recognizable features of the celebration, such as traditional authorities pouring libations or sprinkling the ritual food of *kpoikpoi*. Since the Hɔmɔwɔ-related festivities of different Ga communities take place within the same harvest season but on different dates, in certain years newspapers published more than one article detailing the specifics of the celebration. Consider, for example, August and September of 1965, when the *Daily Graphic* published three announcements: one of them reported on Hɔmɔwɔ in the Ga-Mashie Traditional Area and the other two informed readers about festivities in Teshie, a Ga fishing town adjacent to Accra.[26] The dry cataloging of participants and events in these news pieces leaves much to be desired in terms of descriptiveness and style. However, these terse descriptions, averaging only fifty words in length, are striking for their unapologetic recognition of the Ga nonhuman ontologies, as evidenced by matter-of-fact allusions to the deities and their prominent role in human life. Interestingly, *jemawɔji*—the Ga word for deities—is almost never used, replaced by the English words "gods" or "deities." Articles report on the Ga-Mashie chief sprinkling *kpoikpoi* "to feed the gods," the Teshie priest offering a meal to the deities, and the paramount chief of Teshie "pouring libation for the blessings and guidance of the gods for the nation."[27]

Despite their brevity, the articles call attention to the casual nature of the belief that deities are sentient beings who consume nourishment offered by humans

FIGURE 2.1. The Nai *wulɔmɔ* of Ga-Mashie, Numo Akwaa Mensah III, pours a libation for Hɔmɔwɔ. Photo by author. 2018.

and respond to human actions accordingly. Such explicit references to the sentience of deities start to dwindle in the 1980s. Hɔmɔwɔ was still the time when members of the Ga community "pray[ed] to their gods for success" or "thank[ed] the gods for the abundance of food," but they no longer engaged in the act of feeding them.[28] This subtle linguistic and conceptual shift must be seen in light of the arrival of Pentecostal/Charismatic churches, which were notorious for their hostile rhetoric against traditional religions. The rapid Pentecostalization of public discourse meant that indigenous deities were gradually eliminated from everyday parlance in the media. More important, this shift reflects the frictions between the competing and overlapping epistemologies of secularism, Pentecostal/Charismatic Christianity, and the Ga world view. What unites these early accounts with contemporary coverage of the festival, however, is the depiction of nonhuman beings as collective or national deities rather than local *jemawɔji* in the narrow sense. As we will see in the final chapter, during the culturalization of indigenous belief systems in contemporary Ghana, traditional deities and practices were regularly subjected to such nationalization.

The Hɔmɔwɔ festival acquired a new political function in the 1970s. A 1972 photograph from the *Daily Graphic* shows Colonel Acheampong, then Ghana's military leader, being served *kpoikpoi* at the chief's palace in the Ga-Mashie Traditional Area.[29] In addition to being a testament to the bolstered chiefly author-

ity in the aftermath of Nkrumah's rule, Colonel Acheampong's visibility at the
Hɔmɔwɔ festivities also speaks to his determination to buttress his legitimacy
in the capital.[30] This image encapsulates not only the heightened profile of
Hɔmɔwɔ in public discourse but also Hɔmɔwɔ's importance as an arena for forg-
ing political ties between Accra's traditional authorities and Ghana's political
leaders. In this and other articles, we read of Mantsɛ Nii Amugi II publicly
praying to "grant members of the National Redemption Council long life and
prosperity" or calling on all Ghanaians to support the NRC, which he praised
for "excellence in solving the problems of the nation."[31] The public prominence
of Hɔmɔwɔ as a symbol of forged political alliances also helped spotlight its
historical background. As the number of articles devoted to the festival proliferated, journalists made greater efforts to elucidate its origins.[32] This development, in turn, helped foreground the unique status of the Ga people as the
firstcomers to Accra and therefore as the legitimate caretakers of those lands.

In the 1980s, the number of Hɔmɔwɔ-related stories proliferated. In 1981,
seven separate articles detailed festival celebrations in the Ga neighborhoods
of Teshie, Lante Djan-We, Ga-Mashie, Labadi, and Odorkor.[33] Despite Ghana's
unstable political leadership and frequent deposings in the late 1970s, Mantsɛ
Nii Amugi II appears to have remained influential in the public sphere. He also
used the Hɔmɔwɔ festivities as a platform for voicing politically charged statements. In 1985, for instance, he urged Ghanaians to channel their resources into
supporting Jerry J. Rawlings's Economic Recovery Program, which was failing
to gain popular support.[34] Nii Amugi's high profile and charismatic persona further contributed to the foregrounding of Ga-Mashie as the highest-ranking Ga
community and himself as the paramount chief of the Ga, a misconception that
was first popularized by the colonial administration and has since cast a shadow
over other Ga chiefs who hold identical positions. The inaccurate hierarchization of the Ga traditional leaders is most apparent in the guest lists of the 1980s
Hɔmɔwɔ parties organized by members of the country's top political echelons.
Nii Amugi II and the chief wulɔmɔ of the Ga-Mashie area were often the only
guests from the Ga traditional community at these events. In September 1981,
when Hilla Limann was still president, Nii Amugi II was the only mantsɛ among
prominent political figures invited to the party hosted by I. T. Torto, the Greater
Accra regional minister.[35] In a different setting, at a durbar organized as the culmination of Accra's 1988 festival season, Nai wulɔmɔ, the chief priest of the Ga-
Mashie community, decorated Jerry Rawlings "with a garland of green herbs
which signifies peace in Ga tradition."[36]

Beginning in the early 1990s, the festival emerged as a hotspot of community
organization and publicity for corporations. This trend reflected the Ghana-wide

interest of commercial companies in making their brands locally identifiable through festivals (Adrover 2013). Issues of the *Daily Graphic* from the period are peppered with announcements commending Accra Brewery Limited, GIHOC Distilleries, and the British High Commission, among others, for donating cartons of spirits together with cash gifts to traditional leaders.[37] Since no indigenous festival in Ghana can be successfully observed without the consumption of large quantities of alcoholic beverages that are shared with the deities in the form of libations, alcohol companies remain the most eager sponsors of such occasions even today. Other organizations usually volunteer to sponsor dances and sports competitions that attract large numbers of tourists and residents of Accra.[38]

Emboldened by corporate funding and by mass attendance from both Ga community members and representatives of Accra-based public institutions, Ga chiefs took advantage of the festivals to announce various development programs or seek support from state actors.[39] Hɔmɔwɔ also took on annual themes, incorporating educational programs and workshops to prepare the community to address pressing welfare issues. For example, the 1991 theme of the Ga-Mashie Hɔmɔwɔ was broadly formulated as "war against drug abuse, teenage pregnancies, [...] and other social vices." To sensitize the community to the hazards of these issues, traditional authorities organized lectures and other informational events.[40] The 1995 festival season in the Prampram Traditional Area was a platform for discussing "progress, problems as well as development projects in the area," and the following year, the chief of Prampram, Nene Tetteh Djan, raised funds for a senior secondary school in the area.[41] Beyond the traditional setting, Hɔmɔwɔ-themed parties organized purely for entertainment purposes seem to have been common. My favorite *Daily Graphic* piece that illuminates the burgeoning entertainment and commercial value of the festival is a one-page advertisement for a Hɔmɔwɔ-themed celebration at the Ambassador Hotel in 1985. The announcement promised "a rich package" of events and highlighted "the Homowo buffet," which featured *kpoikpoi* and other Ghanaian dishes, "the cultural explosion" of traditional drumming and dancing, "a folkloric display" of "psychedelic fashion of the past," and a "Homowo jamboree" with a dance party.[42] The Ambassador was the first luxury hotel in Accra to cater to foreigners and upper-class Ghanaians. The planning of a Hɔmɔwɔ party at the hotel speaks to a renewed interest in the traditional festival as a repository of culture and an occasion for entertainment.

In the 1970s, not long after the renaissance of Hɔmɔwɔ in the national media, the first notices about the impending ban on drumming began to appear sporadically in the *Daily Graphic*. Most likely the arrival of these notices was tied to the diversification of Accra's ethnic profile as the city more than tripled in size from 1950 to 1970.[43] These pioneering articles did not target Christian churches for their penchant for making noise but instead concentrated on terminating all forms of "music playing, hand-clapping and whistling" that interfered with ritual silence.[44] A decade later, however, Pentecostal/Charismatic churches figured almost ubiquitously in the announcements of the forthcoming ban on drumming, evidence of their burgeoning public leverage. In the late 1980s, in what seems like a reactionary response to the loosening grip of the ban on drumming on Accra's sonic profile, the Ga Traditional Council took charge of newspaper notices that alerted the public to the onset of sonic abstinence in the city.[45] As a consequence, notices of the ban in the *Daily Graphic* became highly standardized, often including dates of the ban and urging citizens to comply with the regulations. As an illustration, here is an announcement from 1989:

> The annual ban on drumming in the Ga Mashie area and its suburbs begins on Monday, May 8, and ends on Thursday, June 8.
> A statement from the Ga Traditional Council appealed to the general public and identifiable organizations, including spiritual churches, to comply with the banning order by not drumming during the period.[46]

Notices from the 1980s and 1990s repeated the same pattern with only minor linguistic variations. All announcements specified that the prohibition applied to "spiritual churches" rather than the broader category of Christian churches, clearly distinguishing between mainline denominations that had been based in the capital since precolonial times and the Charismatic newcomers to the urban religious milieu.

Many Ga traditional leaders, especially those who identified as Christians, favored a defensive stance aimed at removing prejudice against traditional worship. The most distinctive feature of the statements these Ga community members made is their self-deprecating nature, which reveals missionary and colonial notions about the worth of traditional belief in relation to Christianity. An example can be found in the remarks of the La *mantsɛ*, Dede Kotopon Nii Kpobi Tettey-Tsuru III, at the 1990 Hɔmɔwɔ celebration in the La Traditional Area. In an effort to reconcile his stalwart support for Christianity with his distinguished traditional role in the La community, Nii Tettey-Tsuru maintained that the sprinkling of *kpoikpoi* "agitated" his mind—in all probability, a reaction to the involvement of deities in the ritual. He went on to say that beyond the *kpoikpoi*, there was "nothing heathenic about most African traditions, except that certain aspects of them [were] not polished enough to meet the acceptance of christianity."[47] The idea that traditional religions need to become more polished in order to be favorably received by Christians and modern citizens is a common feature of how they are spoken about in present-day Accra and resonates with an evolutionary vision of religiosity that pronounces Christianity as the pinnacle of refinement to which "lesser" spiritualties should aspire.

The transformation of Hɔmɔwɔ into an occasion for communal entertainment and collective planning in the 1990s did not translate into stricter observance of the ban on drumming. On the contrary, while the format of the ban on drumming announcements remained the same, their numbers waned toward the end of the 1990s and disappeared completely in 1996 and 1997, only to return with a vengeance after the first confrontations between the Ga community and Pentecostal/Charismatic churches in 1998. The vanishing of advisories about acoustic behavior from public media in the two years preceding the clashes could be seen in light of increased state efforts to culturalize the festival, a progression that the N C C led and encouraged. This shift coincided with the formidable public presence of Pentecostal/Charismatic churches, which took advantage of liberalized media to gradually infuse all aspects of daily life with Christian visual and sonic cues. Although a culture of silence prevailed under the authoritarian Provisional National Defense Council, the first signs of press freedom following the 1992 presidential and parliamentary elections significantly improved the flow of information in the country (Smith 2002). From the mid-1990s, the thriving private media enabled the wealthy Pentecostal/Charismatic churches to take possession of the public sphere (Asamoah-Gyadu 2005a; Kalu 2009; Onyinah 2009).

Although the *Daily Graphic* offers some insights into the popularization of Charismatic churches, it also reveals concerns and controversies regarding their deprecation of cultural values. In a 1994 opinion piece, Joe Nyinah deplored the "brainwashed" attitude of "born agains, charismatics and others" who "frown on anything that is traditional describing it as heathen." Nyinah was particularly scandalized by the fact that some born-again Christians opposed the celebration of traditional festivals and that they failed to realize that local traditions "govern people" and if they were obstructed, the social fabric of the community would dissolve.[48] Others expressed concern about the moral uprightness of Pentecostal/Charismatic pastors, stating that although many "good and wonderful things" were happening in these churches, some pastors "charge[d] exorbitant fees for consultation, prayer and rituals, they [slept] with people's wives and engage[d] in activities which are a disgrace."[49] An article published in 1997 echoes the opinion of many of my interlocutors today: "The stunning revelations of the nefarious activities that go on in some of these churches, attest to the fact that most of them are mere smoke screens for those spiritual charlatans who feed fat on innocent and defenceless members of their congregation."[50] In fact, I have often heard that the insatiable desire of Pentecostal/Charismatic pastors for material wealth is what makes them so reluctant to observe the one-month ban on drumming. Allegedly, the lack of vibrant music instills apathy in worshippers and lowers attendance.

When Tired Workers Can't Sleep:
Concerns over Noise Pollution

The newly emerging discourse on noise as a significant public nuisance in Accra was a catalyst in bringing the ban on drumming to the foreground. In addition to the overall rise in urban noise, citizens began to complain that the Pentecostal/Charismatic churches were firmly establishing themselves in the city's soundscape. As we will see later, the grievances the traditionalists voiced in the late 1990s became more prominent than some of the health-oriented pleas of Accra's residents and altered both doctrinal and empirical discussions surrounding the ban on drumming and its regulation.

The first complaints about noise in the *Daily Graphic* appeared in the second half of the 1980s in a column titled "The Voice of the People," which served as a platform for readers who wanted to voice community concerns, who wanted to urge the state and private institutions to solve various social problems, or who simply were eager to engage in conversations about changing social norms. The true magnitude of the acoustic sway of Pentecostal/Charismatic churches shines through; the majority of sound-related complaints in the *Daily Graphic* were either directly concerned with mental and bodily disruptions caused by Pentecostal/Charismatic worship or cited the loudness of those churches as an important source of noise pollution in the capital. Contributors to the newspaper frequently charged Pentecostal/Charismatic congregations with worshipping at unseemly hours and doing so without any regard for the irritated citizens. Godwin Kwashie Mensah of Accra condemned born-again groups for "shouting, shrieking, chanting and clapping very loudly" almost every day of the week.[51] Many readers, especially members of mainline churches, maintained that making noise was not "true" worship, which should be aurally modest and pleasing to the ear. One contributor noted that singing could be a part of worship as long as it was "done in such a way that it [did] not prevent people in the neighbourhood from enjoying their peace."[52] It was not the singing per se that bothered the majority, but the outlandishness of the prayer times and the wide array of human-produced noises that were unusual to the ears of members of the older churches. In 1990, for example, a resident of Teshie criticized Charismatic churches for organizing regular all-night services accompanied by "blowing of horns and playing of musical instruments," as if intentionally designed to disturb people living in the vicinity.[53] In the same year, a resident of Mamprobi complained about a church that had become a source of disturbance for the neighbors after the landlord decided to mount a giant loudspeaker on the roof. "At dawn, to be precise, around 3.00 A.M. everyday, a recorded sermon and religious music are played at the maximum volume. This noise is very disturbing and a nuisance to many," wrote the dismayed citizen.[54] Anyone who has lived in Accra knows that in their quest to please their God, many business owners install large loudspeakers outside their shops or businesses to project religious music. As early as the late 1990s, ear-splitting combinations of gospel music, glossolalia, stomping, and clapping poured out from every street corner of the capital.

Readers never hurled their wrath at mainline churches, and mosques came under fire only a handful of times. In fact, I found only one letter from 1989 that made a fuss about mosques being overlooked in the enforcement of the noise-abatement law. The contributor maintained that dawn prayers remained unaffected by the city's sonic control regulations even though the 4 a.m. call to prayer could easily disturb "the tired worker in his sleep," including those "residing about 1.5Km radius from the mosque."[55]

The few complaints about secular noise in the *Daily Graphic* referred to nightclubs, restaurants, or entertainment centers. As the number of recording studios and music shops in the city increased, residents also began to object to the placement of sound systems in the street. Coincidentally, the neighborhoods most susceptible to unruly sonalities were home to blue-collar workers and low-income families without the social capital to ensure adequate legal protection from noise. Two letters published in the *Daily Graphic* in May 1995 described how The Fish, a drinking establishment, had become a menace to the entire Dansoman neighborhood on account of the loud live music it hosted late at night.[56] "Elderly people complain of stressful noise, students can't study, and children cannot go to school early due to insufficient sleep, all because of the unregulated operations of 'The Fish,'" said one letter-writer.[57] In these locales, residents reported, even policemen rambled around inebriated with no intention of upholding social order.[58] As a matter of fact, the drinking spots where some of the law enforcement officers amused themselves were sites of excessive noise production.

Distraught readers begged the government and community leaders to intervene, and some mentioned failed attempts to seek help from the police.[59] It was from these letters that I learned of a noise-abatement bylaw introduced by the Accra City Council, which was active in the final years of the 1980s. In a letter of gratitude published in 1988, a resident of Adabraka commended the law for bringing "a lot of relief to most residents in Accra from hitherto unchecked and uncontrolled noises from some of our spiritual churches and other night disturbers."[60] I have not been able to find any further information on this bylaw, especially since it was issued under the military dictatorship of the Provisional National Defense Council, which was in power until 1993. It appears, however, that the bylaw was only occasionally enforced. Luckily, we can learn a little bit about its content from another letter in the *Daily Graphic* in which the author appears to be quoting from the bylaw to argue for the unlawfulness of excessive noise—"no person or persons conducting a religious service shall play any music or allow any music to be played loudly to cause annoyance or disturbance of the residents in the area."[61] When I interviewed representatives of various state agencies in 2015–2018, they could only recall noise-abatement bylaws issued during the Fourth Republic (1993–present), which they unanimously claimed were never actually activated or enforced. Indeed, *Daily Graphic* contributors writing after 1992 criticized Ghana's Environmental Protection Agency for failing to address the city's noise problem.[62] In a last-ditch attempt to secure a good night's sleep, and realizing the incompetence of state institutions in ensuring peace, one reader in 1995 even wished that the ban on drumming would apply to his neighborhood because it would provide a long-sought respite from noise.[63] These sentiments of Accra's disgruntled residents must have influenced how traditionalists conceived of the purpose and function of the ban on drumming: it transcended a deity-focused understanding of quiet to include broader communal advantages of peace.

At the beginning of the 1990s, noise pollution had become an issue of national concern throughout West Africa. A five-day workshop organized in February 1991 summoned prominent journalists from Ghana, Nigeria, Sierra Leone, and the Gambia to discuss the subtleties of environmental reporting.[64] Noise in Accra was at the forefront of the meeting, where it was proclaimed the root of numerous health issues ranging from impaired hearing to "headaches and uneasiness." A few months later, Joyce Adjoa Thompson reported on the detrimental effects of noise on human health. Thompson was exclusively concerned with environmental noises such as car horns, airplanes, exhaust pipes, and factories. She noted that according to medical experts, exposure to loaded soundscapes could precipitate "heart diseases, high blood pressure, allergy, nervousness and other ailments."[65] I did not hear these clinical definitions about the consequences of loud noise among the Ga ritual specialists, but in our interviews, they repeatedly stressed the importance of taking a break from the city's soundscape to please the mind and body. I suspect that the growing importance of "fasting" from sound in the framework of the ban on drumming echoed the clinical warnings about the harmfulness of noise in this period.

In religious praxis, these developments were accompanied by a gradual redefinition of the content of noise within the framework of the ban. In the aftermath of the Drum Wars, the ban on drumming became a ban on drumming and noise making or simply the ban on noise making, where noise as a shifting category expanded to encompass urban pollution and condensed around the acoustic profile of Pentecostal/Charismatic churches. Public and state discourse on the detrimental effects of loud sound on human health also significantly affected the ritual function of silence. The increased visibility and prominence of the ban on drumming and noise making transposed the colonial top-down model of acoustic control into a bottom-up venture that was initiated and supervised by an indigenous community, which, as we will see in later chapters, was quite successful owing to unique power-sharing techniques that evolved between the state and traditional authorities.

As an inherently spatial phenomenon, sound or the absence thereof has the capacity to occupy space, change its emotional contours, and enact cultural identity (Sterne 2005; Hervieu-Leger 2002; Tan 2012). In the midst of the convergence of urban identities, the gradual foregrounding of the ban on drumming played a decisive role in fending off the encroachment of outsiders in Accra and, more directly, in territories under the Ga customary supervision. The combination of a sense of entitlement to Accra's urban space, state-led culturalization programs, the sudden ascendance of Pentecostal/Charismatic churches in Accra's religious scene, and persistent poverty pushed the Ga community to performatively fortify the contours of its authority and its threatened sensory order via the "seizure of soundscape" (Oosterbaan 2009, 86). What made the ban on drumming so potent was the fact that it empowered the Ga community to affirm its identity without engaging in a sonic competition with Pentecostal/Charismatic congregations that would require overshadowing their sounds. The traditionalists would have had no chance against the technologically amplified piety of wealthier born-again congregations. Instead, the Ga community weaponized the ban on drumming via the targeted elimination of threatening sonic presence, emerging as unlikely model citizens in the process. Although controlled sound as a source of authority has traditionally been inscribed in the regimes of church and state (Bailey 1996, 53), the ban on drumming rendered the Ga community the primary authority capable of controlling religious and secular sounds in Accra's public space—a status that, as we will see later, was only nominally contested by the Ghanaian state.

3. The Power of Sound

Cross-World Sonic Theologies

The principal streets are lined by small African enterprises, which frequently advertise their commodities and services pictorially rather than graphically. A large alarm clock or wristwatch on the wall of a watch repairer's shop proclaims his trade to potential customers, while the image of a man drinking a glass of beer on the wall of a bar announces the refreshment to be found inside. Women traders either walk through the streets carrying their wares on their heads or sit outside their houses at small tables which display commodities, such as kenkey, tomatoes, combs, cigarettes, and candy. . . . Frequently, a street is closed to motor traffic so that the mourners at a funeral may sit outside the house under the shade of a large tarpaulin. The area is scarcely ever silent—far into the night the flickering kerosene lamps of traders illuminate clusters of people laughing and conversing; the partial stillness of the night is broken by the clank of pails at the standpipes long before dawn.
—MARION KILSON, *AFRICAN URBAN KINSMEN: THE GA OF CENTRAL ACCRA*

Radio and music cassettes blast from taxis and trotros, pavement kiosks and open-air drinking spots—preaching, music, news, jingles; "Radio Gold, your power station." Radio is everywhere

and the sounds of the numerous stations competing for sonic presence merge into each other in the streets. We hear music, singing, laughter, wailing, chattering and preaching from public gatherings, funerals, parties and church services. Talking or quarrelling voices escape from private houses.
—MARLEEN DE WITTE, *"ACCRA'S SOUNDS AND SACRED SPACES"*

My sonic adventures in Accra start at four in the morning when the still of the night is gently stirred by *fajr*, the Muslim dawn prayer that brings me to consciousness with its melodic tone. Before long, I am exposed to a shriller, almost cacophonous, concoction of sounds from a neighboring middle school, where students and teachers gather for early Christian worship. From the shadows of my room, I fathom that the service alternates between preaching, glossolalia, and synchronized stomping. Unable to go back to sleep, I get up and prepare for interviews. As I step out of my apartment in Adabraka, an old central neighborhood of Accra, the city's effervescent energy engulfs me with its striking aural, visual, and olfactory density. Dilapidated cars laboriously cover uneven roads; street vendors advertise their sachets of pure water, roasted peanuts, boiled eggs, *waakye*, and freshly chopped fruits; children play football on the streets; and shops blast their African dance hall and gospel beats.[1] The most outlandish aurality, however, emanates from hundreds of Pentecostal/Charismatic congregations in the city. Their regular worship meetings, all-night prayer meetings, and crusades produce all-encompassing sounds that are simultaneously joyful, anguished, and furious. However, everything changes when the deities visit the city. To guarantee a comfortable environment for the *jemawɔji* who come to prepare the harvest for Hɔmɔwɔ, the Ga *wulɔmɛi* announce a period of peace and deliberation, which means that the city's tourism hubs, outdoor vendors, restaurants, pubs, and religious institutions are obliged to reduce their sonic footprint.

Heated public discussions that followed a series of bellicose encounters between the Ga community and Pentecostal/Charismatic worshippers at the turn of the twenty-first century and continue with less force regularly around the period of the Hɔmɔwɔ festival are notable, as we will see in the next chapter, for their overly legalistic and secularist language. From an ontological perspective, however, the Ga traditionalists and members of Pentecostal/Charismatic churches have almost identical conceptions about the spiritual nature of sound in their respective lifeworlds. One could argue that the two parties understand each other's positions perfectly well in theological terms, yet their distinct legal and political status in Ghana's secular framework demands that they reframe their positions in secular language. To illuminate the sonic dimension of the conflict in more detail, in this chapter, I take the reader on a journey to explore the acoustic worlds of Ga religion and Pentecostal/Charismatic Christianity. I highlight theological beliefs about the power of sound as well as the alleged repercussions of noise and silence for the respective communities. Above all, I describe the positive communal benefits of making noise for Pentecostal/Charismatic congregations and shed light on the potential of flawlessly observed ritual silence to secure a prosperous and healthy year for the Ga community. The affective and metaphysical stakes related to safeguarding these respective sonic world views are often lost in the context of public dialogue. Thus, by probing into the sonic lifeworlds of Ga religion and Pentecostal/Charismatic Christianity, I illuminate the scope of misrepresentation that accompanies the use of legal jargon, which in turn interferes with finding solutions to the ongoing interreligious tensions.

When the Earth Is Heavy with Deities

In chapter 1, I considered the drum as a significant "attribute of power" (Attali 1985) and a conspicuous "sensational form" (Meyer 2006b) in the Ga cosmology. Here, I would like to expand on sound, noise, and the absence of noise in the Ga episteme. Generally speaking, the interpretations and meanings we ascribe to various sonic phenomena across cultural divides are situational. These phenomena take on divergent meanings, both in the way they are labeled sonically and experienced emotionally, depending on the type of interactions that mobilize them. Stressing the flexible nature of sensory classifications is especially important when interrogating sacred contexts, which are prone to fall into the narrative of sensory enchantment that still burdens the investigation of sound in the context of Africa. Like Pentecostal/Charismatic Christians, devotees of the Ga religion perpetually negotiate the meaning of their sonic categories in response to the circumstances.

The theological rationale behind the ban on drumming is the claim that the absence of noise aids concentration. Who is supposed to achieve the state of heightened focus—humans or deities—is another question. But one thing is clear: sound is central to the fine-tuning of the alliance between the two groups. The ban on drumming is a key stage in the Ga ritual calendar that is critical to obtaining a bountiful harvest. The official ceremony that marks the commencement of the ban on drumming in various Ga communities is known as *ŋmaadumɔ*, literally "the rite of sowing millet" in the Ga language. *Ŋmaadumɔ* follows *shibaa*, the preparation of the sacred groves for cultivation, and is part of an elaborate Ga ritual calendar that takes place, with slight variations, in all Ga townships from May to July. While I have observed and documented all stages of the festival, I will not go into detail here.[2] Instead, I will focus on *ŋmaadumɔ*, which I attended across Accra's neighborhoods throughout my fieldwork. One of the common features of the ŋmaadumɔ ceremony as it is celebrated in different townships is a procession from the performing priest's household to the planting site, called the ŋmɔ (farm). The wulɔmɛi, agbaafoi, and wɔyei form a procession and walk in a straight line, singing, "*Awo! Awo! Awo! O, aagbai bleku tsɔɔ, aawo o*" (Mother earth! Mother earth! Mother earth! We prophesy [pray for] a bountiful harvest). Each participant walks barefoot and wears white calico as a sign of purity. The procession, which features prayers, songs, and a festive spirit, is a sight to behold, and community members gather around as a sign of appreciation and support (Ammah 2016, 295, 321; Lokko 1981, 47–48). Holding their staffs, the agbaafoi walk in the front, followed by their female counterparts, who carry brooms to signify the cleansing of the town from evil. The procession stops at various otutu (sacred mounds) to perform prayers and pour libations. As I walked in line with the procession toward the farming grounds of the Sakumɔ deity in 2018, I was struck by the calm that had descended on the normally boisterous Jamestown neighborhood. Onlookers were cordoned off behind cars and motorcycles. Excited, expectant, and deferential, they observed the procession and greeted the priests as they passed by. Once we reached the ŋmɔ, we were strictly warned to stay outside as only male ritual specialists and three or four wɔyei entered the sacred ground to sow the millet that symbolizes the harvest for the entire community. The song performed at the time of planting charts a series of sonically charged activities traditionally prohibited during the ban (Laryea 2011, 88):

Adu ŋmaa fɛɛ.
Akpaa blɛ, akpaa blɛ.
Ofori edu ŋmaa fɛɛ.

Alaaa, alaaa.
Afooo, afooo.
Atswaaa ntonsa, atswaa ntonsa.
Ayiii mi, ayiii mi.
Ajooo, ajooo.
Atuuu ampe, atuuu ampe.
Ashwɛɛɛ adaawe, ashwɛɛɛ adaawe.
Ashiii jama, ashiii jama.
Atswaaa ŋoŋo, atswaaa ŋoŋo.

[They planted all the millet.
They do not whistle.
Ofori planted all the millet.

They do not sing.
They do not cry.
We do not play the *ntonsa* game.
We do not play drums.
We do not dance.
We do not jump *ampe*.
We do not play the *adaawe* game.
We do not play the *jama* game.
We do not play the *ŋoŋo*.]

When the ritual specialists finally reappeared, they stamped the gravel with joy as they walked back to the Sakumɔ shrine. Not far from the *ŋmɔ*, they paused to perform several songs. The *wulɔmɛi* beat their staffs to the rhythm and the *woyei* danced eagerly without leaving their assigned spots in the procession. Upon reaching the Sakumo shrine, the *wulɔmɛi*, *agbaafoi*, and *woyei* circled the ritual tree in the center of the compound three times to conclude the ceremony. Now the ban on drumming was officially in effect, and as the Ga like to say, the earth turned heavy with the presence of the gods (*shikpɔŋ etsii*) (Ammah 2016, 273). Following *ŋmaadumɔ*, specific sounds as well as general noise are prohibited for approximately two to four weeks, depending on the township. Typically, the sonic fast is supplemented by a number of other restrictions. For example, eating peanuts, fresh corn, yams, and *tsile* fish is frowned upon (Laryea 2011, 88); children are discouraged from playing traditional games such as *ntonsa*, *adaawe*, and *jama*; customs and ceremonies that intimate either merriment or spiritual pollution are postponed. Since a deceased body is believed to have a polluting effect, death at this time signals adversity for the family (Amartey 1991, 163–64; Kropp-Dakubu 1987, 516). Significant effort is exerted to maintain an emotionally balanced state within the community, so "debt payments cannot be demanded, oaths cannot be sworn, and legal proceedings cannot be initiated" (Kilson 2013, 91). The ensuing peace and quiet guarantee a hospitable environment for the *jemawɔji* who visit the human world to aid the gestation of the harvest. Ammah (2016) explains that "it is the presence of the gods with a view to watching over the deposited millet that makes the whole period sacred, hallowed, and holy. The gods are not only watching the seed and protecting it, but they are also engaged in prayer to [the supreme] God for rain so that the single grain of millet (*ŋmaa kuli*) may grow in time for the enjoyment of man" (273).

The lack of sonic distractions is also conducive to a productive cooperation between the *wulɔmɛi* and the *jemawɔji*. As intermediaries between the humans and the *jemawɔji*, the *wulɔmɛi* invest significant effort in preparing for this sacred

FIGURE 3.1. The Sakumɔ *wulɔmɔ* places ritual food on the *otutu* (sacred mounds) before the start of the *ŋmaadumɔ* (sowing millet) procession. Photo by author. 2018.

period. They need to be uncontaminated both spiritually and physically in order to obtain messages from the *jemawɔji* and the ancestors (*blematsɛmɛi*), and translate them to the common people who "do not have the ears" to hear the deities (Laryea 2011, 113). With this goal in mind, the *wulɔmɛi* isolate themselves in their shrines (*gbatsui*) during the period of the ban and enter into a state of intensive meditation and prayer. The only physical object found in the shrine is a pot (*kulo*) of water. According to the information gathered by Marion Kilson in the late 1960s, "when a medium invokes spiritual beings, which include not only gods, but ancestral shades and spirits of twins [*haaji*], these beings become localized in the pot of water and reveal their messages from the pot to the medium and through her to other mortals" (Kilson 1971, 69). During my fieldwork, I noticed a tendency among the Ga *wulɔmɛi* to frame the time of deliberation in terms of personal communication with the "god almighty" or his "angels" rather than with the *jemawɔji*, who were traditionally the primary arbitrators between the supreme being and humans in all matters of daily life. The Nai *wulɔmɔ*'s account of the importance of silence echoes the recent emphasis on the creator god. In the course of our discussion, he described how silence prepares "the atmosphere for meditation" and "helps to communicate with your creator inwardly" since "you can't go to the Lord with noise." The ban on drumming was, in his narrative, the time of self-denial, cleansing, and praise of god.[3] The decreased emphasis on the *jemawɔji* in favor of the supreme god clearly signals a Christian-influenced reading of the Ga divine order.

The injunction to eliminate noise and music from the Ga territories makes sense within the context of the profound entanglement of the Ga deities with the worldly sonic realm. Ga devotees maintain that the *jemawɔji* and the *blematsɛmɛi* manifest via meticulously regulated sonic pathways. The *jemawɔji* are mesmerized by human music and delight in listening to ritual songs. In their study of the acoustic representation of the other world in certain African societies, Roseman and Peek (1994, 476) wrote that epistemological contrasts of sound, noise, and the absence thereof are the foundation of cross-world communication. Ritual sound sacralizes mundane space and time, paving the way for the manifestation of the sacred. Ga traditional musicians with whom I spoke described how the core instruments—drums and two iron gongs—invoke or pull (*gbala*) the spirits down into the human world and entice them to enter their priestesses. In the course of the ceremonies, some *jemawɔji* may even ask for certain songs that they especially enjoy (Nketia 1988). This special relationship between nonhuman beings and human music explains the need to eliminate distracting sound waves when it is time to toil over the harvest. Even if secular music and instruments do not have the power to entice the *jemawɔji* to the same extent as ritual music, Christian and popular songs as well as drum beating, clapping, and whistling create a risk that nonhuman actors will become distracted, angered, or irritated.

Following the *ŋmaadumɔ* I observed in Osu in 2017, journalists interviewed a group of priestesses who had taken part in the rite of planting. "By the grace of Lord, we have planted," one of the *wɔyei* said into the microphone as she sat in the company of other ritual specialists in the courtyard of the *wulɔmɔ* of Gua. "We are pleading with everybody, so that they fast and allow the town to be quiet. The beating of drums and other things should not be brought to the town so that the town is quiet. So that everything we are asking should come to pass." What are the other things besides the beating of drums that could unsettle the quiet of the town? As in the Pentecostal/Charismatic context, here too, the terms "noise" and "silence" assume diverse (and often contradictory) meanings depending on the circumstances. For one, against the backdrop of the often unbearable environmental and urban noise that has plagued Accra since the 1990s, the ritual prohibition of sound has expanded far beyond the original restrictions on drumming, clapping, whistling, and sizzling (of frying fish) to include almost all kinds of loud sounds. In addition, there is a significant difference in how Ga community members assess in-group and out-group sound making. The example

I like to cite is the uninterrupted presence of Kpele ritual songs—both live and recorded—in the Ga townships of Nungua and Teshie throughout the period of the ban (Goshadze 2022b). Performed without drums, these tunes allegedly soothe the *jemawɔji* involved in Hɔmɔwɔ because they represent the oldest music associated with their worship (Nii-Dortey 2012). While Kpele ritual songs can be as loud as Pentecostal/Charismatic worship in certain instances, Ga practitioners are adamant about labeling them as not noise during the sonic ban.

On the other hand, Pentecostal/Charismatic music has become one of the primary targets for elimination, especially since the Drum Wars of the late 1990s, a development that cannot be disassociated from the movement's hostility to traditional religions. Music is central to how Pentecostal/Charismatic churches assert their claims to the public sphere (Oosterbaan 2009), which in Accra happens to constitute the Ga traditional territories. When these churches defied the period of silence, Ga people retaliated by giving them a taste of their own medicine, proclaiming their sonic presence—which did not always involve the traditionally prohibited drumming—as noisy. Since the *wulɔmei* not only protect the planted seeds but "are also engaged in prayer to God for rain so that the single grain of millet (*ŋmaa kuli*) may grow in time for the enjoyment of man," any sound that is proclaimed as noise by Ga ritual specialists is detrimental to a successful Hɔmɔwɔ celebration, since it derails communication with the nonhuman world (Ammah 2016, 273). Today, the majority of Ga people feel that the sound of Pentecostal/Charismatic worship is among the noises that throw off the visiting *jemawɔji* and detract ritual specialists from their supplications. This new category of noise has found its way into the Ga community's official guidelines for proper sonic behavior during the ban on drumming and into the public statements ritual specialists and representatives of the state make during the Hɔmɔwɔ season. The annual announcement of the Accra Metropolitan Assembly, which informs the public of the commencement of the ban, confines "the usual form of worship . . . to the premises of churches/mosques" and requires that noise levels "be minimized to the barest limits possible."[4]

The sacred quiet that envelops Ga neighborhoods prior to Hɔmɔwɔ has a peace-generating function. The ban on drumming is meant to usher in a period of social harmony that is free from cacophony, both in an internal and an external sense. Similar practices are not uncommon in other parts of Africa. Writing about the Lele of Kasai, Mary Douglas reports the prohibition of drums and all activities that produce "drum-like" sounds, such as the pounding of grain or work in the forest, on religious occasions and rest days (Douglas [1954] 1999, 12). So strong is the preoccupation with ritual order among Ga people that transgressions, especially sonic ones, were once believed to cause physical pain, especially

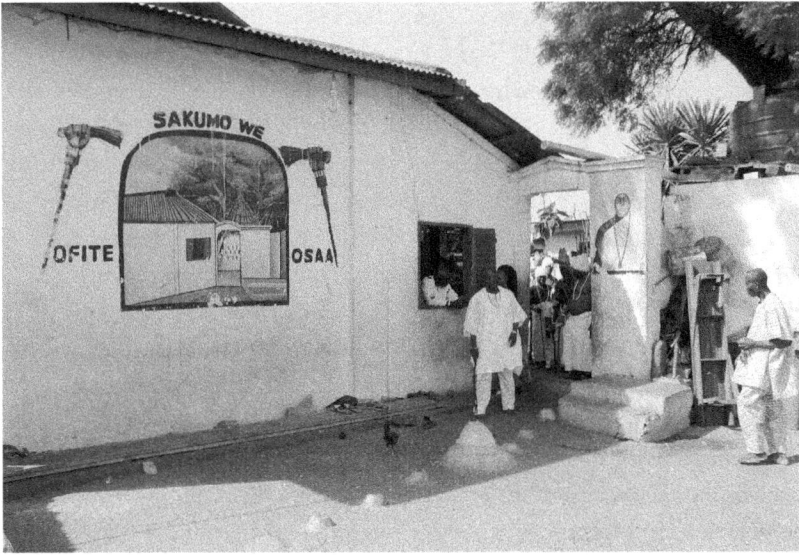

FIGURE 3.2. The *ŋmaadumɔ* (sowing millet) procession is about to start from the Sakumɔ shrine in Ga-Mashie. Ritual food has been placed on the *otutu* (sacred mounds) outside the shrine. Photo by author. 2018.

stomach pain, in the offender (Amartey 1991, 166). In a more ominous formulation, angry gods could even kill human beings for failing to perform the required rites, either directly through a cataclysmic event or indirectly by withholding physical nourishment (Kilson 1971, 24). From a purely functional point of view, one could argue that sacred silence fractures the mundane, gently easing the worshipper into a position of heightened concentration (Wissman 2014, 194). For this reason, the pleas of Ga community members to pay more heed to their most sacred season of the year deserve their share of public and political recognition.

"Shout for joy to the Lord": Pentecostal/Charismatic Theologies of Noise

In the fall of 2017, I walked into the Power Miracle Chapel International, a mid-sized Pentecostal/Charismatic church tucked away on a quiet street behind La Beach Road in Accra. A few days earlier, I had come across a large banner on the side of the road advertising the chapel's Wednesday Jericho Hour. Heavily Photoshopped images of feverish mass prayer were foregrounded with a large portrait of the congregation's leader, Prophet Stephen Mensah, the "Fire Man." Dressed in a black suit and a raspberry-colored shirt, Prophet Mensah gazed into the viewers' eyes as he lightly touched his chin with an index finger. I had a hunch that the Jericho Hour would have the typical Pentecostal/Charismatic acoustic flavor, so I put aside my apprehension about entering an unfamiliar congregation and made my way to the chapel on a Wednesday morning. One of the first to arrive, I surveyed the grounds. A large concrete archway led the visitors into an open space that housed a formidable structure. Massive silver columns supported an unfinished roof over a large seating area that could easily accommodate 150 people. A soft purple and azure color palette dominated the space. Plastic picnic chairs faced a pulpit positioned against an indigo wall. Aside from two sets of massive speakers, stage decorations were limited to two plastic pots of artificial flowers. Once the service began, these human-sized loudspeakers were in the spotlight, occasionally joined by female vocalists and a band of instrumentalists.

During the first hour of the service, the attendees, who were predominantly women, moved back and forth from one end of the room to the other, their steps accompanied by emphatic music, glossolalia, rattling of tambourines, humming, clapping, and clicking. The procession was punctuated by occasional invitations to attendees from assistant pastors to approach the pulpit, raise their hands, and pray "in the name of Jesus." Immediately following these individual prayers, we had to clap our hands three times and shout at the top of our lungs, "Fire, fire, fire!" The routine was eventually interrupted by the arrival of Prophet Mensah. Dressed all in white, he took the pulpit and read from the scriptures for about five minutes before descending from the stage and engaging in practical problem solving with the attendees. The day's service centered on a young woman who, as Prophet Mensah's inquiries revealed, was experiencing a stalled land purchase transaction. The prophet knew the root of the problem in a flash—the land, he proclaimed without hesitation, was haunted by idols, traditional deities who had been mobilized by the woman's uncle to harm her. With the problem identified, it was time to purge these evil spirits. Prophet Mensah poured some olive oil on the young woman's shoulders and placed a hand on her forehead, thrusting it back with rhythmic motions as the church assistants held her down. Soon her body was overtaken by one of the idols, who engaged in a fiery battle with the prophet. The spirit's verbal and physical assaults were countered with intense prayer and the sprinkling of olive oil. The encounter lasted for about twenty minutes until Prophet Mensah approached the young woman one last time, gripping her forehead tightly and howling, "Fire, fire, fire!" Defeated, the spirit fell to the ground.

The Wednesday Jericho Hour described here highlights two elements of Pentecostal/Charismatic services that are essential to understanding the sonic conflict in Accra. For one, the struggle against idols and demonized visions of traditional religions forms the bedrock of these meetings. Paradoxically,

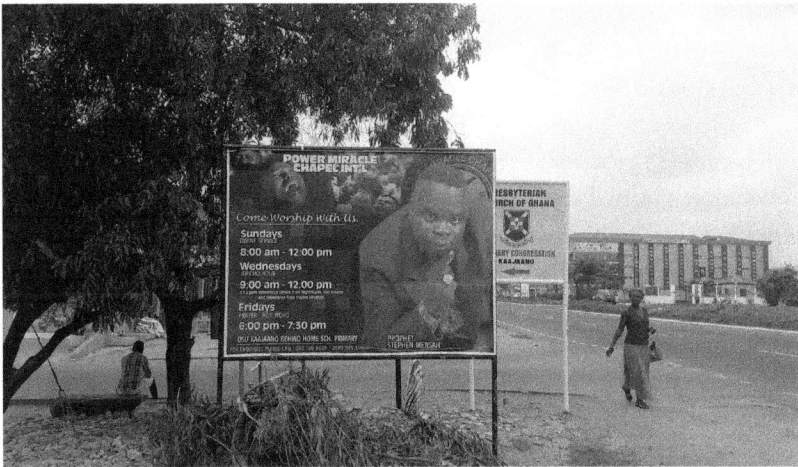

FIGURE 3.3. A signboard for Power Miracle Chapel International. Photo by author. 2017.

the Christian assault on the evil of custom incorporates nonhuman forces associated with traditional religiosity, rendering it essential to the Pentecostal/ Charismatic identity (de Witte 2008b, 13; Gifford 2004). Second, the composition of a typical Pentecostal/Charismatic service leaves no doubt about the relevance of music and sound for the devotees. The worship meetings I attended in Accra typically dedicated at least half of the service to various forms of sonic expression, including performances of a band and a choir, communal chanting and dancing, clapping, and speaking in tongues. Given the incessant sound emanating from the scores of congregations, large and small, that dot the city of Accra, one can imagine the palpable lull that Ga sonic restrictions inaugurate.

To understand the impact of sonic prohibitions on various dimensions of the Pentecostal/Charismatic presence in Ghana, let us first take a deep dive into the history of the movement's enchantment with sound. Today, exuberant worship is the most perceptible attribute of Pentecostal/Charismatic Christianity. Most churches have their own music ministries that are in charge of all matters related to sound and performance. They hire and organize musicians, purchase instruments, develop annual programs, and plan special events (van Dijk 2001, 52). Several Ghanaian scholars maintain that Pentecostal/Charismatic preaching interspersed with loud acclamations, shouts, claps, and singing owes its sonic exuberance to the joy expressed through music and dance in African culture (Asamoah-Gyadu 2005a; Sackey 2001). However, this Afrocentric approach does not fully capture the breadth of the Pentecostal experience. Pentecostal/Charismatic Christianity in Africa has acquired its own acoustic flavor that perhaps involved a metamorphosis and at times an amplification of its individual elements. Yet the aural vivacity of this strand of Christianity in Latin America and more recently in Australia demands that we go back in time to the early Pentecostals and their sonically distinct worship, which in turn connects to the sonic expressiveness of low-church Protestantism. In his exploration of early Pentecostal sound, David Daniels (2008) writes that "historically, Pentecostalism was more often heard than experienced by people. The neighbors would hear Pentecostal voices and music; the radio listeners would have heard Pentecostal worship services and sermons; TV viewers would hear Pentecostal songs, sermons, and prayers" (9). As early as 1906, at the time of the Azusa Street Revival in California, "primal cries with the movement of speech-music-ambient sound in between" were an integral part of the "red, hot, [and] gritty" Pentecostal soundscape (10–11). Daniels posits that the uniquely circular Pentecostal soundways, which began and ended with primal cries and featured "speech-music-ambient sound in between," were meant to promulgate the group's subversive agency in the face of the dominant linear sound of Protestantism, which did not involve primal cries and included silence and sounds "conducive to contemplation and reflection" (11–12). Melissa L. Archer's (2012) work, which draws on the periodicals of the Wesleyan-Holiness and Finished Work traditions in the period 1906 to 1916, offers an alternative interpretation of early Pentecostal worship. Speaking in foreign languages, being moved or "slain" by the spirit, and receiving the gifts of writing and reciting poetry were all tropes that Archer says were inspired by the references to the apocalypse in the Bible. A testimony from China recorded in *Bridegroom's Messenger* in 1915 leaves no doubt that loud Pentecostal worship was born long before the third wave of Pentecostal revival that ushered in Pentecostal/Charismatic Christianity. "At every night's tarrying service," wrote the witness, "the shouts and prayers and singing and speaking in tongues mingled and went up to God in a volume of praise like the sound of many waters" (qtd. in Archer 2012, 94). If one did not know the location and date of the reference, it could easily be mistaken for an account of Pentecostal/Charismatic worship anywhere from contemporary Accra to Cape Town or Rio de Janeiro.

Conversations with my interlocutors about the meaning and role of sound in the Pentecostal/Charismatic lifeworld largely echo the wide array of functional, scriptural, and phenomenological interpretations circulating in the academia at the turn of the twenty-first century. There is an impressive heterogeneity of musical programs in individual churches. Broadly speaking, various forms of prayer have distinct musical profiles. Praise and thanksgiving, the most energetic and upbeat segments of the service, involve clapping, dancing, singing, and playing instruments. Worship, in contrast, is more solemn and is usually accompanied by slow-paced vocals and fewer instruments.[5] When they contemplated the place and role of sound in worship, the majority of devotees said that scriptural references emphasize the merit of exuberant worship. The scriptures that are most often mobilized to encourage loud worship evoke images of warfare and victory. By far the most cherished episode from the Old Testament is Joshua 6:10–27, which details the Israelites' siege of Jericho and the destruction of its walls by the force of Israelite trumpets. Beyond affirming the apparent power of joint prayer, the passage is also believed to suggest that noise is a spiritual weapon for defeating enemies. Another favorite passage of my interlocutors was Psalm 47:1: "Clap your hands, all you nations; shout to God with cries of joy." "Shouting" is the key to grasping the value of the reference in the Pentecostal/Charismatic understanding. "Our shouting becomes a weapon, do you understand?" I was once asked during a conversation on this topic. "It is a weapon that God almighty uses to conquer the enemy. Even in nature, shouts tend to intimidate. When we do a lot of shouting, what we are trying to do is showcase our power."[6] To inspire sonic militancy against evil, preachers also resort to Psalm 98:4, another command to "shout for joy to the Lord." Apostle Samuel Yaw Antwi, who at the time we spoke was the general secretary of the Ghana Pentecostal and Charismatic Council, was kind enough to list all the relevant scriptural references to music and dancing at our 2016 meeting. "If you go through the scripture, you will find that music is an integral part of worship," he told me. "When it comes to presenting a message, it is good to attach it to a song if you can get a song that keeps your message."[7] He then proceeded to list biblical allusions to exuberant worship, among them Psalm 100:1 ("Shout for joy to the Lord, all the earth, burst into jubilant song with music"), Psalm 47:1 ("Clap your hands, all you nations; shout to God with cries of joy"), Psalm 150:1–6 ("Praise him with the sounding of the trumpet, praise him with the harp and lyre. Praise him with timbrel and dancing, praise him with the strings and pipe"), Psalm 96:1–2 ("Sing to the Lord a new song; sing to the Lord, all the earth"), and 2 Samuel 6:5 ("David and all Israel were celebrating with all their might before the Lord, with castanets, harps, lyres, timbrels, sistrums and cymbals").

Determined to get a first-hand experience of Pentecostal/Charismatic soundwaves, in the period 2014 to 2018, I attended services in Accra in churches that ranged in size, affiliation, and prominence. Worshippers and pastors alike frequently alluded to the aforementioned scriptural passages to stoke their sonically heated devotion. "Give a shout to the Lord!", "Let me hear you scream in the name of the Lord!" and similar incantations were frequently uttered with ecstatic joy. As if the sonic heights reached were not enough, church leaders constantly prodded their congregants to join in the celebration with their bodies, arms, voices, and instruments. I once heard a pastor ask his congregation to shout until every one of them had lost their voice as an offering to God.

The scriptural message behind Pentecostal/Charismatic music is decisive in creating the right atmosphere for praising God. Yet my interlocutors often pointed to the embodied sense of joy and hope that the sound waves generate. The music produced in church compounds that traverses almost every street and alley in Accra and enters people's homes through cracked windows and open gates has the power to illuminate the message of God. Belief in the divine power of the gospel and openness to spiritual transformation make people especially disposed to reaping the benefits of sonic messages. I asked Pastor Eric from the Power Miracle Chapel International if it was possible to receive blessings from listening to religious music when I met with him a few days after the Wednesday Jericho Hour. The answer was a resounding yes. "For example, when someone is preaching on radio, and the person tells you if you believe it, you should touch the radio. If you have the feeling, you touch it, and you believe God is gonna touch you, it works!"[8] The benefits of second-hand exposure to Pentecostal/Charismatic worship came up frequently in my discussions with devotees. Beyond the question of belief, interlocutors also underscored the spiritual force of the sound itself. Kwabena Asamoah-Gyadu maintains that the idea of anointing through the airwaves is an extension of a perception of "the mediation of the invisible through the visible" (Asamoah-Gyadu 2005b, 23). I have been told on multiple occasions that "music draws people to God," or that "the Holy Spirit uses the sound to affect whoever is listening at that point in time."[9] Marleen de Witte's work with Pentecostal/ Charismatic congregations in Accra complements these conclusions. Those who follow Pentecostal and Charismatic teachings believe that the senses are routinely disciplined to operate on two levels: first, to establish a relationship with the Holy Spirit, and second, to guard one's spirit against the corrupting power of the devil made perceptible via the senses. "The power of prophecy, preaching, praying aloud and gospel music," she maintains, "rests on the principle of the spiritual effect of the sound of divinely inspired speaking and singing" (de Witte 2008a, 700). In the Pentecostal/Charismatic epistemological framework, the human senses function as conduits for the contamination or sanctification of the soul. What transpires in these acoustic spaces reminds me of Charles Hirschkind's exploration of the ethical discipline instilled by Islamic cassette sermons in Cairo. Hirschkind's interlocutors attuned themselves to the sermons via embodied ethical listening, gradually honing their "ethically responsive sensorium" (Hirschkind 2006, 10). Accra's Christian residents experience a similar yet more spontaneous and instinctive reaction to the rhythms that permeate their being.

Only certain types of noise fit the Pentecostal/Charismatic mold. To start with, the slow and solemn beats typical of mainline churches are clearly inadequate. At the most basic level, the noise needs to be joyful to rattle the attendees, wake them from their slumber, and keep them active in body and soul. Pastor Eric compared the longing for loud and stimulating music to a fire burning in the chest or an irresistible urge to act: "I like to kick, kick, kick, kick. You see, I want the devil to know, I want my enemies to know that I am not a quiet person."[10] Pentecostal/Charismatic epistemology is thus redefining the very notion of noise. With its scriptural label of "noise," loud music, which is traditionally registered as an unpleasant or unwanted sound, becomes a desired experience that can yield a variation of emotional experiences for the listener, from tranquility to utter excitement. I also gathered from my conversations with devotees that the term "noise" often serves as a synonym for "sound" but is favored by virtue of the biblical injunction to make "a joyful *noise*" to the Lord.

My friend Sammy Young, an established minister and an inspirational gospel artist in Ghana, used to be one of the lead vocalists for the Great Fire Pentecostal International Ministry, a prominent megachurch in the country. As a young minister and singer, Sammy is very passionate about the charismatic style of worship and is notably outspoken about its superiority. "We charismatics always say if you want gentle [worship], go to the cemetery," he told me once as we ate chicken wings at Kentucky Fried Chicken, his favorite restaurant in Accra. "What we believe in is that we have to worship and be mad, because David was mad, he danced and he was naked in the Bible. . . . You have to worship and praise because you are worshipping a great God, and a big God. So we believe you have to shout because you have a purpose."[11] To illustrate his point, he first softly mumbled "Hallelujah" to imitate the priests of the mission churches, and then he roared out "Haaaaaaaaalllleeeeeelujah!" in a thunderous voice. When he saw me jump up in surprise, he laughed with satisfaction, "See, even if you are sleeping, you will wake up!"

This "right" kind of noise that spills out from Pentecostal/Charismatic churches, gatherings, and prayer camps is what makes "the spirit flow." "There is stupid noise that does not make sense, but there is some noise that makes sense," the head of the Evangel Church International told me, speaking passionately as I interviewed him in his car to ensure that the "stupid" noise of the street did not interfere with the recording.[12] The noise that "makes sense" invariably brings one closer to God. It is "joyful," both an implement for and a declaration of one's spiritual well-being. The pastor's wife from the same church offered an illuminating account of the power of the right kind of sound: "When the service starts and there is no music, you'll find it difficult to get into the service. The music helps you and when there's good music that uplifts you, it opens the spirit. . . . I don't know how to explain it, the spirit becomes alive. So it makes you enjoy the presence of God."[13]

The most memorable conversation I had about the qualities of agreeable noise was with Victor Yankee from the Evangel Church International. We met in 2017 and found ourselves sucked into a heated theoretical discussion about the nature of sound. As the head of creative ministries, Victor is in charge of an array of performance-related matters at the church, including worship, singing, theater, and dancing. Noticing my surprise at the idea of experiencing joy but above all tranquility from loud sound, he made a point of differentiating between physical and spiritual peace. "I understand where you are coming from, the Orthodox setting, where everything is low key," he said, alluding to my Georgian background, "but once the sound is good it affects you emotionally, it affects your feeling. The end point is that your spirit, deep in your mind, even though the sound might be a little loud, it can be peaceful."[14] This sense of peace and joy, Victor believes, derives from coming together in prayer, praising God, and "serving him with gladness." Listening to Victor's account, I began to realize that what my untrained ears registered as simply loud music could only be appreciated in its full splendor with the right spiritual attunement. Only with the proper sensory and spiritual disposition would the fervid shouts of worshippers become a weapon that, according to Victor, "the God almighty uses to conquer the enemy."

"Give a shout to the Lord!" is an injunction that pastors reiterate dozens of times during each service. It always works like a charm. Immediately, congregation members throw their hands in the air, raise their voices, and double the intensity of their prayer, alternating between shouts, claps, and speaking in tongues. The ensuing "joyful" noise, some tell me, is not always a reflection of their actual spiritual state but is rather their modus operandi for conquering emotional torment and attaining peace. "When you are going through something as a human being and it is eating you up, what you need is to shout out," a pastor told me one evening, comparing the exercise to a psychological release. Others have maintained that multifaceted activations of the sensorium that transpire in the Pentecostal service carry the promise of political as well as spiritual solidarity within the congregation, which in turn is responsible for dispelling the feelings of alienation and desperation that are especially prevalent in large urban settings. Investigating the Cherubim and Seraphim Church in Nigeria, Vicki Brennan (2018) concluded that Yoruba Pentecostals understand "the moral forms of action that constitute Christian practice to be primarily accomplished musically" (7). Accordingly, musical performance is a means of acting on their political and economic circumstances.

In *Sounding Islam*, Patrick Eisenlohr deconstructs the powerful spiritual experience that believers attain via sonic stimulation. He argues that while bodies can be contextually attuned to experience sound in a specific way, sound can be conceptualized as a quasi-objective phenomenon—an atmosphere or energy exuding from its source. To illustrate his point, Eisenlohr dissects the sound of Islam by comparing his interlocutors' semiotic evaluation of a heightened sonic experience with a structurally identifiable concentration of acoustic energy (Eisenlohr 2018, 4, 89, 91). Structural analysis does not fully capture the contextual nuances of a Pentecostal/Charismatic service—the unison of worshipping bodies; the kaleidoscope of somatic stimuli such as clapping, dancing, and speaking in tongues; the energy created by instrumental and vocal performances. Nonetheless, Eisenlohr's allusion to the physicality of acoustic energy experienced individually or in a group can be one way to think about the "touch of God" or the "sense of unity" that some of my interlocutors reported.

The discursive and practical emphasis on technological amplification of sound is the quality that even the tiniest Pentecostal/Charismatic congregation shares with a thousand-member megachurch. When loud worship became the evidence of the intensity and fervor of devotion in contemporary Pentecostal/Charismatic discourse, churches began to compete with each other to install better and louder high-tech speakers, the visual and aural emblems of their spiritual advantage. Such technological intervention generates an "amplified piety" that coats the surroundings in a thick layer of Pentecostal/Charismatic aurality, allowing it to reach a much larger and more diverse audience. I remember walking into the La branch of Christ Embassy Church and being struck by the size of the speakers compared to the size of the room. The small space would barely fit seventy people but was equipped with two sets of five-foot speakers that projected sound far beyond the building. Stacked one on top of another and arranged in formidable rows like domino pieces, speakers occupied a distinguished area in every other church I attended. Larger congregations even build special areas where sound engineers perform their magic.

Irrespective of where it is executed—in a thousand-seat stadium equipped with state-of-the-art sound amplification technology or a streetside tent church with a single battered speaker and a microphone—the production of loud noise is a sign of a fruitful Pentecostal/Charismatic worship service. "Shouting in the name of the Lord" or chanting at the top of one's voice is a common method of emotional release and spiritual determination, while singing and dancing are the glue that binds the congregation members together, giving them a sense of being "united in God." In addition, gospel singers engage in the transnational gospel music scene by becoming adept in the latest genres and styles of singing. As they enact transnational musical and bodily orientations in Ghana, they assert their proximity to the broader Afro-American transatlantic community and their distance from the local cultural background. Against this background, a month-long suspension of a typical service could easily precipitate decreased attendance and less income for a church. If music "can heal, move you in life, and let you get more favor," its absence can also set you back, make you feel less recognized and heard.[15] It comes as no surprise, then, that church leaders are reluctant to turn down the volume in honor of a traditional festival, especially since the rules of the game are dictated by deities who are believed to be an obstacle to Christian salvation and a hindrance to the country's progress. Rijk van Dijk (2001) argues that in contemporary Accra, defiance of the ban confirms that the defiant church "remains in touch with [the] transnational domain and that it has been able to resist successfully the attempt to bring it under the control of local and localizing forces effectuated by chieftaincy" (56).

If we take a step back and look carefully beyond the seemingly insurmountable disagreement between Pentecostal/Charismatic congregations and the followers of the Ga religion over the issue of sound, we will discover that the two communities share the fundamental notion that sound plays a decisive role in religious practice. It can be an agent of spiritual contamination or elevation, a force behind communal well-being or distress, or simply a source of joy for human and nonhuman agents who dare to indulge in it. The Pentecostal/Charismatic distinction between noise that makes sense and noise that does not echoes the Ga distinction between loud sounds that are either noise or not noise, since both are mobilized to bolster the boundaries between an in-group and an out-group.

Essentially, flexible use of these sonic categories permits members of both groups to express their aspirations to define, contest, or transform the "character of the city" (Bijsterveld 2013, 6). These aspirations, in turn, are informed by ongoing sociocultural shifts and the standing of a community in Accra's public domain. If followers of Pentecostal/Charismatic churches blast their speakers hoping to leave their "pagan" past behind, rigorous enforcement of the ritual guidelines allows the Ga to reclaim Accra as the city under their traditional authority. Despite the shared epistemologies of sound, the two conflicting bodies rely on drastically different legal positions as they attempt to translate their concerns to the Ghanaian state. As we will see in the next chapter, the Ga choose to defend the ritual ban by resorting to customary law while Pentecostal/Charismatic Christians insist on their constitutional right to practice religion.

4. When the Deities Visit

Translating Religion into the Language of the Secular

"Those who we call orthodox churches, they observe these things," Nii Shipi mused, leaning back in a plastic chair on his front porch in the Ga township of Teshie. My friend Akwetteh, an accomplished musician, a Teshie native, and a fellow scholar interested in Ga auralities, had brought me to his uncle's compound to talk about the ban on drumming. Seated in shade overlooking a lush, manicured front yard, Nii Shipi, a prominent member of the Teshie traditional community, shared his knowledge of the Ga lifeworld and the circumstances that had led to the Drum Wars. The orthodox churches were never an issue, he assured me: "They sing harmonious songs and the noise is within the chapel. During the ban, they don't drum, they don't clap in the chapel."[1] Although before the 1990s, the ban on drumming was practiced without any significant backlash, Ga authority in the city suffered significantly amid the rapid Pentecostalization of Accra, the influx of migrant workers who had no affiliation to the autochthonous Ga, and the liberalization of the media.[2] Nii Shipi says that the mounting pressure of disparate groups living in the city was the straw that broke the camel's back: "[Pentecostal/Charismatic churches] are in almost every corner of the town. Somebody's house is a church, somebody's workshop is a church. In the '80s, how many Twi speaking people did we have in Accra? How many northerners did we have in Accra? Not many. So then we did not have to announce [the ban] on the air because people observed it naturally. But in the '90s, when Accra became flooded by nonnatives, it became necessary for us to talk about it on air."

The exponential growth of Pentecostal/Charismatic Christianity has been attributed to a lengthy list of variables, including the unwillingness of Western Christianity to cater to the needs of Africans (Omenyo 2005), economic hardships in Ghana (Sackey 2001; Gifford 2004), the strong inclination of Pentecostal/Charismatic churches toward globality and the "sanctified consumerism" of the prosperity gospel (Meyer 1998, 2004a), a particular affinity of Pentecostal/Charismatic Christians for liberal capitalism (Kirby 2019), and the focus of Pentecostal/Charismatic churches on entertainment (Asamoah-Gyadu 2005a). The message proved to be irresistible to Ghana's upwardly mobile youth, who swarmed the new churches to praise the Lord with sonically spirited dedication. Pentecostalization steadily engulfed almost all aspects of public life and took hold of the popular religious imagination, including members of non-Pentecostal and non-Christian groups (Meyer 1999; de Witte 2008b). Intercommunal tensions, the continuous demonization of "traditional religions" by the leaders and congregations of the "one-man churches,"[3] and the sociopolitical hardships the Ga communities suffered in the 1990s soured relations between Ga traditionalists and Pentecostal/Charismatic congregations, triggering a ripple effect of resistance among the former (Asante 2011; Atiemo 2014). In the late 1990s, when the Christian devotees refused to temper their loud worship, the friction culminated in violent physical confrontations and assaults on Pentecostal/Charismatic churches.

This chapter introduces the discourse surrounding the negotiation of the sonic conflict as an illuminating entry point into the nature of secularity in contemporary Ghana. In the heat of the Drum Wars, instances of physical altercations, vandalized property, and injured citizens prompted members of Pentecostal/Charismatic congregations to seek legal action. Despite their shared understanding of the potential of sound to stimulate cross-world relations, the traditionalists and members of Pentecostal/Charismatic churches had to translate their disagreement about whose deities had the right to command the soundscape into the legal language of the secular state. Needless to say, much was lost in the process of translation, since neither that vocabulary nor the legal system in Ghana accommodates the customary understanding of coexistence or the agency of the deities involved in the altercation. The act of translation thus pushed both sides to reduce their positions to different secular discourses: human rights (Pentecostal/Charismatic Christians) and cultural heritage (Ga people). These two discourses reveal divergences in the sociopolitical status of these two communities in relation to secularism.

The freedom-of-worship stance the Pentecostal/Charismatic Christians adopted meant that they entered the dialogue as a religious community. Ga people's mobilization of their right to culture, in contrast, framed them as a cultural community and downplayed their religious identity. This move was conditioned by the dual model of justice that operates in Ghana that marries modern constitutional law with customary laws that have been subsumed under common law (Ngwakwe 2013; Bennett 1995; Emiola 1997). Although practically speaking, the label of culture allowed Ga people more freedom to impose their ritual regulations on the area under their customary jurisdiction, the distinction brought to the forefront the "epistemological ethnocentrism" of Western secularism (Mudimbe 1988, 28). It highlighted the prioritization of Christianity and other world religions over the "lesser" regimes of truth,[4] including indigenous belief systems (Masuzawa 2005; Smith 2004).

This chapter departs from previous work on the Drum Wars by centering the import of the legal references used in the mediations between Ga traditionalists and Pentecostal/Charismatic Christians and the implications of those terms for the place of religion in Ghanaian public sphere. This allows us to apprehend the incongruous positions of Christianity and traditional religions in Ghana and in West Africa more broadly. These positions reflect the deep entanglement of the Christian missionary past, colonial modernity, and modern secularism. A productive reading of the Drum Wars involves disentangling secular discourses and the practices advanced by or ascribed to various religious bodies from the official blueprint of secularism as a political and ideological regime and acknowledging these secularities as viable forms of religious presence (with their own sensory epistemologies) in a modern nation-state. As Nilüfer Göle (2015) writes, as secularism travels outside the West and its Christian wellspring, it is "semantically adopted, politically reinvented, collectively imagined and legally institutionalized" (58). In the process, it diverges from the ideal type, or what Florian Zemmin (2019) calls a "hegemonic elaboration," and transforms into a secularity in practice—differentiations, both practical and discursive, between secular and non-secular spheres that reflect local sensory and epistemological orders. This chapter presents the discursive formulation of the legal positions of the two parties in their attempts to align their respective aspirations with the ideal type of secularism. As we will see, this framework fails to accurately represent Ghanaian secularity, understood not only in terms of institutional arrangements that deviate from secularism as a political order but also as an ontological reality that informs those arrangements.

The Drum Wars

In May 1998, traditional priests accompanied by Ga youth ransacked the premises of the Lighthouse Chapel International, a Charismatic church in the Korle-Gonno neighborhood, and physically assaulted the congregation members.[5] "A group of angry elders and young men suspected to be followers of Ga religion" vandalized churches across Accra exactly one year later. Allegedly, the rationale behind these misdemeanors was the combination of provocative statements made by several radical Pentecostal/Charismatic church leaders on local FM stations and violations of the ban on drumming.[6] *GhanaWeb* reported the incident as follows: "Three busloads of angry traditionalists, armed with clubs and other dangerous weapons, were said to have stormed some churches, including the Church of Pentecost, Dansoman, and beaten up some members of the congregation."[7] The intruders reputedly threw stones at the congregation members and drove away with instruments and loudspeakers that belonged to the churches.[8]

Several attempts at a truce and state-led appeals for peace contributed to the remission of aggression during the 2000 Hɔmɔwɔ festival season as Accra's Christian community collectively reduced its sonic footprint for a few weeks.[9] However, peace was short lived. The Christ Apostolic Church in Osu was assailed a year later, on May 13, 2001, after church leaders refused to stop drumming in response to a request from a Ga *wulɔmɔ*. A young crowd of fifty individuals invaded the church premises, broke glass doors and windows, vandalized vehicles belonging to the church members, and confiscated instruments.[10] People on both sides suffered severe injuries, and police were called to restore order.[11] When I interviewed notable members of the church in 2015, I learned that just before the hostilities, Rev. Annor-Yeboah, the acting chair of the church, had told the Ga community members to go to hell, which set in motion an aggressive reaction.[12] A week later, Ga youth and *wulɔmɛi* gathered at the Independence Square, in the vicinity of the Christ Apostolic Church, reputedly to carry out another attack. However, police present at the scene forced the group to leave "amidst insults and accusation" (Asante 2011). From there, the group moved toward the headquarters of Ghana Prison Service located in cantonments where five churches were housed. In the process of taking musical instruments away, they injured several people and damaged church property.[13]

In 1998 to 2001, similar attacks took place across the city. After finding names of the churches that were attacked from news articles, I located and interviewed the surviving members in the spring of 2018. I spoke with the representatives of four churches attacked at the height of the Drum Wars: the Christ Apostolic Church at North Kaneshie Central, El-Shaddai Ministries in Accra, the Gospel Light Chapel International at Mallam Junction, and the Church of Pentecost at Alajo Central. The sequence of events they described matched in each case: ten to twenty-five young males appeared unannounced, equipped with bottles and in some cases with sticks and cutlasses; they seized whatever equipment they could find (drums, speakers, amplifiers, guitars, and even an organ); and they drove off. At the time of the attacks all four churches played moderate to loud music, including drums. Despite direct appeals to the local traditional councils or petitions submitted to the police, the instruments were never returned. While other attacked congregations stood by or resisted moderately as the instruments were carried off, members of the El-Shaddai Ministries proudly informed me that they refused to be spectators of their humiliation and fought back. Leaving women, children, and the elderly indoors to keep them safe, the men stepped outside to face the Ga crowd. During the commotion, one member was hit on the head with a Coca-Cola bottle and suffered several cuts. "It was scary!" a church elder told me. "Even as a man it was scary because of how they were holding those bottles. And you were not prepared to take the bottle or hurt somebody."[14]

According to public statements and interviews with the Ga community members, the underlying rationale for the attacks was the combination of the Christians' violation of the ban on drumming and publicly voiced disrespectful statements about the Ga lifeworld. Pentecostal/Charismatic pastors were singled out as the instigators of an open confrontation through their "inflammatory remarks and vitriolic attacks on traditional religion and practices."[15] During the transformation of Accra's soundscape in the 1990s, Ga sonic categories also shifted, leading to certain misconceptions regarding the sanctioned forms and levels of noise making. An indication of the changing sonic categories in the print media was the gradual adjustment of the associated terminology. Stories reporting on the Hɔmɔwɔ festival in the *Daily Graphic* slowly transitioned from "ban on drumming" to "ban on drumming and noise making" or "ban on drumming and dancing" when referring to the ritual noise restriction. Simply put, the traditional sonic prohibition preceding Hɔmɔwɔ, most notably of drumming, sizzling, and clapping, was replaced by a broadened secular category of "noise" and "dancing" that consisted of numerous sources of sound production and forms of entertainment that were typically accompanied by music. This change in language enabled Ga people to be more selective about the types of noise they sought to eliminate. During and after the conflict, Ga objections to the churches often went beyond drumming, as had been customary, and encompassed the overall loudness of worship, with or without the instruments. When I lived in Accra, I often asked people from the Ga community what kinds of sounds they thought the ban on drumming encompassed. The range of sonic expressions presented to me—"any form of sound that makes noise," car engines, singing, organs, shouting, speaking into the microphone, "high levels of noise," or "excessive noise"—left plenty of room for interpretation. This refashioning of the ban on drumming reflects a subjective evaluation of noise as something undesirable, unwanted, and irritating and clearly conveys the exasperation of Ga community members with churches that refused to show them deference.

The Drum Wars engendered fervent interest among the Ghanaian public and media in the capital and beyond. As tensions between "tradition" and Pentecostal/Charismatic Christianity plagued all regions of the country, the population recognized familiar tropes and responded either in support of or in opposition to the Christian defiance of the custom. The most striking feature of this discourse was its legal character, which cloaked the conflict in secular garb and concealed the epistemological consonance between the disputing bodies. "Behind the apparent opposition between Pentecostalism and traditional religion," writes Marleen de Witte, "is a difference in religious spatiality, but remarkable similarity in the place of sound in relation to the spiritual" (2008a, 691). Earlier, I proposed that aurality could be an agent of spiritual elevation and contamination, a cause of collective well-being and distress, a resource for communing with the deities, and a means of expressing and negotiating sociopolitical aspirations in the public sphere. While the Pentecostal/Charismatic faction discursively styled its public defense in terms of the right to religion, it was no stranger to thinking about sound as fundamental to crossworld exchange. Nor should we forget that individual Christians who hailed from outside Accra were familiar with similar customary norms in their own regional enclaves.[16] Here, I depart from the argument that Pentecostal/Charismatic Christians reimagined citizenship and territory exclusively in national rather than ethnic terms (de Witte 2008b; Meyer 2010), a claim that has been ascribed to their individualistic model of agency that urges members to sever ties with the past (Marshall 2009; Meyer 1999). Granted, Pentecostal/Charismatic churches champion withdrawal from traditional religions, but practitioners typically distance themselves on the surface and away from the gaze of their ethnic communities. The fact that comparable pre-festival restrictions are consistently observed outside Accra confirms an unbroken devotion to customary practices, or at least a reluctance to transgress customary prohibitions. In the heat of the Drum Wars, Ga community leaders picked up on these regional differences, arguing that it was not fair "to question the ban in Accra on constitutional or religious grounds" when similar practices flourished in other parts of the country.[17] In recent decades, the most striking example of continued devotion to the custom outside Accra was the funeral in Kumasi of Nana Afia Kobi, the thirteenth Asante queen, in 2017.[18] On this occasion, all Kumasi residents were required to stay indoors from 7 p.m. to 4 a.m. so as not to disrupt the queen's funeral rites.[19] Nearly a year later, at the culmination of the ceremony, the Kumasi Traditional Council banned all funeral services, business activities, and "other outdoor social events associated with noise making" for ten days throughout the Asante region, which accounts for one-fifth of Ghana's population.[20] My Ga interlocutors repeatedly insisted that no one—whether Christian, Muslim, or traditionalist—would dare to breach the Asante funeral customs in Kumasi. Yet when these same "ethnic strangers" came to Accra, they gave the Ga chiefs and wulɔmɛi the cold shoulder, an unfortunate development attributed not only to the city's cultural diversification but also to the implicit hierarchy of traditional authorities who represent different regions of Ghana.[21]

The decaying interfaith relations were also linked to the patterns of land ownership inherited from the colonial period and land-related resentments among Ga people. As Accra became Ghana's economic and political capital in the second half of the nineteenth century, the colonial government introduced the Public Lands Ordinance (1876) to facilitate individual and corporate land acquisition. The ordinance prohibited the sale or transfer of land by owners unless the administration had determined its value, effectively obligating families and individuals to alienate their land without proper reimbursement (Sackeyfio-Lenoch 2014). The state's takeover of Ga lands continues to this day. The Public Lands Ordinance of 1951 is especially notable for "leasing" land to the government and religious bodies for ninety-nine years in exchange for a meager annual fee (Quarcoopome 1992). The new Land Act of 2020, which was introduced to create a more modern framework for land administration, maintained the same lease period for residential purposes, but with more transparency in terms of proper documentation and registration of leases. Aggressive incursion into Ga property provoked resistance in the second half of the twentieth century. In the 1950s and 1960s, groups of youths such as the Ga Shifipo Kpee (the Ga Steadfast Association) and the Ga Ekome Feemo Kpee (the Ga Unity Party) called for a collective awakening in the face of the danger posed by strangers who sought to displace the Ga people both physically and socially (Osei-Tutu 2000–2001, 77; Arthur 2017, 175). Although Kwame Nkrumah's administration disbanded the more radical action groups, moderate groups, including the Ga-Dangme Concern Youth Association and the Ga-Dangme Council, remained active. These groups push the government to return leased land or pay a fair price and demand respect from the nongovernmental bodies that occupy their land.

Justice Arthur alleges that the first instance of the Drum Wars in 1998 was largely about Ga indignation over building projects initiated by the Lighthouse Chapel International on land the church had legally purchased from the Accra Metropolitan Assembly in 1995 (Arthur 2017, 115–16). The question of land ownership—understood in terms of Ga collective authority over Accra's territories—is a primary reason why the Ga community insists that the conflict with Pentecostal/Charismatic congregations was not only justified but also required. The land-centered argument shaped the nature of the Ga legal defense in the dispute and is vital to understanding the intricacies of Ghanaian secularity.

Legal Discourse: Culture versus Religion

From a legal perspective, Pentecostal/Charismatic Christians explained their defiance of the ban in terms of their "freedom to practice any religion and to manifest such practice" (Article 21c, 1992 Constitution). Christian contributors to the *Daily Graphic* insisted that since the Ga community identified the ban on drumming as a religious act with "deep spiritual connotation," its forced imposition represented an infringement on their "freedom of thought, conscience and belief" (Article 21b, 1992 Constitution).[22] The Commission on Human Rights and Administrative Justice, an independent government organization in charge of investigating human rights abuses in Ghana, endorsed the legal defense of Pentecostal/Charismatic congregations. In a series of public statements, representatives of the commission invalidated the claim that Ga people could impose their "religious or cultural requirements on others" because that compelled Christians "to forego their constitutional right" to manifest their religion. "Viewed objectively," a 1999 statement by the commission's public relations officer maintained, "the traditional council is not being hindered from practising its religion; on the contrary, the traditional council is seeking to hinder other people from practising their religion."[23]

A statement issued by the Ghana Pentecostal and Charismatic Council, the Christian Council of Ghana, and the Ghana Catholic Bishops' Conference in the aftermath of the initial tensions provides more information about the details of their legal defense:

We strongly believe that the statement from the Ga Traditional Council infringes on our basic human and constitutional rights.

We are being asked to involve ourselves in traditional religious practices, which we do not believe in. We are being forced to avoid something that our religion expects us to do, namely, to sing, drum and praise God.

Our traditional leaders should not force us to do something against our conscience. Such an action is against our human rights. . . .

We hope that the Ga Traditional Council would respond to our gesture by respecting our way of worship.[24]

This excerpt sheds light on one of the characteristics of the postconflict discourse: both sides mobilized the notion of respect. On the face of it, it would appear that the two groups were building on the equality of respect as one of the cornerstones of classical secularism conditioned by a separation of the political and nonpolitical spheres (Maclure and Taylor 2011). In the course of the negotiations, the Pentecostal/Charismatic Christians consistently advocated for mutual respect for "each other's constitutional right" and Ga community members insisted that "ethnic strangers" had disrespected their right over land as enshrined in customary law.[25] Despite different legal positions, both sides conceptually positioned themselves within a discourse of secularization that emphasized mutual respect between various communities (Bhargava 2013).

Thinking of the notion of respect only in terms of the privileges the secular legal framework promises, however, obscures other essential implications of this discourse, namely the African values of intercommunal understanding and harmony. In contrast to the favored paradigm of interreligious encounter in the scholarship on African coexistence (Yakubu 2022; Bediako 2004), media reports and my conversations with Ga community members revealed a tendency to demand respect for "the tradition and culture of the Ga people," "the Ga people and the Ga Traditional Council," or simply "each other" rather than the Ga religion.[26] As I will explain later, the emphasis on cultural rather than religious respect also makes sense given the subsumption of traditional practices under the category of culture. And when Pentecostal/Charismatic Christians and traditionalists demand respect, those on the receiving end of the anticipated recognition are not only humans, as in classical secularism, but are also deities and other nonhuman members of the respective communities (Atiemo 2014, 237). The involvement of deities is usually implicit in the official statements, but some of those statements also make explicit references to nonhuman agents. In the announcement by the Christian community quoted above, they clearly refer to respect for their God, who demands acoustically conspicuous worship.

"Our traditional leaders should not force us to do something against our conscience," argued the members of the Christian bodies. This part is also critical, since according to Jocelyn Maclure and Charles Taylor, freedom of conscience is the second component of secularism after equality of respect (2011, 20). The word "conscience" can be understood as moral knowledge derived from culture or society or as introspectively acquired self-knowledge, both of which determine the human ability to distinguish between right and wrong. Although this philosophical term is relativistic and subjective, it is an oddity in conventional religious language because of its inward-looking nature, which contrasts with the act of accessing moral law from an external entity like God. As such, conscience is a religiously fallible term because it is obtained through human agency rather than from God, and its use by Christian leaders indicates their determination to engage with a secular discourse.

The rest of the statement—"we are being asked to involve ourselves in traditional religious practices, which we do not believe in"—betrays the fear that if God is not worshipped with appropriate sonic fervency, the devotees might become implicated in paying heed to the Ga deities. In the Ghanaian context, I have noticed that the word "believe" signifies paying respect to, venerating, or worshipping one's own nonhuman beings but does not necessarily preclude the existence and sometimes even the spiritual authority of other nonhuman beings. Thus, simply because the statement suggests that Christians do not want to be involved in practices they do not believe in does not mean that they are not aware of the existence of the Ga deities. It could even mean that they are wary of their presence. McIntosh (2019) designates such awareness as "polyontologism," a form of pluralism that acknowledges the ontological reality of various sources of religious authority. The statement thus exemplifies the synthetic nature of the strict banishment of nonhuman agents from the public domain that is typical of the ideal type of secularism and an overlap between secular and theological languages, as it acknowledges the actuality of traditional nonhuman agents while couching the refusal to obey the customary regulations in a state-endorsed secular discourse.

Legally speaking, the traditionalists played the culture card. They argued their case from the perspective of customary law, which Article 11(3) of the Constitution defines as laws that are "applicable to particular communities in Ghana." Article 26(1) sanctions the performance of cultural practices: "Every person is entitled to enjoy, practice, profess, maintain and promote any culture, language, tradition or religion subject to the provisions of [1992] Constitution." The customary law approach differentiates between culture and religion, a choice of terminology that has political implications. Conceiving of groups in terms of their religious rights, explains Elizabeth Shakman Hurd (2015), heightens the sociopolitical salience of whatever national or international authorities label as "religion" (39). She calls this phenomenon the religious rights imperative—the pressure to place oneself in a religious taxonomy designed by the state, which inadvertently privileges certain faith communities over others. Communities that do not fit neatly into these boxes perpetually seek self-identification vis-à-vis the state or other religious institutions, scrambling to adopt the labels most serviceable for establishing their legitimacy. Tisa Wenger and Bjørn Ola Tafjord offer a thorough historical and discursive analysis of how both Pueblo Indians in the US and Bribri people in Costa Rica apply the concept of religion to their traditions and lifestyles to better defend them in the political arena (Tafjord 2016). Wenger maintains that although such a redefinition did not always fit well with older cultural norms, it allowed Pueblo Indians to fight against government suppression. By classifying their ceremonies as worship, they fashioned an image that was familiar and acceptable to the American Christian mainstream (Wenger 2009, 5, 164). In his exploration of the dynamics of religious coexistence in Kenya, Erik Meinema (2021, 102) suggests that traditionalists sometimes claim the label of religion to gain access to civil society organizations that take an interfaith approach.

The Ga people geared their politics of language in an opposite direction, choosing to defend their cultural rather than religious rights, but with the same goal of ensuring the greatest possible benefit for the community in terms of its religious self-expression. The Ga traditionalists I spoke with were quick to stress that Ghana's customary law officially recognized Ga people as the custodians of Accra's lands. Accordingly, their demands were modeled after "a custodian's point of view."[27] Numo Akwaa Mensah III, the Nai *wulɔmɔ* of Ga-Mashie, illustrated the implicit expectations of the arrangement through the analogy of the landlord-tenant relationship: "if you are a tenant in an apartment you have rented, you have many rights but there are laws governing the tenancy agreement, which are set by the landlord."[28] Once these laws are violated, he went on, the landlord has every right to take the transgressor to the court. Even if this formulation sounds convincing, in practice, it is inaccurate due to the messy terrain of legal pluralism in Ghana. While Ghana's hybrid legal system was designed to accommodate multiple political, legal, customary, and religious authorities, "the reality of postcolonial society is that the State superimposes its laws on other legal structures of society, a situation that pushes chiefly laws into the margins of the legal orders" (Tweneboah 2019, 70). Customary law is only one of the legal systems of Ghana along with the Constitution, "enactments made by or under the authority of the Parliament," and "orders, Rules, and Regulations made by any person or authority under a power conferred by Constitution" (Article 11[1], 1992 Constitution). The Constitution is recognized as "the supreme law of Ghana" and "any other law found to be inconsistent with any provision of the Constitution" is void (Article 1[2], 1992 Constitution). In other words, in the case of tensions between the two legal systems, customary regulations are to be subordinated to statutory law. Ambani and Ahaya (2015), who examine an identical clause in the Kenyan constitution, write that the Constitution is the "most important yardstick against which the relevance of all other laws, religions, customs, and practices are measured" (49). This means that legally speaking, customary regulations, such as the Ga period of quiet, cannot be enacted in contravention of citizens' constitutional rights, in this case, their right to religion.

"Because the contemporary Ghanaian nation-state emerged from diverse sacred traditional polities whose legal norms and institutions were legitimated by spiritual forces of nature," writes Seth Tweneboah (2019), "there is a continuous role of religious and customary normative systems in the public sphere" (1). Although the legal plurality established in Ghana seeks to balance overlapping state and nonstate rights, it is also cumbersome because secularism as a Eurocentric epistemological and institutional regime cannot accommodate the complexity of the customary system with its inclusion of nonhuman entities in the public sphere. Thus, Ghana's legal system does not always correspond to how things are done in practice, and actors stretch regulations to fit historically accepted norms. The legal position the Ga community adopted proved effective because it validated the imposition of Ga customs on all residents of Accra. This would have been constitutionally implausible had they operated as a religious entity, since freedom of worship does not sanction the entanglement of one faith group in the religious directives of another. Strictly speaking, the translation of Ga claims into the language of customary law still imposes limits on Ga authority. However, the accuracy of the translation is not paramount to the involved actors, as both the Ga community and Pentecostal/Charismatic Christians are compelled to engage in what Birgit Meyer calls theological reductionism to adapt to a legal system that does not capture their respective ontologies (Meyer 2020, 162). Interestingly, the meaning behind Ga claims framed as customary rights seems to remain intact not only for the Ga but also for some Pentecostal/Charismatic Christians.

The discussion boils down to the traditional understanding of land custodianship, which encompasses more rights over the land than modern constitutional law sanctions. While researching Ghana's dual law, I was fortunate to speak with Isaac Lartey Annan, the director of human rights at the Commission on Human Rights and Administrative Justice. Dr. Annan, who also teaches land law, sees the issue of land ownership as a minefield for the Ghanaian state:

"In the Western world, the land belongs to the state. Here, the land that you are practicing your religion [on] as a charismatic does not belong to you. They will tell you 'This is our land', [but] meanwhile the state is sitting on that land. Land tenure gives people that right to dictate to you what to do."[29] In principle, the state of Ghana does not own land. "The very land upon which Ghana is built and on which every socioeconomic, legal, and political activity takes place," notes Tweneboah (2019), "is recognized as the sacred property of the chief's ancestors" (49). Communal rights over land extend to nonhuman entities anchored in that territory. State actors are aware of traditional sovereignty over the land, even if the system of legal pluralism does not capture their ontological entirety. In Accra, for instance, state officials often tiptoe around the Ga chiefs, who maintain custody of the land, when they need approval for various construction projects. The awareness-raising programs of the National Commission for Civic Education in violence-prone areas also stress the traditional understanding of land ownership, according to which customary jurisdiction cannot be overridden even if the land is physically in the hands of another party.[30] Although nonhuman entities are never mentioned in official discourse, they must be taken into consideration because the ritual prohibitions implicit in customary jurisdiction also cater to their needs. When members of the Ga community position their legal claims in customary law, they mobilize this traditional understanding of land ownership, paying no mind to the fact that in strictly legal terms, constitutional rights to religion override their customary rights. The Nai *wulɔmɔ* of Ga-Mashie articulated Ga expectations: "You are here on the Ga land, you go by the law. When you go to Rome, you do as the Romans do. It is our right by culture and by custom. If we have constitution supporting custom, it should support us, because that is who we are."[31]

The line of reasoning that accompanies the culture-based defense of the Ga community echoes recent scholarly critiques of secularism as a Western political doctrine. Authors in this camp question the universal applicability of the model because of its epistemological implications and insist on historically and culturally informed alternatives that reckon with the uniqueness of local circumstances (Cady and Hurd 2010; Casanova 2001). These secularities—which depart from classical constitutional, institutional, and ideological systems—are informed by regionally relevant processes of defining, mediating, and remaking the role of religion in the public sphere. In the midst of negotiations, the Ga community advocated for culturally informed decision-making that paid heed to the reality of "plural, shared, overlapping and competing authorities in the governance space" that was akin to the Foucauldian notion of multiple governmentalities (Tweneboah 2019, 46).

Although Ga people interpret the rights guaranteed by customary law generously, they are much more rigid about the 1995 bylaw on noise abatement. They complement their insistence on their right to culture with an equally pronounced claim that the Pentecostal/Charismatic right to religion is powerless in the face of the bylaw, which seeks to establish "public peace and social tranquility" for the entire city.[32] In 2001, K. B. Asante cited the failure of the Accra Metropolitan Assembly to enforce the bylaw the previous year as the reason for the ongoing clashes.[33] The year before, a prominent Ga public figure, Dr. N. Josiah-Aryeh, had complained that Pentecostal/Charismatic church leaders were overlooking the nuisance control bylaw in favor of their "freedom to practice any religion." He argued that such behavior was unacceptable because one could not choose "which law to obey and which to ignore."[34] It is clear that a double standard exists about interpreting who is law abiding in the context of the Drum Wars. On the one hand, the Ga defense rests on the claim that blind compliance with human rights provisions is not beneficial to the country, but on the other hand, they insist that the nuisance control bylaw be strictly enforced. The selective approach corresponds to the perception of the ban on drumming as a communal practice of nuisance abatement that is beneficial not only to the Ga community but to the city as a whole.

The Culturalization of Traditional Religions

As discussed in previous chapters, the juxtaposition of custom or culture with religion communicates the larger symbolic system that structured missionary and colonial discourses of modernity, development, and progress and continues to structure contemporary discourses on these topics (Steegstra 2005). The positioning of traditional lifeworlds within the domain of culture dates back to the precolonial phase in the late eighteenth and the early nineteenth centuries and evinces the failure of missionaries and travelers to recognize the existence of religious sensibilities among Africans. Reports of "nonreligion," explains David Chidester (1996), sent a political message that indigenous people lacked "any recognizable human right or entitlement to the land in which they lived" (14).

Practices that did not neatly satisfy the modernist expectations of proper religiosity were reframed in terms of cultural heritage. Cati Coe's illuminating study of Ghana's education system traces the roots of this romantic-nationalist conception of culture to the Basel missionaries who transported notions of the European "folk" to the Gold Coast (Coe 2005). Coe acknowledges the tensions that arose from this approach. On the one hand, the missionary project "created a sense of the nation based on language and ethnicity," but on the other, it "generated a notion of modernity based on a rejection of the lifeworld of tradition" (31). The colonial government continued to pursue the exploration of African heritage as a foundation for indirect rule (de Witte and Meyer 2012, 47). After independence, beginning with Kwame Nkrumah's national movement in the 1950s, culture, expressed primarily through various art forms, was redefined as the essence of Ghanaian identity to be promoted and preserved. The symbol of this revival was Sankofa, a mythical bird with its head turned back in the direction of its origin. This state cultural propaganda had political implications. In a country where ethnic loyalties trumped a sense of national belonging, the state's curation of certain cultural practices emerged as a shrewd method of legitimizing power (Coe 2005). Nkrumah's regime famously expropriated various traditional symbols of authority, weaving them into the fabric of his own personality cult (Hess 2001; Birmingham 1998; Amoah 2007). As subsequent governments sought to maintain power after Nkrumah was deposed in 1966, the state's interest in nation-building waned. In the 1980s and 1990s, Jerry John Rawlings reinvigorated cultural nationalism with some modifications; he put more emphasis on the modernization of traditional festivals (Schauert 2015; Lentz and Wiggins 2017). In the first decade of the twentieth century, President John Kufuor, a neoliberal politician, saw culture primarily as a potential business model. Kufuor is known for the introduction of the National Friday Wear program that encouraged Ghanaians to "wear Ghana" on Fridays (Asare 2022, 34; Schauert 2015, 20). The Pentecostalization of the public and political spheres around this period—the active deployment of Christian symbols and the increased visibility of Christian public officials—also weakened the appeal of Sankofaism as a national project (de Witte and Meyer 2012). Although interest in arts and culture has waxed and waned with successive political leaders, Sankofaism has maintained its vigor as an ideology that aims to create favorable conditions for development by fostering social inclusion and a sense of unity (Lentz and Wiggins 2017; Asare 2022). The culturization of traditional practices has been accompanied by the simultaneous reification of Christianity and Islam as the country's religions.

When Pentecostal/Charismatic churches entered the public sphere in the mid-1990s, they quickly capitalized on the dichotomy between tradition/custom/culture and modernity in order to lay claim to the latter (Corten and Marshall-Fratani 2001). More than any other group, Pentecostal/Charismatic Christians have adopted and popularized the basic components of secular modernity, most notably individualism and consumer culture (Kirby 2019). The "reversed paradigm" of religiosity, in which a religious movement is widely recognized as a bastion of modernity rather than a sign of bygone times, is largely responsible for the political and social eminence of Pentecostal and Charismatic churches in Ghana. Since its inception, the movement's promise of success and prosperity has been coupled with the vision of African culture as the realm of the devil, a localizing force that is detrimental to Ghana's development (Gifford 1998). This is despite the fact that Pentecostal/Charismatic Christianity is to a large extent defined in dialogue with traditional religions. As Marleen de Witte (2008b) puts it, the new churches "implicitly incorporate the logic, spiritual forces, and ways of worship of local religious traditions as media through which Christian spirituality is communicated" (13). Since the deliverance praxis of Pentecostal/Charismatic churches emphasizes "breaking" ties with the past, many devout worshippers ardently avoid involvement with the culture (Coe 2005; Meyer 1999).

The distinction between Christianity and culture is thus maintained in the contemporary vernacular. As Marijke Steegstra (2005) puts it, "the contrast between 'culture' as something of 'the past' and Christianity as 'modern' and 'civilized' determines the discursive space within which Ghanaians have to organize their view of the world, even though different values are attached to culture in local usage" (317). When the Ga commitment to "heathen" deities came under attack in the heat of the Drum Wars, it became an excuse for some Pentecostal/Charismatic leaders to label the community as backward and therefore unfit for the "evolved" monotheistic sensibilities of Accra's emerging urbanites (Arthur 2017, 142). Even in its ahistorical and depoliticized form, traditional culture attracts charges of unsophistication, ignorance, and backwardness in a Pentecostalite city like Accra (van Dijk 2001, 36).[35] Not surprisingly, Ga traditionalists often try to normalize their practices for mostly Christian interlocutors and state representatives by reframing the ban on drumming as a standard period of spiritual deliberation and "the atmosphere for meditation" as something akin to the Easter fast or Ramadan, downplaying the active role of the deities in the process. In a 1998 statement, the Ga Traditional Council emphasized the "deeper spiritual connotations" of the ban, characterizing it as something "bordering on the purification of the mind and soul."[36]

Writing about nation-building in Nigeria, J. D. Y. Peel (2016) observed that traditional religion had to be desacralized by taking it out of the category of religion and moving it to the category of culture that all citizens could be proud of (154). (I will look at similar state-led initiatives in chapter 6.) However, when the discursive culturalization of traditional religions is carried out by traditional communities, as in the legal defense examined here, it rarely means their actual desacralization. In fact, for Ga traditionalists, the use of the words "culture" or "custom" does not exclude the presence of religious elements. In part, this has to do with the semantic ambiguity of religion as a concept. In the Ga language, "religion" is commonly translated as *jamɔ*, or worship, and is used in reference to Christianity and Islam. By contrast, my interlocutors rarely referred to the ban on drumming or other associated rites strictly as religion, because it is difficult to disentangle ritual practice from a broader system called custom, or *kusum*. *Kusum* refers to the overall character of a community that permeates all aspects of life. It incorporates the traditional philosophy of the communal religion as well as beliefs about land ownership and the place of nonhuman actors in relation to human life. In addition, labels like "religion," "culture," and "custom" are never carved in stone; actors may use them interchangeably or deliberately mobilize them to achieve particular ends. I have witnessed the Hɔmɔwɔ festival being described as both religion and culture, as a combination of the two, and as a form of religion that is not institutional.[37]

The Perks of Being a Culture

Irrespective of how we approach the incremental culturalization of traditional religions—as a "cultural innovation" (Lentz 2001), a "restatement" (Odotei 2002), or a commodification—the initial impression is that this process stems from the marginalization of traditional religions. I have shown how the long history of denial of African religiosity, the hybrid legal system of Ghana, Sankofaism, and the fundamental challenge of squeezing the traditional world view into the Western notion of proper religiosity contribute to an environment where traditional communities are forced to resort to defending their cultural rather than their religious rights. While I fully acknowledge the drawbacks of culturalization, I suggest that in certain instances, the label of culture can be advantageous for traditional communities. First, it enables the practitioners of traditional religions to exit the hierarchy of religions in which Christianity embodies the "civilizational matrix" (Wenger 2009). Second, the identification of certain practices as culture makes it possible to circumvent some of the legislative restrictions imposed on religions in the secular public domain.

I should note that even if the culturalization of traditional religions is the most common discursive strategy, there are also instances of religionization of traditional religions, especially when Ghana is cast as a multifaith secular society. Officially speaking, Ghana takes pride in its triple religious heritage—Christianity, Islam, and traditional religions. Even here, however, traditional religions are placed at the bottom of a hierarchy that is dictated by the world religions paradigm and is embedded in secularism as a political regime (Ambani 2021, 8; Masuzawa 2005).

The latent Christianity of secularism is partly due to the nationalization of Christianity in Europe, which rendered it "coextensive with the nation[,] in contrast to other religious traditions that [are] perceived as foreign" (Oosterbaan 2014, 592). Because the historical superiority of Christianity in the Euroamerican context is encoded in the institutional model of secularism transported across borders, other religions end up unfairly disadvantaged.

The transposition of the Christocentric paradigm in the Constitution of Ghana and the uneven appropriation of Ghana's religious traditions in popular discourse has fostered a public space in which secularism and Christianity are conflated as indicators of modernity. The Eurocentric ranking of regimes of truth is evident in the legal and discursive positioning of Abrahamic religions at the top of the hierarchy. Although the country's secular Constitution prohibits the elevation of any faith to the status of a state religion, other mechanisms are in place that marginalize traditional religions. For example, the Constitution grants tax exemptions to churches and mosques and the privilege of participating in constitutional bodies only to representatives of Christianity and Islam (Quashigah 2010, 332–35). The tax exemption applies to registered religious organizations; traditional religions are not eligible because they are not registered as separate religious entities. Traditional religions are also less visible at national ceremonies, especially in contexts that foreground the country's religions rather than its cultures. Whereas Muslim and Christian prayers are consistently recited at major state functions, most notably at the Independence Day celebration, libation pouring is occasionally banned at these occasions (Goshadze 2022a). Traditional religions are also rather absent from school, university, and military chaplaincies (Arthur 2017, 105). Similar patterns of religious prioritization exist in other parts of Africa, as evidenced by the fact that to date no African country has recognized a traditional festival as a national holiday, even when Christian and Muslim celebrations, such as Christmas or Eid al-Fitr, are ordinarily observed on a national scale (Mazrui 1991). The fact that traditional religions are commonly branded as culture, even if in the context of preserving and rejuvenating Ghana's national heritage, suggests a belief that they are incompatible with the modern nation-state.

Legally speaking, however, being a "nonreligion" is not always disadvantageous because culturalized religious practices can more easily seep into secular institutions. In the current legal framework in Ghana, it would be constitutionally impossible for a religious entity to force another faith group to participate in its religious directives. What has worked in favor of the Ga community is the insistence that their custom needs to be maintained. Because the Ga custom implies a convergence of religious and civic identities, defending one's right to culture as permitted in customary law also entails defending one's religion. The promotion of customary regulations alongside civil law structures, in turn, ensures the presence of nonhuman actors in the public sphere.

The possible advantages of culturalization are often considered with respect to Christianity in Europe (Astor et al. 2017; Joppke 2018) but not in relation to indigenous religions. Instead, several authors have documented the repeated efforts of indigenous communities, especially in the context of the Americas, to "religionize" their practices in order to gain access to various forms of capital (Tafjord 2016; Kraft 2009). The culturalization of traditional religions in Ghana is comparable to the culturalization of Christianity in Europe, where it has retained a position of privilege that it had lost under the status of religion (Martinelli 2020; Brubaker 2016). What renders the Ghanaian case distinct, however, is that culturalized traditional religions embody an episteme that runs parallel to secularism as a political regime that accommodates culturalized Christianity. Traditional religions become beneficiaries of certain privileges only at the expense of their legally and discursively underprivileged status in the contemporary state. This form of culturalization illustrates the layering of epistemologies in the postcolonial context. While the top, official institutional and legal layer mimics the Euro-American model of governance, lifestyle, and discursive profile, below that layer is the less publicized but no less consequential layer where culturally specific modes of existence thrive.

The appropriation of the cultural label by the representatives of the Ga community should not be interpreted as necessarily strategic. The actors who believe in the authority and relevance of custom are also convinced that it is fundamentally different from religions such as Islam and Christianity. Even though custom harbors ancestral wisdom and an ancestral way of life, traditional communities consistently question the compatibility of its religious dimensions with modern personhood. The ambiguous impulse to simultaneously cherish and doubt customary lifeworlds was communicated, verbally or affectively, by every Ghanaian I spoke with, whether they were a traditionalist, a Christian, or a Muslim. Missionary education, institutionalized colonial Christianization, the Sankofaism of the Ghanaian state, and the demonization of culture by Pentecostal/Charismatic Christians facilitate a concept of custom that is not religious. This has enabled the majority of Ghanaians to reinterpret traditional epistemology and to continue performing ritual practices dictated by their traditional communities without appearing uncivilized—an insult that Pentecostal/Charismatic Christians commonly hurl at traditionalists. A senior official at the National Commission for Civic Education captured the eagerness to strike a balance between Christian faith and the importance of performing traditional duties: "You see, we all believe in Christ, but before Christ came there were traditions. So you can't do away with it, although we believe that Christ came to die for us, but at times we don't do away with our traditions, you understand me? Most of us are all Christians today, but still when you go back home and there are traditional things, you can't take yourself out."[38]

CONFRONTATIONS OVER SOUND, writes Karin Bijsterveld (2013), express a disagreement over the ultimate "character of the city" (6). Followers of Pentecostal/Charismatic churches blast their loudspeakers in the hope of leaving their "pagan" past behind, and strict enforcement of the ritual guidelines allows the Ga to reclaim Accra as a city under their customary authority. More important, however, the controversies, agendas, and negotiations surrounding the imposition, regulation, and practice of the ban on drumming divulge the "shared sovereignties" of Ghanaian public space in which different communities, represented by their human and nonhuman members, compete for their authority (Tweneboah 2019).

Cultural analysis assumes that legalistic language is employed when there is a need to translate conceptual differences in a negotiation. Subjects often articulate their identity through the use and interpretation of law, which serves as a kind of lingua franca used to facilitate communication between different parties who lack a common language for negotiation. Religious groups are particularly vulnerable to legalized communication because their vocabularies and world views are considered inferior to the political metalanguage. Ga traditionalists and Pentecostal/Charismatic churchgoers understand each other's concerns because they perceive sound as a vehicle for transforming human beings in their relationship with the otherworldly as a physical force that "makes the spirit flow" and as an energy that manifests the presence of deities. In the Pentecostal/Charismatic world view, obedience to the sonic regulations of the Ga community directly threatens the sovereignty of their God. For the Ga faction, on the other hand, the imposition of the ban on drumming blocks out sounds that could adversely affect the ritual specialists and disrupt the *jemawɔji*.

The two conflicting bodies must appeal to the state to navigate Ghana's legal hybridity. The state's involvement demands that each party's concerns be translated into a secular language that cannot accommodate the relationship between human and nonhuman forces that are central to the conflict. The linguistic switch recasts the two positions in a way that obscures their original common conceptual ground. As the Ga community defends its ritual ban within the framework of customary law and Pentecostal/Charismatic Christians insist on their constitutional right to religion, they are engaging in a process of simultaneous "religio-culturalization" that requires that certain concepts be stripped of their religious meaning while others are shaped into religious forms.[39] Consequently, they have created "religionized" Christianity and "culturalized" traditional religion, a configuration reminiscent of the Christocentric orientation of secularism as an epistemological and institutional regime, on the one hand, and the culturalization of traditional lifeworlds in missionary, colonial, and nation-building contexts, on the other.

5. Sacred Acoustic Inspectors

The Ghanaian State and Noise Abatement
during the Hɔmɔwɔ Festival

If you happen to visit Accra in May or June, you may encounter a group of men trooping about in the central neighborhoods. Several times per month, they venture out on a mission to monitor sound levels amid the cacophony of the city. In residential areas and educational and health facilities, they are expected to hunt for sounds that exceed fifty-five decibels—roughly, the amount of noise the drone of an air conditioner makes at a close distance. In entertainment centers, churches, and mosques, they listen for noises above sixty-five decibels.[1] These vigilantes with alert acoustic sensibilities are trained and paid by the political and administrative authority of the city, the Accra Metropolitan Assembly (AMA). The group, Accra's Nuisance Control Task Force, works to ensure that urban noise levels do not exceed the limits prescribed by the Ga Traditional Council (GTC), the main body that oversees successful execution of the annual Hɔmɔwɔ festival. When I first started working on this topic, my curiosity about the task force skyrocketed upon discovering that it was led by a Ga *wulɔmɔ*, Numo Blafo III, who served as the head of the AMA Public Affairs Office. This meant that in addition to being a ritual specialist in the Ga community and therefore a direct participant in Hɔmɔwɔ festivities, Numo Blafo III supervised the city's acoustic levels during the ban on drumming in the name of the AMA.

The AMA is the political and administrative authority of Accra, a constituent of Ghana's local government system and part of the state apparatus. It is responsible for, among other things, "the overall development of the district," "the maintenance of security and public safety," and the "preservation and promotion of cultural heritage" (Section 12.3, Local Governance Act 936). As such, the AMA's actions are always planned in coordination with state policies. State-sanctioned acoustic control is a relatively recent development in Accra. The Nuisance Control Task Force is part of the state's response to interfaith confrontations between Ga traditionalists and representatives of the Pentecostal/Charismatic churches when the latter refused to comply with the ban on drumming. The initial steps toward a settlement were modeled after the AMA's 1995 metropolitan noise abatement bylaws. Previously, those bylaws had been used to regulate noise in nightclubs and industrial areas, but only in a handful of cases and with limited efficiency. Public outcry over the Drum Wars and sustained pressure from the GTC impelled the AMA to entrust the task force with enforcing the bylaws in 2001.[2] The ensuing aural control was publicized as a remedy for the city's pressing noise-pollution problem.

State involvement in the Drum Wars is attributable, in part, to the sonic quality of the conflict. While somatic expressions of worship can be confined within a fixed physical space, sonic communication transcends spatial boundaries. In the words of Brandon LaBelle (2010), "the temporal and evanescent nature of sound" enables it to disregard "the particular visual and material delineations of spatial arrangements, displacing and replacing the lines between inside and out, above from below" (xxi). Significantly, sound breaches the divide between public and private realms, which forms the essence of the secular demarcation of religious and nonreligious institutions. This is particularly evident when sound is amplified through loudspeakers, which have become integral to Pentecostal/Charismatic worship.

This chapter focuses on the implications of the establishment of a state-governed noise-control task force in constitutionally secular Ghana and its use for the benefit of the Ga celebration, with Numo Blafo III serving as the symbol of state patronage. At first glance, one is tempted to interpret the acoustic inspectors as the embodiment of the Ghanaian state in its struggle to institute and enforce technologies of biopower. The emphasis on the health hazards of urban noise pollution testifies to the scientific scrutiny of citizens and corresponds to state-led practices in postcolonial and postsocialist contexts to rely on science in efforts to legitimize its authority (Petryna 2002; Foucault 2007, 2013). The establishment of the Nuisance Control Task Force in 2001 seemed like the ultimate solution to intercommunal tensions, as it guaranteed impartial application of the ban, addressed public concerns about noise pollution and the grievances of the traditional community without blatantly favoring any of the parties involved. In practice, however, the task force serves as a place for traditional authorities to maintain their influence in the administration of Accra's soundscape, sometimes in contravention of constitutional law. The state's mediation of the ban on drumming sheds light on Ghanaian secularity as a blending of customary political authority that preaches mutual sharing of space yet grants special benefits to the custodians of the land, on the one hand, and secularism as a Christocentric institutional and ideological regime that pushes traditional lifeworlds either to the bottom of the religious hierarchy or outside it, as nonreligion or culture, on the other.

The Sacred Acoustic Inspectors

As tensions escalated between Ga traditionalists and Pentecostal/Charismatic churches in the late 1990s, the state devised a two-pronged intervention to neutralize the situation. First, in the immediate aftermath of the 1998 tensions, it established a seven-member committee and recommended that the GTC raise awareness about Hɔmɔwɔ by officially announcing the dates of the annual ban (Arthur 2017, 115). Second, it promised to begin regulating excessive noise in the city. In order to stay within the bounds of the Constitution, however, the state had to launch a general noise-control campaign rather than a periodic intervention targeted specifically at the ban on drumming. To that end, it revived the noise-abatement bylaw the AMA had issued in 1995.[3] Section 8(1) of the bylaw states that "a person conducting a religious service shall not play or cause music to be played so loudly so as to cause a nuisance to the public and residents in the area." When the bylaw was drafted, sonic clashes were still a thing of the future, so the regulations were primarily aimed at decreasing the level of urban noise pollution. Mass prayer groups, crusades, and sermons amplified by cutting-edge sound systems had already become the trademark of Pentecostal/Charismatic congregations throughout the country. Although the 1995 bylaw was not intended to police the ban on drumming, it included a clause targeting loud religious services. In the context of the Drum Wars, the constitutionally secular state had no legal right to intervene in the regulation of a ritual ban in the name of a customary community, nor could it condone the implementation of that ban at the expense of the religious rights of others. Article 56 of the 1992 Constitution clearly prohibits Parliament from enacting a law "to establish or authorize the establishment of [a] body or movement with the right or power to impose on the people of Ghana a common program or a set of objectives of a religious or political nature." The secular language of the 1995 bylaw was an ideal entry point for securing the customary ban in the name of curbing urban noise pollution. Several state agencies were mobilized to enforce Accra's aural order, namely the Accra Environmental Protection Agency (EPA) and the Nuisance Control Task Force affiliated to the AMA. The AMA's official procedures for monitoring excessive noise were identical for religious and secular contexts. The EPA also accepted complaints from individuals and groups about all types of noise pollution in the city, much of which was emitted by Pentecostal/Charismatic churches.[4] With church noise in the same category as noise from factories, airports, and nightclubs and with an emphasis on year-round control, the campaign was publicized as a remedy for the problem of noise pollution in the city.

Justice Arthur provides a timeline for the activities of the Noise Control Task Force. He suggests that until 2008, the fourteen-member crew did not feature representatives of the GTC and consisted of police and officials of the AMA and the EPA. The group was disbanded from 2009 to 2012, when the National Democratic Congress came to power and eliminated the Greater Accra Permanent Conflict Resolution Management Committee, one of the architects of the task force. The GTC took advantage of the opportunity and monopolized the administration of the ban on drumming during that period (Arthur 2017, 127–28). In 2013, when the Greater Accra Regional Coordinating Council restored state control of the ban and nominated a new task force, GTC members had replaced EPA representatives. When I started my research in 2014, it was clear that the GTC had taken a leading role in the revamped task force.

At its inception, the task force was responsible for ensuring that music stores, nightclubs, religious institutions, and other parties complied with the mandates of the EPA. When the task force was inaugurated in 2001, Greater Accra Regional Coordinating Director F. T. Nartey stated that its function was to enforce the law and educate the public regarding the perils of noise pollution. He emphasized that the task force was not designed to force churches to comply with the orders of the GTC.[5] Media reports and my interviews with state, church, and Ga community representatives, however, indicate that the task force came together during the period of the ban to address the concerns of the GTC regarding possible transgressions of the ban on noise (Arthur 2017, 229).[6] "The task force cannot watch the whole [of] Accra at a particular time," the Nai wulɔmɔ told me, "so they have vantage points that they go around [to]. Once there is a church who is violating, just make a call and within a few minutes you will see the task force arriving."[7]

An exponential growth in public concern over noise-related health hazards in the 2000s is evidence that the urban noise problem had not been adequately addressed. The *Daily Graphic* includes numerous narratives of ordinary citizens struggling with often-insufferable noise from neighborhood churches and drinking spots. "The Church Won't Let Us Sleep," "Enforce the Law on Noise Making in Churches," "Noise Everywhere," "AMA, Deal with Noise Pollution," "Is Our God Deaf?"—these are just a handful of examples of articles published in the 2000s that implored the state to attend to the problem of noise pollution that was often attributed to Pentecostal/Charismatic churches.[8] Below is an excerpt from an embittered reader bemoaning the persistent lack of state initiative in regulating extreme cases of sonic nuisance: "Even though there are bye-laws which prohibit excessive noise-making, it looks as if they only exist on paper as nothing is being done to bring this nuisance under control. One wonders what the Accra Metropolitan Assembly (AMA), and other assemblies are doing about the menace as officials are more concerned about other things than about the health and well-being of the citizens."[9]

In 2002, Dr. Geoffrey Kwabla Amedofu, a Ghanaian otolaryngologist, emphasized the correlation between high noise levels and an array of medical conditions, including physiological disruptions, cardiovascular ailments, mental health issues, and stress.[10] Two years later, audiologist and speech pathologist Moses A. Amihere linked various degrees of hearing loss with frequent and intense exposure to noise.[11]

When conducting research for this book, I witnessed the protracted and fruitless process of seeking legal remedies against excessive noise in a residential area in the city center. Almost every morning for the period of six months, my neighbors and I fell victim to the ear-splitting dawn service of a nearby Charismatic congregation. I have numerous audio recordings of loud stomping, clapping, and howling at five in the morning. At last, our landlord resolved to take action and lodge a complaint with the AMA. Dozens of unanswered letters and daily phone calls later, matters had to be settled directly between the church and the neighbors, without any third-party arbitration.

I could only find two instances when noise-related punitive measures were enforced by the AMA independent of the ban on drumming, and these interventions were oddly severe. In 2011, the AMA closed down the Accra branch of Ebenezer Miracle Worship Center on the grounds of excessive noise nuisance.[12] In a similar disciplining act, in 2013, the AMA and the Accra Police Department demolished the building of Fruits of Life Ministry at Bubuashie for a breach of the permitted noise levels.[13] According to Simpson Anim Boateng, director of the Public Health Department at the AMA, the wooden structure had to be taken down because its sonic output caused significant cardiovascular problems for the neighbors.[14] An interesting piece of information, which was given only secondary mention, is that both of these churches operated without an AMA permit, which is usually procured for a fee. Could it be that the noise abatement bylaw was instrumentalized to settle financial scores? It is difficult to answer this question since the official AMA statements defended the measures imposed with loose references to public health, suggesting that strict measures were necessary to ensure the mental and physical well-being of Ghanaian citizens.

The sporadic nature of noise regulation prior to the establishment of the task force was at odds with the consistent intercession of the task force in the administration of the ban on drumming. Each year, the AMA issues a notice a few days before the ban begins that informs the public about the relevant dates and terms. Among other directives, the initial statements urged Christians to "confine their worship to church premises" and warned the public to refrain from making noise.[15] Since the mid-2010s and following complaints from Christian churches, the statements have been modified to include both Muslims and Christians. For example, in 2018 the AMA recommended that the ban on drumming be observed under the following guidelines:

1 During the period of the ban, the usual form of worship should be confined to the premises of churches/mosques and noise levels be minimized to the barest limits possible.

2 Religious bodies and the Traditional Authorities must show respect for one another and restrain their followers from making derogatory and inflammatory remarks about the beliefs and practices of one another.

3 The positioning of loud speakers outside the premises of churches, mosques, and pubs are banned. Roadside evangelists are to cease their activities during this period.

4 Apart from the identifiable task force which consists of AMA personnel, the Police Service and Representatives from the Traditional Council with tags, no other person or group of persons should be seen or found enforcing the abatement of noise in the metropolis.[16]

The language and tone of annual statements suggest the AMA's reluctance to delineate the directives as mandatory. This has to do with the hierarchy of legal systems in Ghana, which renders the universal imposition of ritual guidelines unconstitutional, even if they are authorized by customary law. Instead, they are labeled as "guidelines" that are developed "in the interest of peace, harmony and national security."[17] Furthermore, while the press releases declare that it is the task force that will monitor and enforce the noise regulations, no mention is made of how that enforcement will be carried out and what repercussions transgressors could face. Such discretion in public statements leads to the belief that state officials, embodied by AMA representatives and the regional coordinating director, tiptoe around the implications of the state's enforcement of the ritual ban, for example by assuring citizens that the police and the district assemblies are instructed to "ensure that the laws on public nuisance [are] enforced throughout the year and not just during the period of the ban."[18]

What I learned in my visits to the AMA and my interviews with the penalized congregations and members of the task force offers a different order of events. Numo Blafo III described a routine noise inspection conducted by his team:

> We go around in the metropolis, we check people who are disobeying the law, and then we arrest them. What we normally do is that we take their sound system and we take it to a particular place. Sometimes we bring it to our security office. When we are taking these, we list the names and after the ban is lifted, we will send you to any of our traditional houses where the chiefs will deal with you, maybe they will fine you. It normally consists of drinks and some amount of money. Then they will call us and we will release things. They are kept in a security office across the road.[19]

According to this account, not only does the task force come together during the ban, it also allows Ga traditional authorities to impose customary penalties within their discretion. Numo Blafo III's successor at the AMA, Gilbert Ankra, also confirmed that the GTC metes out punitive measures.[20] Fulfillment of the obligations outlined in the customary penalties determines whether the confiscated instruments will be released by the security office. This dynamic illuminates how the task force operates as an auxiliary in relation to Ga community leaders, which is rarely emphasized and is even concealed in official AMA statements.

What distinguishes the Nuisance Control Task Force from the Ga traditionalists who took the matters into their own hands in the late 1990s is its collaboration with the police and its alleged reliance on the EPA-mandated acoustic code.[21] Yet when it comes to actually measuring noise, the task force almost never relies on proper equipment. Until 2005, the AMA was "handicapped in dealing with noise" since it had to borrow noise-measuring instruments from the EPA. This meant that routine checks were hardly ever conducted.[22] By 2008, the AMA had purchased six noise meters to help reduce noise in the city.

Simpson Anim Boateng, director of the Public Health Department, said that staff "went out twice every week especially at night to assess the situation on the ground."[23] Letters of complaint and my conversations with citizens, however, make it clear that the AMA is reluctant to become involved in cases of noise pollution unless there are additional incentives. Some citizens find it curious that traditional leaders are more competent in curbing noise than local authorities and the EPA: "When it comes to noise making and applying sanctions, why is it that during every Homowo season, the traditional authorities in some parts of the Ga state are able to effectively enforce a ban on noise making which includes drumming by churches and playing of sound systems indoors? Yet our local authorities and the EPA, with all the administrative power they wield, are not able to apply stiffer enforcement of noise pollution when it is abundantly clear that such noises have consequences for those at the receiving end."[24]

These examples show that although the state's involvement in regulating the ban on drumming was justified as an initiative to combat the noise epidemic in Accra, in reality the bylaw and the associated EPA guidelines are hardly relevant to the operation of the task force. There is reason to believe that the state's public health approach was instrumental in redirecting public attention from its tutelage of the Ga festival to the threats to health urban noise causes. Gilbert Ankra told me that the imposition of the ban "had nothing to do" with the Constitution but rather was "traditional in nature" and had to be observed for that reason.[25] In 2017, a controversial addition was made to the noise-abatement bylaw. Article 10 states that "the Assembly [AMA] shall enforce the ban on drumming and noise making as shall be imposed by the Ga Traditional Authority."[26] In addition to giving the GTC state-sanctioned tools for imposing noise restrictions on all citizens, regardless of their religious or ethnic background, the language of Article 10 also suggests that the AMA task force, which supposedly is advisory, is empowered to delegate the issue of punishment to the GTC. Furthermore, the inclusion of this article in the noise-abatement bylaw implies that enforcement is subject to EPA decibel guidelines, which is not the case in practice. In 2018, Gilbert Ankra assured me that the ban on drumming does not have to comply with official guidelines: "The ban is about drumming and noise-making. For the noise of course we should be using some levels to check it out, but we cannot identify when there is noise, is it loud enough?"[27] This means that even as they walk the city in their special AMA uniforms with official IDs pinned to their shirts, the task force members must intuitively recognize sounds that violate the ban on drumming. This act requires fine attunement to the sensory intelligences of the Ga community and its nonhuman associates, the primary beneficiaries of the ritual quiet.

Arbitrating the Secular: Numo Blafo III

The core characteristic of Western secularity, wrote Charles Taylor in 2001, is its insistence that the world is not an enchanted place, a view that effectively strips spirits of the ability to shape human life by relegating them to the domain of the mind. In Western secular understanding, the mind is a freestanding, buffered self that can countenance beliefs about gods and other beings without allowing them to spill into the clearly delineated realm of nonreligion (Taylor 2001). As we are starting to recognize that "religion" and "nonreligion" are structured by historically informed practices, laws, and discourses, it is becoming impossible to speak of strictly defined sacred and profane domains (McCutcheon 2007). The task is especially daunting in postcolonial contexts, where the Western dichotomy of the religious and the secular cohabits with historical understandings of the relationship of these two realms. In Ghana, the interaction of the regional episteme with Western secularism produced a modernity in which African traditional religions are only occasionally framed as religions alongside Christianity and Islam in discursive contexts that highlight the image of Ghana as a multifaith secular society. However, given the Christocentric orientation of many modern secular democracies in Africa, which were inherited from colonial legal systems, Christianity is at the top of a religious hierarchy and traditional religions are positioned at the bottom (Ambani 2021, 8). Simultaneously, traditional practices that we would typically associate with religion are continuously redefined as part of culture. Marleen de Witte and Birgit Meyer (2012) argue that Ghana's national culture project has ambiguous implications. On the one hand, it is a postcolonial strategy to affirm "the African self so as to shake off British administration" (47–48). On the other hand, it appropriates colonial and missionary constructions of culture and tradition that resonate with the Pentecostal/Charismatic demonization of tradition. Despite the ambivalent implications of culturalization, there is an agentive quality to the ways in which traditional authorities (and sometimes state actors) mobilize dereligionized "culture" in their own favor. Ultimately, then, Ghanaian actors normalize the customary enmeshment of the religious and the nonreligious in the public sphere by tailoring secularism, as a political and ideological regime, to their own needs. The outcome challenges modernist ideas about the "proper place of religion" (Kallinen 2016, 56). Numo Blafo III personifies such careful arbitration between religion and custom/culture in contemporary Ghana.

I first heard about Numo Blafo III in 2015, when I started interviewing Pentecostal/Charismatic congregation members in Accra to discover more about their involvement with the ban on drumming. On several occasions, I was told

FIGURE 5.1. Numo Blafo III (second from the right) participates in traditional rites performed in Ga-Mashie. Photo by author. 2016.

about a certain Ga priest who held a high-ranking post at the AMA. Traditionally, traditional priests do not work outside the Ga community because the Ga tradition imposes numerous ritual constraints on their lifestyle. I was curious about the Ga priest who had managed to hold down an important office at a state agency. Following some online research, I decided to simply turn up at the AMA headquarters and try my luck at meeting Numo Blafo III. I walked into the gated area and was directed to the second floor of a two-story building. The room was crammed with oversized desks and two soft sofas for visitors. To my right was a man I recognized from the news articles as the AMA public affairs officer, a priest of the Ga-Mashie community, and the person in charge of the Nuisance Control Task Force. Straight ahead of me, two heavily built men were eating their lunch of *waakye* served on palm leaves. I did my usual introductions as I eyed the man behind the desk. In accordance with Ga custom, he was dressed in white from head to toe—a knit beanie, a linen two-piece set, and no shoes on his feet.[28] "It's a pleasure to meet you. I am also a scholar, so I'd be happy to talk to you," he said with a warmhearted smile. Thus began our friendship that would introduce me to the Ga ritual scene. Numo would often take me along when he performed his *wulɔmɔ* duties or attended traditional ceremonies or I would sit in his office at the AMA, asking questions about the task force and the Ga ritual life. The rundown of Numo's life I present in the following pages is based on multiple conversations that we had in 2015 to 2018. The ease with which Numo Blafo III balanced state and customary offices illustrates the selective incorporation of Western ethical, sensory, aesthetic, and discursive forms by Ghanaian actors in the production of Ghanaian secularity.

Born in 1968, Numo Blafo III always had a penchant for learning. His family could barely afford clothes and food, yet he insisted on walking two hours to school every schoolday until his family could no longer pay the fees. Determined to earn a living, he learned how to DJ and performed at social functions. By 1996, he had saved enough to buy his own sound system, and just four years later, he opened his own music shop in Accra, where he sold electronics, CD players, and cassettes. The business was just starting to boom when the shop was robbed clean. Numo says that this was the most challenging period in his life: "I was in debt with people who were bringing items for sale. Most of them were harassing me with police. Taking me to the police station. I got to the point where I had to relocate to run away from my debtors." Desperate to get his life back on track, Numo moved to his grandfather's house in the heart of Jamestown, one of the oldest Ga communities in Accra. One day, on his uncle's advice, he decided to visit a shrine to seek help from a spiritualist. It was there, as he was waiting in the line, that his life was turned upside down. Out of nowhere, three priestesses (wɔyei), who had become possessed minutes earlier, approached him and put beads over his neck. Before long, they were slaughtering a ram and pouring the blood on Numo's feet to betoken his initiation into priesthood. Numo was dumbfounded, "I was like, ahh, is that the way they acquire a priest? They don't inform the person, the person's family does not know about anything. How is that?" Although Ga priesthood is hereditary, Numo Blafo III grew up without knowing that he was next in line, and at first he had no desire to give up his life and his dreams for priesthood. After some deliberation, however, he realized that if he was enstooled, his debtors could not harass him. He was also fearful of the spiritual repercussions associated with fleeing the priesthood, so he agreed to enter his new life. Today, he believes he would have perished if he had not become a wulɔmɔ.

Soon after, a long-lost aunt reappeared in Numo Blafo's life and offered to enroll him in a newly opened African Institute of Journalism and Communication. At first, both the Ga traditional community and the school's admissions office were unnerved by the prospect. It was the Ga community's responsibility to offer sustenance to ritual specialists, so priests were not allowed to be employed. However, Numo was uncomfortable with this arrangement, so he defied the accepted norms. Once, while we were leafing through an old photo album in his backyard, he spoke words that shed light on his decision: "Those who don't work, they have a lot of issues. That's why some of them will sell lands which don't belong to them because they also have to live as humans. But I don't want to go into selling lands. In fact, I don't want anything from anybody."

At the institute, many students were put off by Numo's priestly white attire and would not even want to sit next to him. In due course, however, everyone recognized his hunger for knowledge, which earned him the nickname Walking Encyclopedia. "Before the end of the first semester," he recounts with nostalgia, "I think I had too many friends. Everybody was my friend. People got to like me how I am because they started seeing me as just a simple person." However, practical challenges remained. Although for the first few years he was allowed to study free of charge, some lecturers were reluctant to have him attend their classes. In those hours, Numo would seek sanctuary in the library and do his own research. Soon, Accra's journalists started to take note of him. *The Spectator* published a feature article presenting him as the first *wulɔmɔ* to go to school. That article secured him patronage from the chief executive of the AMA, who paid his school fees and offered him a national service position at the Public Relations Department. In 2008, when he completed his national service, Numo was made a senior information assistant, and two years later, he was promoted to the public relations officer position. In the meantime, he received a degree in communication studies, trained in alternative dispute resolution, and completed a master's degree in customary issues.

As the only *wulɔmɔ* with considerable political and social capital beyond Ga traditional life, Numo Blafo III is a visible symbol of the complex relationship between Ghana's secular state and its system of traditional authority, which cannot be divorced from the Ga belief system. In addition to serving as the spokesperson for the AMA and the secretary of the Ga State Council of Wulomɛi in Accra, Numo was in charge of the Nuisance Control Task Force in 2013 to 2018. It is curious that throughout his appointment, neither he nor his AMA coworkers considered his double allegiance a clash of interests or a sign of favoritism on the part of the assembly. "When you see me or a police officer, you know that anything that is taken from you will be given back," he told me once proudly, referring to the trust he enjoys from Accra's residents when instruments are confiscated during the ban. It is unclear, however, whether this sense of trust derived from Numo's secular appointment or his religious appointment, since he did not clearly differentiate between the two. When he discussed the ban on drumming and the Nuisance Control Task Force, his self-positioning seemed to suggest that he was speaking in the name of the Ga traditional community. For instance, although confiscation of instruments during the ban clearly violates

FIGURE 5.2. Blafo *gbatsu* (shrine) in Ga-Mashie. Photo by author. 2017.

the citizens' freedom of religion, he insisted that implementation of the ban, which he frequently referred to as the law, fell within the scope of the Ga traditional authorities since that had been the case for centuries.

Re-Formations of the Secular

There have been significant theoretical shifts in the scholarly examination of the secular. One of the strongest critics of the category, Talal Asad (1993, 2003, 2013), has argued that the secular episteme was shaped by Eurocentric cultural hierarchies conceived in terms of civilizational progress. Triloki N. Madan (1987) notes that the paradigm of modernization that bled through borders and nations elicited a narrative that non-European nation-states were deficient and inadequate. Jose Casanova (2001) points out that the concept of secularization became deeply problematic once its Eurocentric undercurrents became obvious—namely, the implication that the Western model engenders the perfect secular habitus characterized by rationality that ultimately leads to unbelief. This shift in how the secular is analyzed was consistent with a growing interest in the historical idiosyncrasies at play in the production of European secularity (Gorski 2000; McLeod 1995). The historical positionality of secularism as an ideological project meant that it was never entirely attainable outside the European continent unless an amalgamation of similar historical events was replicated elsewhere. The notion that secularism has a generalizable formula has also been criticized in view of the fact that the classical model is entrenched in the Christian historicity of Western Europe, in particular in the dialectic between Protestantism and modern science (Casanova 2001; Berger 2008; Davie 2002).

The theoretical lens I use in order to make sense of secularity in Ghana is a hybrid of two prominent orientations in the study of the secular. To fathom the knowledge regime that underlies the process of religio-culturalization of epistemologies in Ghana, I draw on the Asadian idea that the political project of secularism is informed by an understanding of modernity that derives notions of human development from the Enlightenment (Asad 2013; Scott and Hirschkind 2006). The presence of missionaries and colonial officials in the Gold Coast and the centrality of Christianity in the project of national state-building served as fertile ground for the idea that Christianity is most compatible with Ghana's modernist aspirations and should enjoy a privileged standing in the secular public domain (Dovlo 2005). Traditional religions, in contrast, have experienced two forms of marginalization in modern secular Ghana. First, they emerged as residual categories in a political environment that mirrors the religious hierarchies of the world religions paradigm (Masuzawa 2005; Shaw 1990). Second, as residual religious categories, they have been habitually demoted to the realm of culture, a process that is accompanied by a simultaneous legal and discursive religionization of Islam and Christianity.[29] In an ideological framework that displaces, outlaws, and penalizes indigenous lifeworlds to make way for modernity, the Nuisance Control Task Force, which works to the advantage of the Ga traditional religion, is a remarkable initiative.[30]

While the Asadian perspective sheds light on secularism as a hegemonic regime, it overlooks the reality on the ground that it often remains unspoken. The second theoretical camp I resort to, which crystallized around the Multiple Secularities research project, is wary of "undue generalizations about the ideological power of Western secularism" and suggests that the differentiation between the secular and the religious has also existed in premodern and non-Western contexts (Wohlrab-Sahr and Burchardt 2017, 11, 6). Although I disagree with the idea that the ideological burden of Western secularism as a political doctrine is overstated in postcolonial or postsocialist frameworks, I find that the multiple secularities approach creates room for the grassroots mobilization of traditional lifeworlds as culture, as exemplified by the Ga insistence on subjecting the city of Accra to strict acoustic control despite the limitations of customary law. The bottom-up perspective expands our purview to include parallel narratives and realities of local secularities that operate alongside the political and ideological project of secularism, an idea inspired by Shmuel Eisenstadt's (2000) hypothesis that specific cultural imprints generate different ways of being modern.

An emphasis on the multiplicity of secularities introduces two important corrections to the Asadian framework. First, it helps preserve the concept of modernity and steers clear of the essentializing discourse on the alterity and perpetual religiosity of the non-Western world (Wohlrab-Sahr and Burchardt 2017, 2012). Recognizing the existence of traditional modes of regulating the public status of religion is especially relevant in the study of Africa, which has long been portrayed in the literature on the secular as the "slanted and enchanted" land (Engelke 2015, 87). Second, by shifting attention to secularity, we can investigate the historical path dependencies that condition modes of interaction with official state guidelines (Kleine 2018). My work contributes to this line of thinking by paying special attention to what Wohlrab-Sahr and Burchardt (2012) call "cultures of secularity," a concept that denotes "the *meaning* [their italics] that is attached to the institutions, practices or discourses of differentiation and distinction with regard to religion" (884). An example of a culture of secularity is the importance members of a traditional community attach to their customary rights over land and the underlying interreligious and state-religious relationships that transcend constitutional constraints, namely the subordinate status of customary law to constitutional law. In the Bourdieusian spirit, however, it is difficult to separate the meaning of the concept from its structuring dimensions, and thus it is important to recognize that the grassroots, culturally shaped dispositions toward religious and secular spheres in non-Western contexts are formed in a dialogue with Western epistemologies (Dressler 2019).

The coexistence of secularism and secularities also translates into the coexistence of two sensory intelligences: one that does not recognize the presence of deities in the public domain and another that recognizes and responds to their agency. We can think of the copresence in terms of Claire Decoteau's (2013) term "hybrid habitus," a combination of Bourdieu's term "habitus" and Homi Bhabha's concept of hybridity. "Hybrid habitus" does justice to the epistemic disjunctions and contradictions that accompany the postcolonial condition. When the head of the AMA tells me that the ban on drumming has nothing to do with the Constitution but is rather a tradition that simply must be followed, he reveals his hybrid habitus, which can accommodate and switch between two sensory intelligences. Similarly, when a Ga Christian assures me that the deities do not eat the food offered to them, he foregrounds his Christocentric secular habitus, which in a truly Protestant spirit is averse to the materiality of the non-human, especially in the public sphere. In the same conversation, however, that person will casually mention that the gods are around only to protect humans in the biblical sense, thus acknowledging the presence of immaterial, angelic beings that are more compatible with modern Ghanaian identity.[31]

The epistemic stains of Christocentric "modernity" as a hegemonic project are ubiquitous, whether in public discourse or in the secular habitus that both Christians and adherents of traditional religions adopt unevenly, yet unanimously (Hirschkind 2011). This ideological and bodily orientation is especially manifest among the modernist elites who are concerned with bringing Ghana up to international standards of modernity. "In an interdependent modern world," writes Talal Asad (2003), "'traditional cultures' do not spontaneously grow or develop into 'modern cultures.' People are pushed, seduced, coerced, or persuaded into trying to change themselves into something else, something that allows them to be redeemed" (154). Even the most mundane conversations about religion with individuals from distinct religious, economic, or cultural backgrounds made me understand that Ghanaian secularity is continually being forged out of the push and pull between the determination to preserve and appreciate what is truly Ghanaian and the need to keep up with the times, an orientation beset by implicit normative understandings of religion in a modern and democratic polity (McCutcheon 1997; Fitzgerald 2007).

Regardless of their religious identification, members of the Ga community were particularly careful to distinguish their traditional practice from fetish worship and to present it as ethically and aesthetically compatible with the ideal type of modern religiosity. The details of the presentation varied. In the wake of the first major attacks on Christian churches, a number of Ga leaders insisted that Ga ritual specialists were priests of the monotheistic god, that customary practices were not premised on "heathenism," or that there were numerous Hebrewisms in Ga practices.[32] The latter claim derives from the Ga origin story, which asserts strong cultural links with ancient Israel. Every Ga ritual specialist I conversed with during my fieldwork was quick to emphasize the resemblance of Ga practices to ancient Judaism, as if hoping to communicate their value, especially in relation to Christianity. In general, Christian and Jewish terminology was routinely used to describe Ga beliefs. I once spoke with a Ga official from the Ga-Mashie Development Agency who emphasized that the Ga religion is spiritual since the *jemawɔji*, or angels on earth, mediate between the people and the supreme god.[33] The emphasis on spirituality is similar to the faith-based orientation of Protestant Christianity. However, in contrast to the latter's aversion to material mediation, my interlocutor did not find it the least bit problematic that the Ga angels live among humans and intercede on their behalf. The aspiration to trim down the Ga traditional religion to the Abrahamic model is the result of the discourse on civility and barbarity in which Christian identity is commensurate with matured humanity (Fitzgerald 2007).

The equivocal institutional and ideological status of the Nuisance Control Task Force is also a testament to the entanglement between those two epistemic regimes in Ghana. Ghanaian secularity, which seeks to reconcile Western secularism and traditional modes of being in the modern nation-state, permeated public statements state officials made in the aftermath of the Drum Wars. In the wake of the first major attack on a Pentecostal/Charismatic church in May 1998, Minister of the Interior Nii Okaija Adamafio made an official statement that generated significant controversy, especially in Christian circles. Instead of condemning vandalization of the church property, Adamafio, a Ga man, encouraged citizens to respect the ban and urged the AMA to pass bylaws to effectively enforce it. On June 3, 1998, the front page of the *Daily Graphic* was emblazoned with the minister's statement that it was "wrong for certain people to assume that such practices, such as the ban on drumming, is fetish and therefore of no significance to society."[34] Adamafio's statement ruffled the feathers of many Christians who questioned the rationale behind the ban and challenged the constitutionality of the announcement. In a letter to the editor, Pastor Kojo Osei-Wusuh delivered a strong critique of state officials who advocated for the violation of the citizens' right to religion: "As a Minister of State responsible for law and order, and who controls the internal security forces, his call that apparently ignores the tenets of the constitution has a veiled threat of show of arbitrary power and can only cause confusion and conflict in religious circles."[35] Other Christian leaders interpreted the AMA's regulation of the ban as evidence of its endorsement of the GTC. In a clear evocation of the Hegelian vision of Christianity as the herald of secular reason, Emmanuel Enoch Agozo, the leader of the Ghana Evangelical Society, alleged that the AMA's actions were an "abuse of authority" and an attempt to "obstruct the movement of the spirit of God that brought liberation of the church and the people from idolatry and captivity."[36]

The vehement pushback from Christian worshippers did not fall on deaf ears. Soon after Adamafio's statement, the Ministry of Local Government and Rural Development denied that it had any intention to issue a model bylaw requiring churches to defer their worship to "traditional customs and cultural practices." Minister Kwamena Ahwoi declared that such bylaws would be imprudent since the relationship between the state and traditional religions is not subject to legislative oversight.[37] However, as relations between Pentecostal/Charismatic Christians and Ga traditionalists deteriorated, AMA officials abandoned concerns of legislative correctness and pleaded with Christians to practice "religious tolerance in the interest of peaceful co-existence."[38] The call for tolerance was effective because it was commensurate with ideals of mutual respect present both in secularism and the customary world view. On a separate occasion, the National Commission on Culture chair, Nana Akuoko Sarpong, who also served as the presidential staffer on chieftaincy affairs, called on the Charismatic churches to compromise and follow the traditional edict since "traditional authorities are not asking too much if they demand that in one out of the 12 months churches stop drumming." Because such a compromise would require that Christians give up their legal rights and respect the Ga custom, Sarpong felt obliged to emphasize that compliance with the ban on drumming did "not in anyway [sic] suggest that the churches stop worshipping or join the traditional religious practice."[39] Following this progression of events, twenty-eight churches in the Ga-Mashie neighborhood, led by the Christian Council, the Catholic Bishops Conference of Ghana, and the Ghana Pentecostal and Charismatic Council, signed an agreement stating that their churches would comply with the ban.[40] The agreement was struck in consultation with local assembly members and amid considerable pressure from the AMA and the National Commission on Culture, which in turn paid heed to the GTC. In a joint statement, the three Christian organizations denounced the ban as "an infringement on the human and constitutional rights of members of churches" yet expressed their readiness to cooperate providing that the GTC responded by "respecting [their] way of worship."[41]

Beyond Religious Tolerance: Culturally Grounded Cohabitation

When I was investigating the phenomenon of the task force, I talked to dozens of people about Numo Blafo and his office at the AMA. I often asked Christians and individuals who did not identify as Ga what they thought about a Ga traditional priest acting on behalf of the state to regulate noise during the Ga harvest festival. In light of the epistemic tangle that evolved from superimposing two separate, historically determined differentiations between religion and nonreligion, it is natural that some people would not be pleased with Numo Blafo III's involvement in the Nuisance Control Task Force. Many of my Christian interlocutors argued that his appointment distorted the neutrality of the law by servicing Ga religious convictions at the expense of Christians' constitutional right to worship as they pleased. Without a doubt, Numo's physical appearance made it easier to present the appointment as incoherent in secular terms. His performance of his secular duties in priestly garb detracted from the idea that the Nuisance Control Task Force was a secular, health-oriented enterprise. The ambiguity was further aggravated by the fact that AMA's annual announcement of the ban never failed to spotlight religious congregations and roadside evangelists as the primary sources of urban noise.[42] A former high-ranking member of the Christian Council of Ghana articulated the perceived incongruity of the matter in a conversation we had in 2016: "Laws are laws, and they must be applied whether you are Christian, whether you are Muslim, whether you are doing entertainment, laws must be applied to all. We as a country must say that noise pollution is a problem, and we have agencies that are supposed to control noise from January to December, not only Hɔmɔwɔ, or Lent, and so on."[43]

Looking back on the conversations I had from today's vantage point, I find my approach crass, but I understand where I was coming from; I was hoping to tease out a conflict that I felt was clearly present even in the most guarded interviews. Today, I am much more appreciative of the subtle ways Ghanaians navigate the concept of custom. Opinion pieces published in the *Daily Graphic* in the wake of the Drum Wars captured the conundrum of becoming modern while taking pride in tradition. In an op-ed piece titled "To Drum or Not to Drum," British-educated lawyer Nii Armah Josiah-Aryeh criticized the "ill-considered intervention" of the Commission on Human Rights and Administrative Justice that declared that the ban on drumming was unconstitutional. Human rights, writes Asad, function only within the boundaries of a nation-state and are concerned with the individual as a citizen rather than as a human being. Therefore, the secular state can and does exploit human rights discourse to coerce its own citizens (Asad 2003, 135). Because I situate human rights discourse within the framework of secularism as a political project, I interpret views that question human rights talk and favor a more culturally grounded orientation as articulations of Ghanaian secularity. Josiah-Aryeh's piece exemplifies this stance. He warned against striding into modernity and adopting "all the mechanisms of foreign countries" in complete abandonment of Ghana's cultural soul and stated that "constitutional rules alone" are not sufficient for addressing complex societal issues.[44] K. B. Asante, a prominent Ga scholar and the former head of the GTC, articulated the same position in his opinion piece on the matter, suggesting that "when age-old practices divide society on mutual rights, it is unwise to bury one's head in the constitution and the laws of the land."[45] Reservations about Western secularism and the presumption that culturally grounded approaches have more to offer are, of course, nothing new. We find similar discourses in other social and geographic contexts. A common feature of these anxieties is the belief that the mere transfer of foreign structures and discourses of modernity is not only futile but also pernicious, whether because it engenders "gaps, inconsistencies, and deficiencies" (Göle 2010, 43) or because it causes "the loss of one's soul" (Madan 1987).

As is often the case in non-Western contexts, underneath the prima facie Western secularist position, my interlocutors creatively engaged in the process of translating secularism with culture-specific epistemes in mind (Kleine 2018; Madan 1987). The word "tradition" invariably served as the core of the conversations I had with Ga and Akan individuals, with mainline Christians and Muslims, with government officials and small business owners. I recall chatting with Emmanuel Baah at the National Commission for Civic Education. Despite his Ashanti background and his professional dedication to educating people about the country's laws, he prioritized tradition over the constitutionally proclaimed freedom of worship. "Freedom of worship is there," he said with conviction, "but all those things came to meet the tradition. Freedom of worship came as part of the constitutional mandate, but the leaders and the chiefs were there as traditional authorities way ahead before we came to accept our independence. Out of our independence came all these freedoms, but before these freedoms there were still freedoms in our homes where the king was the head of authority within every community and every clan. And these laws are preserved!"[46]

Although saturated with a different set of affective attitudes, the emotive charge of tradition is also present among Pentecostal/Charismatic Christians, who in recent decades have become more aware of the "rules of the land" and the concessions that are required of them in order to live in harmony. Many members of the churches that were attacked refrain from proclaiming the absolute primacy of the statutory law over customary law. This may have to do with a reluctance to make controversial statements after reconciling with the Ga traditionalists and coming to terms with the customs of the land. Particularly memorable is a conversation I had with a prophet from the Mallam branch of the Gospel Light Chapel International, in which he extolled the virtues of customary dispute resolution: "When you sit down and have a peaceful settlement nobody is fined, it brings peace. We believe it is good to sit down because we respect our elders. When the elders sit down and settle this issue, it dies, but when you send somebody to the court, the issue will never die. So there will not be peace. So we never pursue it to court or try to have anybody fined."[47] It is debatable whether the preference for peaceful resolution amounts to the domestication of Pentecostal/Charismatic Christianity by traditional religions, to use J. D. Y. Peel's terminology, since that would require Christian actors to be imbued with traditional values of cohabitation (Peel 2016, 149; Sanneh 1980). Even if these values are important to some Pentecostal/Charismatic Christians, they are not enough unless the state enforces the ban on drumming in accordance with the provisions of the noise-abatement bylaw. "Because of the law, there is sanity," a member of one of the attacked churches explained as we compared the unannounced

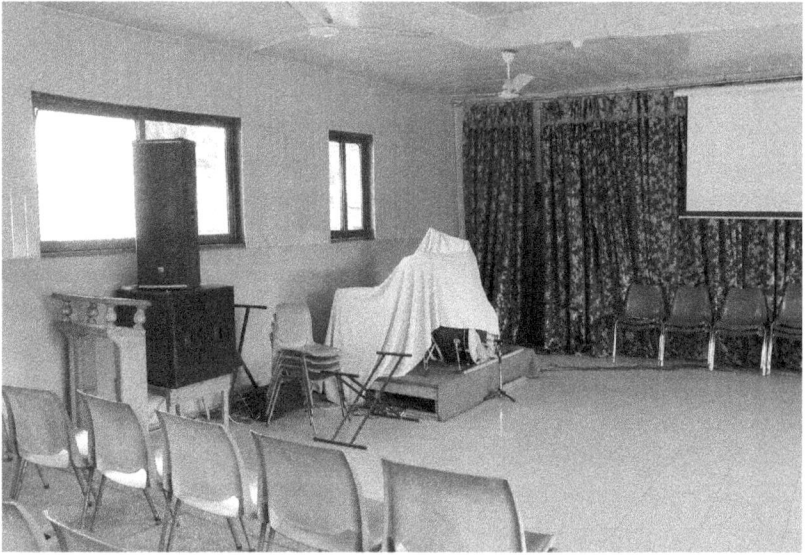

FIGURE 5.3. Instruments in a Pentecostal/Charismatic church in Accra are covered to signal compliance with the ban on drumming. Photo by author. 2018.

attacks of the late 1990s with the current official calls to reduce noise.[48] Another interlocutor, a member of the International Central Gospel Church, suggested that state intervention had become inevitable so that people would not "kill themselves over whose god is superior.... Because it looks like my god is saying this, my god is saying this."[49]

More than two decades after the initial conflicts, I still stumble across reports of clashes over the ban on drumming during each Hɔmɔwɔ season. All the same, a greater commitment to dialogue is clearly evident among Pentecostal/ Charismatic churchgoers. It helps that all Accra residents have become versed in the guidelines that follow the announcement of the ban. The director of Christian education for the Christ Apostolic Church International, the church at the center of the controversy for refusing to submit to the Ga directives, described the measures taken during the festival season: "The Ministry of Culture knows about the ban and they send a warning every year right before the Hɔmɔwɔ season starts. There should be no drumming in Ga areas, sound systems must be turned down, no loud music should play in the neighborhood."[50] When that interview was conducted in 2015, the church leaders seemed far more receptive to the idea of collaborating with Ga traditionalists than they had been in the late 1990s, as long as the state monitored the terms of the ban. "Render to

Caesar the things that are Caesar's; and to God the things that are God's" (Romans 13:1)—my interlocutors recited these words again and again to stress that living in harmony on Ga land required sacrifice. "We are staying among them, we are living among them, so we have to forget about it," another member of an attacked church said with a certain air of resignation when I asked why they did not seek an official settlement.

These conversations are illuminating because they reveal the lived reality of Ghanaian secularity, the idiosyncratic ways two understandings of the role of religion—one inherent in secularism and the other in the customary world view—are balanced, negotiated, and institutionalized in everyday living. The coexistence of the two epistemes means that at times one is more palpable than the other, while at other times they both occupy the same public stage. Individualism—along with a legal emphasis on human rights—largely shapes the Western episteme while communality as a value seems to be integral to Ga custom. Numo Blafo III's involvement in the task force summons the view that communal responsibility is entwined with the land and its rules and runs counter to the idea of a neutral public domain that is common in secularism. I have spoken with individuals, both in the state apparatus and in Christian churches, who see service to the community as the primary responsibility of any official, whether that individual is a priest or a civil servant. A member of the National Peace Council who is also a linguist of the We Traditional Area advocated a golden mean between the two epistemes regarding respect:

> I don't think the task force works in [a] vacuum. . . . For them to maintain sanity as far as that aspect of culture is concerned, it is appropriate they make sure the task force moves around. . . . I think it's in place so that we all obey such laws. After all, it's just for four weeks and that's it. . . . These things, they come and go as when the demand arises and it's not for any lengthy period, sometimes a day or two, sometimes a week, so we go by it. It is misunderstanding and misconception and the miseducation that come mostly from the people who are bent on believing that once I'm not part of the people I don't have to respect them.[51]

The notion of respect is constructive because it conjures the traditional understanding of cohabitation and the idea of pluralism in democratic contexts. What distinguishes the two world views, however, is that in the traditional framework actors are willing to give up more of their essential rights to religion and culture in order to maintain peace. The very existence of the task force represents a concession of sorts in customary terms, since it takes the right of enforcement out of the hands of the traditional community and gives it to a state-governed task force that consists of representatives from multiple groups.

The state's receptiveness to the traditional religion of a given locality occupying the public sphere under the guise of culture stems from precolonial principles of religious freedom. According to Abamfo Atiemo (2014), in precolonial Ghana, freedom of religion "included the choice to accept and express new beliefs but not the freedom to renounce state religion," which was interchangeable with citizenship (242). Since both religious and civic identities are imbricated in the customary context, rites associated with political office or community more broadly were obligatory for all residents, regardless of their religious affiliation. Even so, powerful shrines and deities were welcome in the state pantheon as a means of harnessing energy and promoting communal prosperity. "It is clear . . . that a distinction was always maintained between the religious elements formally linked to the state and all others. All other shrines in the state were regarded as subjects of the state and therefore were expected to be loyal to the state," observes Atiemo (162–63).

The fact that many African countries maintain the institution of chieftaincy alongside the Western model of governance means that the two ideas about the place of religion in the public sphere coexist. The question of chieftaincy is critical to political decision-making in the postcolonial context. Traditional governance, initially the darling of many Afrocentric public figures and scholars who sought to counteract the imposition of foreign administrative systems, has now entered the mainstream discourse. Some argue that chieftaincy can reintroduce alternative sources of power in order to breed a truly African democracy (Gyampong 2006; Wiredu 1995), while others see it as a remnant of the past that runs counter to democratic principles and should better be eliminated (Tsikata and Seini 2004; Ubink 2007). Some domestic and international proposals also urge African governments to make good use of the existing system of local governance (Mamdani 1996; Piot 1999; Kallinen 2016).

In Ghana, chieftaincy has weathered the storms of major political transformations and is one of the most enduring institutions. During the colonial period, chiefs were integrated into the system of indirect rule, which granted them relative autonomy in the realm of customary affairs (Quarcoopome 2006). Samuel K. Gyampong (2006) argues that indirect rule was a comfort zone of sorts for the colonial authorities because it relieved the administration "of the burden of having to place expensive judicial and law enforcement structures in every community to maintain law and order" (185). Wary of chiefly authority, the leader of Ghana's First Republic, Kwame Nkrumah, opted to keep it under control through strict legislative measures (Rathbone 2000). Since then, the power of chieftaincy has waxed and waned in response to political transformations in the country, but it remains a significant mechanism of co-governance. Chapters 271–277 of the 1992 Constitution as well as the 2008 Chieftaincy Act stipulate that chiefly authority shall not extend beyond customary law. However, as the Nuisance Control Task Force illustrates, the dynamics of power-sharing on the ground are far more complex. Because the institution of chieftaincy is hard to disengage from traditional calendar and ritual responsibilities, the uninterrupted leverage of chiefs has ensured the presence of traditional deities and ritual specialists in the public sphere (Tweneboah 2019, 60).

Contemplating Christianity's strong foothold in secular Europe, Martijn Oosterbaan maintains that historical relations with the state are a decisive factor in determining the degree of public visibility accorded to a religious tradition in its "culturalized" form (Oosterbaan 2014). Although the standing of traditional religions in modern Ghana is often questioned, especially in light of the upsurge in Pentecostal/Charismatic Christianity, they nevertheless retain a historically established relevance, albeit in a modified form. The lack of compartmentalization between the public sphere and custom, the unbroken institutional and emotional relevance of traditional authorities, and the customary conflation of civic and religious identities enable traditional religions to slip through legislative restrictions. In customary terms, when Ga ritual directives are conceptualized as part of the state religion, they do indeed supersede the right of Charismatic devotees to worship as they wish. However, Ghana's secular establishment derives from the Western model, which comes with its own set of ideas about the place and function of religion. As a constitutionally secular state, Ghana guarantees religious liberty to all citizens and pledges to defend citizens' freedom to manifest their religious beliefs (Quashigah 2010). With this in view, the activities of the Nuisance Control Task Force are unconstitutional since they elevate customary law above statutory law when customary law is constitutionally subordinate. It is no wonder that many Ghanaian Christians believe that culture is a Trojan horse of sorts that is used to smuggle traditional religions into the public sphere (Kallinen 2016, 120). In the early stages of the conflict, many Christians asserted their constitutional right to "freedom of thought, conscience and belief" and by extension, their entitlement to resist the ritual restrictions imposed on them.[52] In the aftermath of state intervention and extensive public debate, however, the Pentecostal/Charismatic faction toned down its accusations, as evidenced by the fact that the human rights violations that occurred during the Ga attacks on Christian churches were settled out of court and with state mediation.

This course of events would have been inconceivable had the state not packaged and presented the AMA Nuisance Control Task Force in secular terms. In public discourse, the task force is a health-oriented enterprise with the primary goal of alleviating noise pollution and raising awareness of its dangers. In the same vein, the measures the state took in the immediate aftermath of the conflict, which included the mass training of environmental health officers and the establishment of submetro stations to control sound, fit neatly into the idea of secularism.[53] In accordance with this narrative, the task force exemplified the Ghanaian state's acoustic policing of the city. What news agencies and public announcements failed to convey, however, was that the task force functioned in tandem with the Ga community. What is more, noise control in Accra was introduced primarily as a means of enforcing customary norms of land custodianship that serve human and nonhuman members of the Ga community. Numo Blafo III's persona is fascinating precisely because it embodies the cohabitation of customary and state authorities in Accra. Instead of seeing the task force and the negotiations over the ban on drumming as expressions of a failed secular state—a conclusion that would be unavoidable if we were guided by the Western model—I suggest that they allow us to contemplate Ghanaian secularity as an entanglement of customary and state power structures, along with their historically determined roles for religion. The task force is thus another example secularism, laden with its own religious hierarchies, is being appropriated to better serve Ghana's geocultural reality (Chatterjee 1993; Guha and Spivak 1988).

6. Let Us Offer Thanks for the Nation of Ghana

Hɔmɔwɔ as a Civil Ceremony of Thanksgiving

In August 2016, I attended a thanksgiving event at the Presbyterian Church of Ghana in Osu, one of the central neighborhoods in Accra. The event, "Remembering the Living Dead: A Christian Response to the Offering of Kpokpoi to the Departed," was organized in celebration of Hɔmɔwɔ. Rev. Dr. Philip Laryea, one of the most prominent Ga scholars of religion, was invited for the occasion to deliver a lecture on revisiting past values and salvaging tradition. The assorted audience included both Ga and non-Ga members of the Ebenezer Presbyterian Church. The space was decorated with a large colorful poster commemorating the occasion. Photographers, journalists, and camera operators were strategically positioned to document the event without interruptions. Prominent visitors were seated to the right of the speaker's platform; to its left, the church choir was preparing to launch the event with a musical introduction. The prized guest of honor was the paramount chief of Osu Traditional Area, where the ceremony was taking place. In his short address, Nii Kinka Dowuona VI spoke of his dedication to bridging the gap between tradition and God, referring to the long-standing schism between traditional religions and Christianity.

In addition to the conflict-resolution interventions the state launched as a response to the ban on drumming, I observed subtler governmental and nongovernmental initiatives targeting the Hɔmɔwɔ festival. In 2015, one of the country's leading ecumenical bodies, the Christian Council of Ghana (CCG), inaugurated the Hɔmɔwɔ Thanksgiving service and other associated events in some of the oldest churches in the Ga traditional area. The goal of the venture was to contribute to building peace through intercommunal commemorations. In the same vein, the Ministry of Tourism, Arts & Culture initiated Homofest in 2014, an undertaking that unified Hɔmɔwɔ celebrations across the six Ga townships and combined them with other annual festivals observed by the Adangbe people.[1] The name of the initiative is ironic in view of the recent, muchdiscussed clampdown on sexual minorities in the country and the infamous draft bill that seeks to criminalize LGBTQ+ persons.

Homofest denotes a celebration that "homogenizes" the four main festivals of the Ga-Adangbe people: Asafotufiam, Ngmyaem, Kplejoo and, most important, Hɔmɔwɔ. Designs for both of these undertakings—Hɔmɔwɔ Thanksgiving services and Homofest—had appeared in the late twentieth century in embryonic form. As early as 1972, Mantsɛ Nii Amugi II read a sermon to the congregation of the Wesley Church in Accra at a thanksgiving service that rounded off the Hɔmɔwɔ season.[2] An embryonic vision of Homofest, on the other hand, was articulated by Deputy Minister of Tourism Nana Akomea at a Maggi Homowo Cook Out Competition in 2002, who proposed to convert Hɔmɔwɔ into a more attractive national event.[3] While proposals to repackage the annual festivals have been voiced at intervals since the 1980s, no practical steps were taken in this direction until the mid-2010s.

There is no publicly articulated link between these initiatives and the social anxieties the ban on drumming triggered at the turn of the twenty-first century. The two ventures the Ministry of Tourism and the CCG launched are largely cataloged as an outcome of the country's burgeoning multicultural and multireligious profile. Even so, the two initiatives to upgrade the Hɔmɔwɔ festival continue to typify Ga traditional cosmology in Accra as a belief system in which two sensory regimes coexist. What unites the two seemingly disparate initiatives is their preoccupation with deconstructing, classifying, and reassembling the past to forge a respectable domestic and international presence for Ghana, an endeavor commonly associated with modernity (Baudrillard 1994; Elsner and

Cardinal 1994; Bennett 1995; Harrison 2013). Within this frame of reference, the modernization of Hɔmɔwɔ contributes to the national project of cataloging and displaying heritage in order to bolster a modern Ghanaian multicultural identity. This idea of modernity has a complicated relationship with traditional lifeworlds that varies between rejection, demonization, and partial preservation. In a highly Christocentric political environment, the perceived advantages of culturalization transcend the Western discourse of heritage, in which preserving culture means safeguarding the fundamental core of a transforming society (Oakes 2010). J. D. Y. Peel has argued that secularization, which involves working with "a highly reified concept of culture," is yet another means of rendering traditional religions safe (Peel 2016). This safety is to be understood in spiritual terms. Practices that are rendered safe no longer pose a spiritual threat to the Christian community because the associated nonhuman powers are neutralized. However, as we will see in this chapter, the approaches of both the Ghanaian state and the mainline churches in Accra value certain dimensions of traditional culture, and the culturalization of those values does not necessarily involve their complete desacralization. This approach is drastically different from the Pentecostal/Charismatic perspective, which rejects tradition on spiritual grounds because of the spiritual forces that remain attached to it (de Witte and Meyer 2012).

The state's choice of communities to be targeted for deconstruction and re-evaluation speaks to the prominent cultural and religious policies in the country. The culturalization of traditional religions should be distinguished from the culturalization of Christianity in Western contexts. The latter process is motivated by the need to make room for religious pluralism in order to legitimate the continued influence of a majority religion in the public sphere (Zubrzyciki 2012). The culturalization I investigate here, in contrast, stems from the historical marginalization of traditional religions as nonreligions or as deficient religions. In other words, the state's decision to rebrand Hɔmɔwɔ rather than Christian or Muslim religious festivals reveals a great deal about the ambiguous status of traditional religions in Ghana.

I would like to counter the potential conclusion that the Ga religious capital is managed by other cultural communities in Ghana by highlighting the agentive role of the Ga people in both tourism-oriented self-commodification and Christian proselytizing. David Mosse (1994) reminds us that in missionary contexts, converts become "active creators and manipulators of symbolic and ritual systems which serve indigenous social and political ends" (85). Given that Homofest and Hɔmɔwɔ Thanksgiving services occur in addition to, rather than as an alternative to, Hɔmɔwɔ proper, the Ga community retains almost complete authority over Hɔmɔwɔ proper. In addition to controlling the ritual cycle of Hɔmɔwɔ, the community is actively involved in approving various adaptations of the festival. As a symbol of their approval, Ga traditional authorities are present at the organized events of such adaptations. For their part, the actors behind the two recently developed celebrations exhibit a resolve to generate alternatives without directly engaging with Hɔmɔwɔ proper. This design speaks to the unbroken hold the Ga community maintains over its traditional domain, even when operating in the name of culture.

In this chapter, I argue that the modification of Hɔmɔwɔ, whether to foster pride in Ghanaian culture or to bolster intercommunal allegiance, is an ambivalent enterprise. On the one hand, it champions acceptance of the meaning behind traditional celebrations, promotes greater comprehension of traditional knowledge, and reinforces communal harmony. On the other hand, it renders traditional practices safe for general consumption by secularizing and repackaging some religious aspects as culture (Peel 2016, 224).

Before delving into the details of the Hɔmɔwɔ Thanksgiving service initiative, I should situate the endeavor within the broader Christian interfaith practice. The born-again denominations were heralded as the long-awaited harbinger of non-Western Christianity in Africa (Asamoah-Gyadu 2014; Kalu 2008), as a "vitalistic" movement (Dovlo 1998), or simply as a religion that was "more responsive to contemporary needs in Africa" (Omenyo 2002, 264). Although the Pentecostal/Charismatic movement romanticizes its rupture with a past fraught with misbelief and sin, its very identity is defined against traditional religions, a stance that inadvertently marks it as Africanized. Here, my interpretation of Africanization aligns with Birgit Meyer's and denotes both the positive and negative incorporation of traditional elements into the process of identity formation (Meyer 2004a). After all, the anti-traditionality of Pentecostal/Charismatic churches derives primarily from their recognition of spiritual forces that operate within a shared ontological framework (Gifford 2004). This, of course, is no reason to ignore the deleterious effects of the othering that Pentecostal/Charismatic Christianity engages in, an exercise that consumes everything cultural in the broadest sense—traditional music, language, dance, religious practice, dress, and so on.

While the lack of constructive dialogue with traditional lifeworlds was also a notable feature of the so-called mission or mainline Christian churches that came before, those churches did not outwardly reject the traditional world view in its entirety but instead targeted its selected, highly religious features, such as pouring a libation, worshipping multiple deities, venerating ancestors, and making ritual sacrifices. They labeled the rest "culture" and deemed it worthy of preservation or placed it at the beginning of the sequence from primitive to civilized and viewed it as the potential foundation upon which Christianity could flourish. The continued policy of many mainline churches of using the Ga language when operating in Ga traditional areas is a testament to the priority given to communal dialogue. In the twentieth century, the tolerance for traditional cosmology increased, a shift that can be ascribed to African leadership in the postindependence mainline churches and to major competition from African Initiated Churches, which condoned and celebrated African world view. Indeed, the amalgamation of Christianity and African culture—particularly the idea of community, joyful music and dance, and the recognition of witchcraft—constituted a keystone of the unique identity of African Initiated Churches (Sackey 2001, 42).

The honeymoon of Christianity and traditional religions came to an end with the rise of the Pentecostal/Charismatic churches. Against the backdrop of constant verbal attacks on traditional practices by leaders of born-again denominations, the active denunciation of culture as fetish on the part of leaders of the new churches, and the rapid Pentecostalization of all forms of public discourse, some hardline Ga traditionalists interpreted the sonic transgressions of the late 1990s as a full-blown Christian assault on their lifeworld. The ensuing lumping together of all Christian churches in an us-versus-them discourse was facilitated by a concurrent process of charismatization in mainline denominations. The unprecedented prominence of Pentecostal/Charismatic churches and the ensuing erosion of youth interest in the older churches led mainline churches to develop survival strategies that mimicked some of the charismatic modus operandi, such as exuberant worship, Christocentrism, and an emphasis on healing, speaking in tongues, and deliverance (Omenyo 2005; Sackey 2001). Although the majority of Ga people continued to distinguish between the more respectful mainline churches and the insolent Pentecostal/Charismatic offenders, the interfaith initiatives of the CCG in the 2010s should be seen as a gamble that sought to mend the tattered trust of the Ga hosts.

"This festival is about solving problems"

Hɔmɔwɔ Thanksgiving services were the idea of Rev. Dr. Kwabena Opuni-Frimpong, who at the time was the general secretary of the CCG. The council was formed in 1929 to provide official representation for the majority of the country's mainline churches, especially in their dealings with other religious bodies, traditional communities, and the state. Its mission is "to contribute to achieving Justice, Unity, Reconciliation and Integrity of Creation among various sectors of Ghanaian society and [to] provide a forum for joint action on issues of common interest."[4] Today, the council includes more than thirty churches, including the

Methodist Church of Ghana, the Evangelical Presbyterian Church, the Ghana Baptist Convention, the Evangelical Lutheran Church, and others. Its annual meetings are designed to identify and negotiate a common position on national and local issues and to coordinate interdenominational, interfaith, and intercommunal collaboration programs.

After the first Hɔmɔwɔ Thanksgiving event in 2015, I met with Rev. Opuni-Frimpong at the headquarters of the CCG in Osu. My goal was to understand how the contentious traditional festival would be received by those who subscribed to Christian cosmology. Opuni-Frimpong is a charismatic individual with an extensive knowledge of traditional religions and a strong vision of their role in contemporary Ghana. As a fellow scholar, he welcomed my inquiries and allowed our exchange to go well beyond the allotted time. He insisted that instead of downplaying the ideological tenor of the festival, Ghanaians ought to integrate its wisdom into their daily lives. "The festival is about solving problems," he said. "Now there are modern problems—unemployment is a problem—these are modern-day challenges that must be solved in order to have meaningful Hɔmɔwɔ."[5] Opuni-Frimpong was alluding to a narrative that links the origins of the festival to the Ga people's victory over a terrible famine that occurred when they settled the territory of present-day Accra. Since then, the Ga community has gathered annually to offer thanks to *jemawɔji* for delivering their ancestors from imminent death and to celebrate yet another prosperous and peaceful year.

Since the primary aspiration behind the thanksgiving initiative was to mend the deteriorating relationship between mainline churches and the Ga community, the organizing committee set out to find viable models of similar collaboration from the past. As it turned out, variations on the thanksgiving theme had existed as early as the nineteenth century, yet they had been publicized as Christian ceremonies unrelated to Hɔmɔwɔ that were dedicated to expressing gratitude to God for a bountiful harvest. Although these services established no direct connection to Hɔmɔwɔ, they frequently coincided with the festival calendar. When I researched past thanksgiving ventures at the National Archives of Ghana, I found that even in the past, some people were puzzled by the conjunction of the two events. Troubled by the possible entanglement of Christianity with traditional religions, a reporter for *The Gold Coast Leader* in 1912 wrote: "One thing I wish to point out is, that the annual Harvest Festival of the Wesleyan Church here always falls on the very Sunday as the Homowo. I do not see how these can coincide as the Harvest is of a christian origin and not fetish: how can the two festivities then come in together, when the one is christian and the other fetish?"[6] A few years later, a journalist for *The Gold Coast Nation* shared his concerns about the wisdom of the "duplicate-festival," suggesting that efforts to "raise funds for chapel and other building or repairs, or to support the poor members of the church" could fail because God would be displeased by the church's acceptance of the "fetish."[7] However, these precursors of Hɔmɔwɔ Thanksgiving services had their apologists who attempted to separate Hɔmɔwɔ from its religious connotations, suggesting that it had "very little to do with Custom" and could thus be integrated with Christian celebrations.[8]

Interdenominational thanksgiving services continued throughout the twentieth century with little direct engagement with the Hɔmɔwɔ festival. The *Daily Graphic* routinely reported on thanksgiving observances at various mainline churches in and around Accra, packaging them as special Christian services dedicated to giving thanks for the harvest. However, in isolated instances, a mainline church explicitly organized a thanksgiving service to conclude the Hɔmɔwɔ season. This happened exclusively in the traditional section of the Ga *akutsɛi* (quarters) where both the congregation and the church leadership were from the Ga community. As noted above, the politically prominent *mantsɛ* of the Ga-Mashie Traditional Area, Nii Amugi II, read the first lesson at an interdenominational thanksgiving service at the Wesley Church in Accra in 1972. The *Daily Graphic* reported that in a sermon delivered for the occasion, Rev. Stephens urged the Ga community "to enhance their traditional [*sic*] and culture and develop a spirit of unity, love and harmony," a position that continues to resonate with the state-led discourse on national culture.[9]

As it happens, Opuni-Frimpong's interpretation of the purpose of the Hɔmɔwɔ Thanksgiving ceremony—particularly the desire to tap into the collective consciousness to solve national challenges—is consistent with the dominant paradigm of "culture with progress." With a compelling timbre in his voice, Opuni-Frimpong elaborated on his vision during our conversation: "They are saying that if you want to attract the blessing of the unknown, the God, the ancestors, we must go through it in their terms, and we must have a moment of silence. . . . Which makes sense if you want to solve the problem!" As he spoke these words, emphasizing the urgent need for reflection in order to transition into a problem-solving mode, his suggestion made sense. When I asked whether this meant making the festival national in character, Opuni-Frimpong agreed that Ghana needed a collective Hɔmɔwɔ to engender the right mindspace for solving national problems such as unemployment, lack of discipline, the energy crisis, corruption, and economic obstacles. This is undoubtedly a commendable position for the former head of a countrywide Christian ecumenical body to take. In practice, however, Hɔmɔwɔ Thanksgiving services are an exclusively mainline Christian initiative rather than a national endeavor and continue to be observed by only a handful of churches.

This brings us to the second motivating factor in the advocacy for Hɔmɔwɔ Thanksgiving services. In our conversations, the organizers explicitly articulated their aspiration to bring the traditionalists closer to the Christian faith. Although the immediate plan is to hold the program in parallel with the traditional celebration, Opuni-Frimpong indirectly communicated the ultimate expectation of absorbing "the idea, the wisdom, the intellectual weight" of the Hɔmɔwɔ festival, just as the Christmas holiday of today recasts pre-Christian celebrations and beliefs.[10] The head of interfaith relations at the CCG, Abraham Opoku-Baffour, was more explicit about the ramifications of the thanksgiving venture he sought. While recognizing that the healing of interfaith wounds was the primary concern, he acknowledged that the fundamental aspiration was to bring traditional people closer to the church. "Perhaps there are some who want to become Christians and they are not, so we have our own evangelistic agenda behind this," he told me as we sat in his office at the headquarters of the CCG.[11] Since evangelism is a significant component of the Christian faith, it is only natural that in their perfect world, Christian leaders in Ghana would seek more than just peaceful coexistence. It is curious, however, that this aspiration does not appear in public statements of the CCG and the participating churches regarding the intentions of the Hɔmɔwɔ Thanksgiving venture.

Despite this motivation, the permissibility of joint church services remains a delicate issue for many mainline Christians. The roots of the argument go back to a theological concern with the corruption of absolute truth as embodied in Christianity. While the Protestant Reformation unsettled the notion of a single source of truth, anxieties about acceptable deviations surface when synergy with traditional religions is on the table (van der Veer 1994). The CCG generously shared with me its template for the invitation to the Hɔmɔwɔ Thanksgiving service it sends annually to various Christian stakeholders. The tone and wording of the text suggest an almost apologetic rationalization of Christian involvement in traditional practices: "Our involvement in the Homowo celebrations, among others, is premised on Colossians 1:15–20. We believe that if all things were created by Christ, through Him, and for Him, then we the Christians in the Ga state must join in the celebrations with the message that it is our God the Jehovah Jireh who provides for us abundantly. Moreover, the Church Service will promote peaceful coexistence between the church and the Ga Traditional Councils."[12]

As the letter demonstrates, the belief behind the initiative is that it is Jehovah who provides for humanity, both spiritually and materially, and hence, offering gratitude in his name is not to be regarded with contempt. This interpretation builds on the premise that Christian epistemology takes precedence over Ga cosmology, at least those features that are readily recognized as religious. This allows organizers to be guided by their own account of an abundant harvest while turning a blind eye to the eminent role of Ga deities and ancestors in securing communal prosperity. In other words, the theological validation of Hɔmɔwɔ Thanksgiving services demands an alternative interpretation of the story behind the festival. "They know of one God but they tell us that God can be reached through *jemawɔji*," said Daniel Lankai Lawson, the second minister of Osu Presbyterian Church in 2017. "Now we are saying that, okay, that same God that we are referring to, the scripture says that he can be reached through Jesus Christ. So, if we want to celebrate Hɔmɔwɔ, you want to do that through *jemawɔji*, we want to do it through Jesus Christ."[13] While intercommunal dialogue is a noble endeavor, the insistence of mainstream Christians that the Ga are simply misguided in their belief in *jemawɔji* can be seen as yet another instance of the victors rewriting history. A press release that the CCG published in 2015 illustrates this view. It proposes that the Hɔmɔwɔ Thanksgiving service was designed to "offer Ga indigenes and residents who are Christians, and their leaders the opportunity to thank God for the year and also commit the coming years into the hands of God as it seeks for God's prosperity and abundance in the land."[14]

Abraham Opoku-Baffour told me stories of Ga Christians from royal families who sprinkle the Hɔmɔwɔ ritual meal of *kpokpoi* while also attending church.[15] Indeed, many prominent Ga traditionalists are staunch Christians. For example, the late acting chairman of the Ga Traditional Council, Nii Adotey Obuor II, and the paramount chief of Jamestown, Nii Kojo Ababio V, were well-known Anglicans, and the La *mantsɛ*, Nii Kpobi Tettey Tsuru III, was a Roman Catholic (Arthur 2017, 243). The porous nature of traditional belief, its openness to synchronous worship and rejection of religious boundaries, and its inherently nonproselytizing nature primes many mainline Christians not to be threatened by the Ga rendering of Africanized Christianity. This disposition is tied to a deep-seated conviction that traditional epistemologies are at best flawed and inconsequential and at worst primitive and diabolical and thus can never truly challenge Christianity. There is no doubt that the late-1990s discourse on Hɔmɔwɔ also lent itself to the ease with which traditional rites and beliefs were incorporated into the Christian context. Deeply affected by a history of culturalization and the intermittent national policies of heritage-making, the Ga community recognized the benefits of downplaying religious language in favor of the more flexible label of culture. The combination of the reality of overlapping religious loyalties and the Ga insistence that their custom has nothing to do with worship convinced leaders of mainline churches to allow exceptions or deviations from what had previously been considered unbiblical. For instance, the Presbyterian Church in Akropong allowed a traditional chief to receive communion.[16] From a mainline Christian perspective, similar concessions bolster coexistence and increase the appeal of Christianity.

Elsewhere, I have expressed concern about the long-term effects of Christianization on Ga cosmology—in particular, the risk of condensing Ga *jemawɔji* into a collective god and trivializing their overall role in Hɔmɔwɔ (Goshadze 2019). However, I have come to appreciate the communal benefits of the Hɔmɔwɔ Thanksgiving service initiative, especially the eagerness to understand rather than condemn, which is a welcome response to the clashes of the late 1990s and truly resonates with the view of many mainline churches. Indeed, in his treatise on the alliance of indigenous knowledge and Christianity, Opuni-Frimpong (2012) advocates for replacing the theology of tabula rasa, which placed Africans in a religious vacuum that needed to be filled, with the theology of accommodation, in which "the Indigenous Knowledge Systems in Africa's cultural heritage must set the agenda for mission theology and praxis" (205). It is also important that the Hɔmɔwɔ Thanksgiving initiative was discussed from the outset with the chief of Osu, who welcomed the idea partly as a means of building peace with the Osu Presbyterian Church, the main host of the previous Hɔmɔwɔ Thanksgiving events. High-ranking church officials had previously referred to Ga traditionalists as idol worshippers, so with this gesture of inclusion, Ga traditional leaders felt compelled to bury the hatchet. Even beyond the leadership, the proposal was well received by the Ga community for its generous, conciliatory tone.

Alas, the efforts of the CCG have not been successful in ameliorating the intercommunal politics of Pentecostal/Charismatic churches. My inquiries at various Pentecostal/Charismatic prayer houses around Accra revealed their reluctance to engage with traditionalists because of the presumed futility of such endeavors. Sensing their hostility, mainline churches are less likely to extend invitations to representatives of born-again denominations to hybrid religious events akin to Hɔmɔwɔ Thanksgiving services, which of course rubs salt in the wound of already strained relations of Pentecostal/Charismatic churches with the Ga community. The overwhelming majority of Pentecostal/Charismatic Christians do not believe in the benefits of cooperation beyond cohabitation. A conversation I had with the leader of Victory Bible Church International was the most memorable manifestation of this sentiment. When asked why his branch did not offer special Hɔmɔwɔ Thanksgiving functions, he seemed puzzled by the absurdity of my inquiry: "You see . . . we are Charismatics and I ask myself, to what effect? If it has effect, then I should have seen this effect. So you see that it is just like coexistence, but not really changing their philosophy because to change culture, it is something beyond man. I don't think that meeting is having any effect on Hɔmɔwɔ and whether it has changed their thinking."[17]

Pentecostal/Charismatic Christians find the efforts at joint initiatives futile, believing that cosmetic changes cannot erase deeply rooted beliefs. From their perspective, inclusion is not enough motivation to harness change, and therefore only strong government policies against poverty can combat the "mediocrity" that, in the words of one of my interlocutors, feeds "the culture of darkness."

Culturalized Ancestors

The Hɔmɔwɔ Thanksgiving program, which has been held with varying degrees of fervor since 2014, normally includes a series of events at select mainline churches. It culminates in a special service dedicated to expounding the value of Hɔmɔwɔ beyond its standard theological implications. The 2019 Hɔmɔwɔ lecture titled "Sparks of Divine Revelation: Ga Folklore and Tradition as Witnesses to God's Faithfulness" directly engaged with the idea that Christianity can be disguised as traditional religiosity. Other events that are typical of the program include Hɔmɔwɔ-themed Bible quizzes, praise and worship, prayer bazaars, and crusades.[18] These events use Pentecostal/Charismatic terminology and devotional forms, a clear sign of the mass charismatization of mainline churches.

The Hɔmɔwɔ-themed lectures delivered at the closing service aim to educate Christians about the benefits of the festival and the ideology behind it. "We want to see how best we can Christianize some of the things they do," reasoned Andrew Odonkor, the district minister of Osu Presbyterian Church, who, as a Ga man, believes that some customs should not be abandoned but should rather be celebrated in a Christian context.[19] The lectures serve as a gateway to traditional religiosity for many Ga Christians who either refrain from engaging in the rituals associated with Hɔmɔwɔ or do so with a sense of self-reproach. According to the organizers, Philip Laryea and other prominent guests who deliver lectures on this day are often approached after the ceremony by Ga Christians who confess that they have been wary of partaking in the Hɔmɔwɔ festivities, even refusing to consume the "idol food."[20] It is precisely this demonization of the festival that the organizers of Hɔmɔwɔ Thanksgiving services reproach. They suggest viewing the event as a celebration of deliverance and abundance following a time of crisis. "And who gave us the abundance?" asked Abraham Opoku-Baffour in the name of all Christians. "It's God. So, why can't we celebrate with them?"[21]

Before I discuss the details of the 2016 Hɔmɔwɔ lecture I attended, it may be instructive to consider the overall theme of these presentations. Most of the lectures were delivered by Philip Laryea, a distinguished Ga scholar who has dedicated his academic career to melding Ga customs with Christian faith. Embodying strong devotion to both Christianity and his Ga background, he believes that rescripting tradition is a matter of personal urgency. In 2011, Laryea published a monograph—*Yesu Hɔmɔwɔ Nuŋtsɔ* [Jesus, the Hɔmɔwɔ Lord]—that describes his Christian take on Hɔmɔwɔ. The book epitomizes the position of many Christians who comprehend the importance of conserving the cultural values inherent in traditional cosmologies but are wary of violating the basic tenets of the Christian faith. J. D. Y. Peel (2016, 224) has observed a similar trend in Nigeria, where mainline Christians and Muslims resort to the culturalization of the Òrìṣà religion in order to preserve its redeemable elements. Yoruba intellectuals, in particular, promote the idea of Ifa as Yoruba philosophy. In the same spirit, Laryea's strategy for cloaking Hɔmɔwɔ in Christian garb is to identify the core of the celebration and to proclaim it as a universal human issue. He maintains that the rationale for Hɔmɔwɔ is professing and promoting the human aspiration to live a long life; hence the appeal for food, water, fertility, longevity, health, and peace.

Laryea's 2018 Hɔmɔwɔ lecture elaborated on some of the themes advanced in his book. The title of the lecture, "Yesu Anokwale Wala Ŋmaa [Jesus, the True Food of Life]: The Significance of Ŋmaadumɔ for the Christian Faith," played on the dual meaning of the Ga word *ŋmaa*, which broadly refers to the food people eat and narrowly to the millet planted before the festival (Laryea 2011, 86). Laryea argues that in the contemporary context, the planted millet signifies long life, progress, and development. "From my point of view, there is nothing wrong with the Gas seeking these things," he writes. "My belief as a Christian tells me that the life we seek is in Jesus" (29). To corroborate this, he cites John 10:10 and 1 John 5:11–12, claiming that the knowledge that human life comes through Jesus may have escaped the Ga ancestors but it can certainly be grasped today.

The lecture also contemplated a possible link between the harvest thanksgiving some Christian congregations celebrate and the traditional Hɔmɔwɔ festival. Laryea introduced the harvest thanksgiving as *ŋmaakpamɔ*, or "harvest of the millet," and claimed that conceptual similarities between the two holidays and the shared idea of *ŋmaa* as the source of life means that Hɔmɔwɔ contains God's testament. In the book, Laryea supports this hypothesis with the fact that Christian hymns often refer to Jesus as *ŋmaa wala*, or "the food of life," citing as an example the words of this hymn:

Bo, anɔkwale wala ŋmaa [You, true food of life]

Hii wɔŋɔɔ, ni efiŋ wɔ kwraa! [Stay with us, and we will not be in need forever!][22]

Recognizing these parallels as an opportunity to bring the two world views together, Philip Laryea and other organizers of Hɔmɔwɔ Thanksgiving services were convinced that it would be a grave mistake to ban Hɔmɔwɔ enthusiasts from Christian ceremonies.

Another point of convergence between Ga culture and Christianity at these events is the commemoration of ancestors. Philip Laryea's 2016 lecture was essentially a tribute to the founding fathers of the Ga community. He explained that the act of feeding the *blematsɛmɛi* with the ritual food of *kpokpoi* is performed solely as a symbolic sign of respect and in no way suggests that the dead can impact the realm of the living. This is a prominent opinion among Ga scholars who identify as Christians. In a 1939 essay, E. A. Ammah argued that Christians should participate in Hɔmɔwɔ since it is "never celebrated in honor of the dead," who are instead "simply remembered" and are "asked to join the living in the participation of the feast" ("Ancestors," in Ammah 2016, 408). In another article, he elaborated on the role of the ancestors: "We do not worship them, we remember them on public and private occasions. If we do not pour libation for them, nothing will happen. Before we eat, we put some food down for them; we remember that in the past he or she was eating with us. We think that the essence of the food is enjoyed by the ancestors even though the practical thing is still on the ground" ("Ancestors," in Ammah 2016, 123).

While the role of the deceased in Hɔmɔwɔ is ambivalent in these pronouncements, one claim is constant—ancestors are never worshipped. In his 2018 lecture, Laryea maintained that the relationship between the so-called living dead and the living could be transferred to the Christian context as long as the former are simply remembered as indispensable in the process of community building. He was careful to point out that *blematsɛmɛi* could only be remembered as departed relatives and not as powerful beings in the lives of the living. "It appears that the power and authority that the ancestors held in the past do not exist any longer," Laryea maintained. "Otherwise, how do we explain the near-breakdown of our traditional societies?" He chronicled undeniable signs of dwindling deference to ancestors: "Such a thing could not be imagined in the past, that anyone could sell the sleeping places of their ancestors, let alone desecrate their tombs, because people are looking for jewelry or something of value, or worse still, remove coffins and resell them, or crush the remains, the bones, and use the powdery substance to sell dangerous drugs like cocaine."[23] The only way to maintain admiration for the ancestors in a modern nation, Laryea said, is to view them as prominent members of society who exercised selfless devotion to the community during their lives. He pointed out that the commemoration of prominent Ga individuals on the plaques of the Osu Presbyterian Chapel does not denote their postmortem potency but rather their dedication to the progress of the nation while they were alive. The Ga word for ancestors, *blematsɛmɛi*, lends itself to this kind of interpretation because the literal translation suggests that the ancestors are the fathers/elders (*tsɛ*) of olden times/ancient days (*blema*).[24]

The active integration of ancestors into Christian cosmology can be traced back to the mid-twentieth century, when mainline denominations began to prioritize theologies of continuity to ensure a smooth transition from traditional religions to a Christian future (Westerlund 1985, 45). This approach was popular among many African scholars who were preoccupied with finding similarities between African religions and Christianity. In 1955, the Christian Council of the Gold Coast organized a conference titled "Christianity and African Culture," where the African regard for ancestors was made intelligible in the framework of the fifth commandment, "Honor thy father and thy mother" (Christian Council of the Gold Coast 1955, 65).[25] A few years later, in 1962, the First International Congress of Africanists, which was held in Accra, brought together the Presbyterian Church of Ghana, the Methodist Church, and the Evangelical Presbyterian Church. Ancestors were a prominent topic on the agenda, but the nature of the relationship with them was strictly set apart from "worship" (*jamɔ*), which was reserved only for the deities (Ammah 2016, 271). Much like the coordinators of Hɔmɔwɔ Thanksgiving services, conference participants claimed that adopting African culture would not threaten Christian values (Parsons 1962, 2–3). On the contrary, echoing some of the themes Philip Laryea raised in his 2016 lecture, conference participants presented ancestors as worthy role models for the younger generation.

Recasting ancestors in a secular light by downplaying their material involvement with the human world through exchange and communication may well prove to be a fruitful method of redeeming traditional religions in the eyes of mainline Christians. Peel (2016) documents an analogous development in Nigeria, where Yoruba deities (*òrìṣà*) are reconfigured as "kings, heroes, and great men" whom Christians can honor as ancestors and founding fathers (154). The trend allows for a greater fluidity of traditional ideas, but it also obscures the fundamental role of ancestors in the pantheon of African religions (Opoku 1978; Pobee 1976; Zahan 2000). Ancestral spirits are commonly listed among the primary elements of traditional religions (Parrinder [1962] 1976; Idowu 1973). While there is no consensus concerning the actual relationship between humans and ancestors, it is generally recognized that rites performed for ancestors are acts of devotion and that the association between humans and ancestors is continuous and reciprocal. Bolaji Idowu (1973) even argues that although ancestors are on a lower footing than deities, they "receive veneration that may become so intense as to verge on worship or even become worship" (186). In his 2018 lecture, Philip Laryea stressed the urgency of incorporating cultural values into Ghanaian national identity: "We need to salvage as much as we can from our past cultures."[26] While culturalization of Hɔmɔwɔ makes it possible to communicate its worth in broader national terms, it is important to remember that "cultural objectification" (Handler 1988, 14) and selective mobilization of traditional ideas it entails spring from the nonreligion discourse that is fundamentally invalidating.

"The carnival is the traditional exposé of our culture": Homofest and Domestic Tourism

Building on the idea that tradition must be refined in order to become adequate in the modern context, the enhancement and modernization of culture are prominent goals of Sankofaism and current cultural policies in Ghana (Asare 2022).[27] An essential component of this orientation is what Rosalind Hackett (2022) calls the festivalization of traditional religions; that is, the reliance on the format of the commercialized festival to popularize traditional practices. In 2014, the Ministry of Tourism launched another initiative to boost the public visibility of local festivals and to enhance Ghana's allure as a tourist destination. Homofest was part of this endeavor, designed to "create value for happiness through entertainment and pleasure [and] forge tourism partnerships with neighboring sister countries in a bid to promote multi-destination tours."[28] The effort showcased the rich culture of the Ga-Adangbe, with Hɔmɔwɔ at its core, as evidenced by the name and timing of the initiative right after the Hɔmɔwɔ season. Much like Hɔmɔwɔ Thanksgiving services, Homofest was designed to bring Ghanaians together in celebration of their cultural identity. As the only nationalized traditional celebration, Homofest may have been devised not only to showcase the capital's cultural wares but also to defuse tensions that have marred Hɔmɔwɔ's reputation over the past decades, whether due to chiefly disputes that tarnish the Ga townships or clashes with Pentecostal/Charismatic churches over the ban on drumming.

Intrigued by the initiative and its possible ideological parallels to the Hɔmɔwɔ Thanksgiving service the CCG promotes, I visited the National Commission on Culture, the cultural wing of the Ministry of Tourism and the co-organizer of Homofest. I was fortunate to run into the commission's head of programs, Bernice Deh-Kumah, and was delighted when she eagerly agreed to enlighten me about Homofest. Bernice is an endearing and hardworking soul dedicated to the mission of sharing Ghana's artistic treasures with the world. She believes that it is critical to preserve cultural values and pass them on to the next generation, but with certain adjustments. The organizers of Homofest appreciate the idea behind Hɔmɔwɔ but find that the way it is traditionally celebrated is disjointed. "If you look at the promotion of the traditional Hɔmɔwɔ," Bernice explained, "each clan or each town will have it in [a] different time and different section. They don't unify it where it would be at one central position where they will celebrate it. So the ministry thought that it is good to put all these people together."[29] When I asked Bernice what she thought about omitting religious elements from Homofest, she suggested that religion was already taken care of in the standard, traditional rendition of the festivals. Instead, the organizers of Homofest sought to create a platform for national cohesion in the hope that it would help resolve intercommunal disagreements and tensions. The second and the more pronounced rationale for rebranding Hɔmɔwɔ was to open it up to a wider audience, including tourists interested in the aesthetic and entertainment side of the event. Homofest features a wide range of events, including parades through the major streets of Accra, clean-up exercises, photo exhibitions, food bazaars, cooking competitions, lectures, beauty pageants, and durbars with chiefs.[30]

Bernice told me that Homofest is always held with the approval of the Ga-Adangbe chiefs, many of whom attend the festivities. Their involvement is not surprising, given the assurances of the Ministry of Tourism, Arts & Culture that Homofest will "encouraged [sic] business development and promotion through sponsorship" and will "bring Ga-Adangbe together to foster unity and development."[31] Undoubtedly, the prospect of investment and the allure of making Ga-Adangbe culture more exciting for future generations contributes to the desire of members of the Ga community to collaborate with public authorities. In 2018, Homofest was even chaired by Nii Kinka, the chief of Osu who attended and spoke at the 2016 Hɔmɔwɔ Thanksgiving lecture.[32]

The commercial appeal of large public festivities like Homofest is substantial. I remember attending the Twin Day festivities in Ga-Mashie in August 2016. Twin Day is the most beloved ceremony in the Hɔmɔwɔ festival season, attracting large crowds of curious observers. Spectators stand transfixed as twins donned in their best outfits walk the winding, narrow streets of Jamestown, followed by various youth groups (asafoi) who gesticulate joyfully.[33] Large tents of various colors are set up around the procession, where merrymaking continues well into the night. Signs and billboards scattered throughout the neighborhood congratulate people on the new year as they promote different products and services. Loudspeakers of all sizes are brought out onto the streets to entertain friends and families sitting in plastic chairs and eagerly consuming food and drink from street vendors. Star and Club Beer, Alomo Bitters, locally made akpeteshie, sweet and savory popcorn, meat on skewers, palm wine, and other snacks and refreshments are readily available.[34] This abundance is not limited to Twin Day; feasting and jubilation follow all major traditional celebrations. Because of their mass appeal, large corporations vie with each other to fund festivals such as Hɔmɔwɔ and cash-strapped chiefs are forced to accept and even solicit corporate support. Such arrangements with corporate sponsors foreground images of commodities and brand-name logos, markedly reconfiguring the context and content of ritual events (Adrover 2018, 236).

The Ga historian Irene Odotei describes the appeal of festivals as a lucrative source of publicity for local companies: "To make sure the sponsors gain economically from their investments[,] activities are planned that would enhance the consumption of their products. Food fairs, dances and beach parties are additions made to traditional festivals. Star beer, ABC and Club beer with their 'T' shirts, banners and other products are now familiar items during festivals. The banner with the Star beer advertisement 'Our Culture, our Heritage, our Festival, our beer' blows across the streets. Conspicuous consumption as a feature of Ghanaian festivals is fully exploited by modern commercial enterprises" (Odotei 2002, 27). The audience for the Hɔmɔwɔ ritual celebration consists primarily of Ga community members since it is held in accordance with Ga customary law and many of its components are closed to the general public. Thus, Homofest, a nationwide, government-organized celebration, presents a more enticing marketing opportunity for sponsors.

Rodney Harrison (2013, 39) asserts that the desire to preserve the past stems from an overwhelming sense of uncertainty about the present. It is no coincidence that heritage and culture programs thrive in transitional periods accompanied by the need for a strong national identity. The culturalization of traditional lifeworlds through the commodification of indigeneity has a long history in Ghana, encompassing missionary practices, colonial policies, and the Sankofa movement that marked the cultural turn in postindependence state policy. The modern politics of institutionalized nostalgia rarely recognizes its colonial antecedents (Boym 2001, 15). Instead, as Tim Oakes (2010) posits, cultural policies are articulated in direct correlation with modernization and development objectives. As it happens, since the establishment of the Fourth Republic, Ghana's discourse on culture has gradually aligned with the worldwide preoccupation with heritage that is so entwined with Western modes of commodity production (Phillips and Steiner 1999; Lentz 2001). Alexis Bunten (2010) suggests that the most successful cases of indigenous tourism "reference Western paradigms of cultural representations drawn from popular images of 'the Other' usually cast from colonialist, orientalist, exoticizing tropes and reproduced through consumer driven media" (52). These representations of culture are specifically designed to ensure a more alluring display. Years before launching Homofest or other similar initiatives,[35] the minister of chieftaincy and culture, Sampson Kwaku Boafo, announced that as Ghana was promoting tourism to the position of the source of the country's primary foreign exchange income, "cultural activities such as passage rites, festivals, traditional dances, funerals among others if well packaged and promoted [could] play an important role in increasing the country's tourism potential."[36] Almost a decade later, ideas voiced by Minister Elizabeth Ofusu-Adjare, the architect of the Homofest initiative, strongly echo this view: "Rebranding of our culture and festivals is important because it will not only boost investment, but will also create business opportunities that will make the local industries thrive."[37] Whereas mainline Christians often support these state initiatives, Pentecostal/Charismatic leaders insist on the dangers of populating the public sphere with spiritual forces that could be detrimental to the country's spiritual and economic progress (de Witte and Meyer 2012, 51).

Jacob K. Olupona (2011) assesses the nationalization of traditional celebrations positively in the Nigerian context but links the process to the dwindling influence of traditional religions in their current form. The "actions, rituals, and mythologies" extracted from traditional celebrations, he postulates, create unity among disparate societal factions through what he calls civil religion (11). He describes the gradual association of the Yoruba Ọdún Ọba ceremony with the national interests of postindependence Nigeria as community development became one of the main features of the festival: "Sons and daughters return to the city to raise funds for development projects, clubs, and community associations in the city and try to outdo each other in their expressions of solidarity and support for their community" (141). These activities are consistent with Homofest, yet Homofest is a very different phenomenon. First of all, Homofest was intentionally created by the Ghanaian state as a counterpart to Hɔmɔwɔ and other Ga-Adangbe festivities, which continue to be celebrated in an unabridged form. While in Olupona's case study, it is the ọọ̀ni, the traditional ruler of the Yoruba kingdom, who strives to transform a traditional ceremony into a symbol of nation-building, Ga traditional leaders have very little to do with Homofest beyond sanctioning its existence. Second, the label of civil religion cannot be applied to Homofest since it is deliberately designed as a nonreligious counterpart to Hɔmɔwɔ, which maintains its religious elements. Instead, the Ministry of Tourism envisions Homofest as a religiously neutral festivity that all citizens can enjoy, including Pentecostal/Charismatic Christians, for its entertainment value.

WHAT INITIALLY DREW my attention to Hɔmɔwɔ Thanksgiving services and Homofest was their "culture with progress" branding, promotion, and coverage. I was especially disconcerted by the Hɔmɔwɔ Thanksgiving services. I wondered if the enterprise was yet another clandestine instrument for reasserting the Christian monopoly over Accra in the aftermath of the Ga pushback against the ascendancy of Pentecostal/Charismatic churches and the Ga community's ensuing command over Accra's soundscape. Initially, I thought that interviews with representatives of the mainline denominations confirmed my speculations because of their willingness to speak openly about their aspiration to fully Christianize Hɔmɔwɔ in the future. Over time, however, I have come to discern the true commitment of organizers of Hɔmɔwɔ Thanksgiving services to building bridges rather than waging wars. There is no doubt that both Hɔmɔwɔ Thanksgiving services and Homofest are organized with the best of intentions. They highlight the value of tradition for all Ghanaians and preserve and cherish the customs of various communities. The central goal of both ventures, from the perspective of their key actors, is to bring the nation together around their shared allegiance to national welfare and progress.

More broadly, the two initiatives offer a glimpse into the layered epistemologies that structure contemporary attitudes toward traditional religions in Ghana. On the one hand, they convey an appreciation of traditional celebrations as platforms for civic cohabitation. In this rendering, traditional religions are imagined as "hospitable religious spaces" (Yakubu 2022, 246), or spaces of communal devotion and maintenance, in contrast to the Euroamerican idea of religion as a private domain of individual reflection (Wenger 2009, 6). On the other hand, the production of these spaces subjects traditional religions to practices of selection and classification, activities premised on the belief that traditional religions must be religiously neutralized in order to become serviceable in the contemporary secular state. Reflecting on the future of Hɔmɔwɔ in 1967, Ghanaian scholar Alfred Kofi Quarcoo (1967) wrote that festivals are social events and that "when freed of the religious content, [they] will be effective functions that will foster modern social solidarity" (36). This is a popular opinion governed by an implicit belief that traditional religions can be forged into instruments of social solidarity only if they are unmoored from their matrix of associations, purged of threatening and outdated features, and refined for the modern Ghanaian nation-state. One might argue that these attitudes are common in secular frameworks, where the growing demand to remove religion from the public sphere dictates its reframing as culture. However, in the African context, the culturalization of traditional religions is accompanied by the religionization of Islam and Christianity and is propelled by the perceived incompatibility of traditional religions with modernity. The words articulated by the Osu Presbyterian minister Andrew Odonkor illustrate this point: "How can we still celebrate Hɔmɔwɔ as a traditional festival in a Christian context?

That is what we are working on now. It is not only about Hɔmɔwɔ but also about other traditional rites, which have been Christianized now—like child naming. Because there are good things in those celebrations, they do not need to be abandoned, but they need to be celebrated in the Christian context."[38] The understanding that there are good things in these celebrations is central to both Hɔmɔwɔ Thanksgiving services and Homofest. This understanding also implies that there are bad things that should be discarded or customized to enhance their value to both the Christian community and the Ghanaian state at large. The badness of these elements is understood both in terms of their backwardness and uselessness and in terms of their spiritual threat and potential to corrupt. The ease with which the actors involved speak of doing away with religious elements in traditional celebrations points to the normalization of the epistemological framework in which traditional religions are a likely target for bricolage, while Christianity and Islam, as part of the sacrosanct domain of religion, cannot be subjected to the same modifications.

Conclusion

Layered Epistemologies of Contemporary Accra

On a typically hot day in late January 2018, I was sitting in the palace of Sempe Maŋtsɛ, the chief of one of the quarters in the Ga-Mashie Traditional Area, where I was conversing with the *wulɔmɔ*, Numɔ Kpakpo Oyeeni. At that point, I had spent about nine months in Accra, researching the ban on drumming. "The Ga and Israelis," stated Numɔ Oyeeni, "we are the same people. The customs we perform here are exactly the same that they perform in Israel: like when we celebrate Hɔmɔwɔ, they do the same thing in Israel." Although such kinship with Israelis or, in alternative formulations, with Egyptians, had been intimated in passing in earlier conversations with others, this was the most straightforward declaration of what I would later learn is a widespread theory of origin among the Ga community of Accra.[1]

Even if the correlation has not been explicitly verbalized elsewhere, I could not help but draw parallels between the popular enthusiasm for the Israeli theory of origin and the prevalence of Pentecostal/Charismatic Christianity in Accra. In particular, I was reminded of the discriminatory rhetoric against traditional modes of religiosity that I witnessed on numerous occasions while attending Pentecostal/Charismatic services. Ga people are numerically concentrated in the capital, the hub of the Pentecostal revival in Ghana, and the community has borne the brunt of the growing prejudice against traditional religions and traditional culture more broadly. In these circumstances, the increased visibility of the Ga story of origins in Israel appears to be an ideological response to the Pentecostal/Charismatic hostility against Ga traditionalists, as it links the Ga people to the Old Testament and thus exempts them from being demonized as fetish and idol worshippers. The statement of Numɔ Oyeeni corroborates the argument that runs through this book: the Ga community relies on its traditional religion to buttress its position and maintain its authority in the face of the epistemic marginalization it experiences in the conspicuously Pentecostal city of Accra. Ultimately, the ideological work performed by the ban on drumming or the Israel origin story demonstrates that tradition is what shapes the community's effective engagement with modernity.

The history of noise restriction in Accra—from nineteenth-century colonial sonic hierarchies to the current prominence of the Ga ritual quiet—was the primary lens through which I conveyed the resilience and functionality of the Ga religion in the contemporary context. Subsumed under this framework were two central arguments. First, I maintained that the impact of the Ga ban on drumming on Accra's contemporary soundscape represents an inversion of earlier top-down noise abatement efforts. The former were state-initiated techniques to curb and control the indigenous lower-class population, whose "heathen" aural tastes were juxtaposed with the "evolved" sensibilities of the Christian elite. The ritual ban on drumming instituted in contemporary Accra is at odds with the established paradigm because it represents a blend of secular sensibilities and the dictates of Ga lifeworld, mobilized against the most "progressive" Christian movement in Ghana. The Ga takeover of Accra's soundscape signals the group's determination to consolidate its authority, especially in the context of the Pentecostal/Charismatic Christianity that is spreading like wildfire across the continent.

Second, I approached the agendas and conflicts surrounding the imposition and regulation of the ban on drumming as an entry point into a critical analysis of secularity in Ghana. On the one hand, the state seeks to maintain an aura of religious neutrality. At first glance, its management of the Drum Wars and its establishment of the Nuisance Control Task Force appear to be signs of institutionalized noise control, in which both Christianity and traditional culture are subjected to the governmentality of the Ghanaian state. However, the state-led public discourse communicates that Christianity holds an elevated status as the religious tradition most consistent with the post-Enlightenment vision of modernity. The blending of the Christocentric evolutionary taxonomy of religions implicit in secularism as an epistemological regime, the copresence of customary and constitutional law, and the customary lack of compartmentalization between the public sphere and state religion create favorable conditions for the culturalization of traditional religions, whether discursively, by the Ga traditionalists themselves, or in various state-led cultural policies such as Sankofaism. The continuous relevance of the Ga traditional religion is made possible by the conflation of religion and culture that enables Ga religious authorities to collaborate with state officials in policing Accra's soundscape. Under the guise of culture, Ga religion is able to seep through the cracks of the secular institutional framework and maintain its weight in the lives of modern urbanites. Since secularism as an ideological and political regime cannot fully accommodate the intricacies of Ghana's socioreligious landscape, it is gradually being modified to reflect regional specificities. The resulting secularity demonstrates that contemporary forms of government are deeply enmeshed with the localities in which they function. In acknowledging Ghana's own model of modernity, I stand with scholars who insist on the existence of multiple modernities that are unmoored from the Euroamerican ideal type.

Beyond the primary focus on Ghana's secularity, this book is also a history of religious pluralism, human rights, culturalization initiatives, and minority politics. It counters the epistemological subjugation of traditional religions of Africa in particular and contemporary African lifeworlds in general by highlighting knowledges from below and accentuating contexts in which the agency of those lifeworlds is unmistakable. As a scholar of African religions, my priority is to reintegrate subaltern epistemologies into the mainstream narrative while simultaneously challenging the hierarchies that continue to haunt the study of religion. Researching a community that is recognized as quintessentially urban due to its proximity to the economic and political hubs of the region was a convenient starting point for observing how traditional religions are entangled with urbanity as legitimate components of African modernity. Yet when I first took up this topic, I could not even imagine the extensive and often invisible reach of the Ga religion in Accra's urban fabric.

The collaboration between Ga traditionalists and the state in curbing Accra's soundscape flies in the face of the common portrayal of African cities in urban studies as chaotic and dysfunctional. African cities are routinely conceptualized as places of speculation rather than intense planning that operate along informal, invisible, and decentralized pathways (Simone 2008, 104) and as unruly forces of failing infrastructure (de Boeck and Plissart 2006). In contrast to these visions, the driving motivation behind the ritual ban on drumming is a desire to imprint order on public spaces by disciplining Pentecostal/Charismatic churches, the unruly actors who fail to respect the customary notions of the role and place of traditional religions.

My engagement with the sensory orders inherent in noise regulation practices has been a fruitful avenue for theorizing the subversive power of quiet. Noise as a category has attracted considerable scholarly interest in recent decades (Attali 1985; Bijsterveld 2008; Schwartz 2011), often in the context of sound studies (Bailey 1996; Picker 2003; Sewald 2011; Sterne 2005; Thompson 2002). However, the antipode of noise has received less attention, leaving the category significantly understudied both in the context of religious studies and in sound studies more broadly. My research begins to fill this gap by furnishing the field with new material on quiet and by theorizing a model of noise regulation that challenges previous top-down approaches. I argued that noise-abatement initiatives tend to follow the same pattern: they are state-imposed, often secular ventures modeled on the normative Euroamerican sensory hierarchy that places certain senses and experiences below others. Not coincidentally, sensory experiences placed at the lowest level of "evolution" tend to be the province of the marginalized. In contrast to this paradigm, the ban on drumming—conceptualized as a ritual noise-control technique that has propelled secular noise-regulation initiatives since 1998—is a bottom-up venture that stems directly from religious taboos. Moreover, it is instituted by a group that has been sidelined in public discourse and it is used against the trendiest Christian movement. The ban on drumming also represents an inversion of the classical associations generated by the categories of noise and not-noise. Protestantism, as the religion of modernity, used to be the global trendsetter in sensory discourse. In the context of the Drum Wars, however, it is the Ga religion that advocates silence to stifle the sonic pandemonium of Pentecostal/Charismatic Christianity.

I contribute to the study of the secular through my emphasis on marginalized alternative modernities that develop alongside Western modernity. Varieties of secular forms have attracted considerable scholarly interest in the past decade, but engagement with the topic often occurs on a theoretical rather than a practical level. The theoretical framework I use to examine the Drum Wars emerged in response to observing power-sharing between various state, religious, and customary authorities. These interactions deviate from the power dynamics anticipated in the classical model of secularism, yet they are perfectly functional and compatible with the region's history. The patchwork quilt of intercommunal engagements described in this book testifies not only to shifting religious boundaries but also to the alternation, interplay, tension, and overlap between local and global and European and indigenous regimes of truth that produce a hybrid epistemological and sensory order. Against the backdrop of long-standing historical ties between traditional communities and mainline Christians, religious boundaries become permeable as the epistemologies harmonize. In conflictual scenarios like the Drum Wars, in contrast, the boundaries become rigid and insurmountable as the emphasis shifts to epistemological hierarchies that highlight differences rather than similarities.

By looking at the particularities of Ghanaian politics—its plural legal system that harmonizes customary and constitutional law, the legacy of Christian missionary work, and the unbroken relevance of custom—I endeavored to transcend the narrative of deficient secularism and instead emphasize multiple secularities. As a blend of two discursive and sensory regimes—one inherent in secularism and the other in the customary world view—Ghanaian secularity remains ambivalent about the status of traditional religions. Actors who believe in the relevance of custom, a category broad enough to include religious elements, are also convinced that it is fundamentally different from religions such as Islam and Christianity. The ambivalent impulse to cherish and dismiss traditional lifeworlds and the historically pronounced discourses that proclaim custom as not quite religious have enabled Ghanaians to tolerate or even endorse the presence of traditional practices in the public sphere. Custom dictates that inhabiting a traditional territory comes with communal responsibilities that run counter to the idea of a neutral public sphere that is common to secularism. Whether sobered by the pushback from the traditionalists or influenced by the state's endorsement of the Ga community, even some Pentecostal/Charismatic Christians are opting for communal peace. An elder from the Christ Apostolic Church was touchingly magnanimous toward the traditionalist view: "The traditionalists are not saying that we should come and worship with them; [they are saying that] we should have quietness. This is what we Pentecostals do not understand. But we are starting to understand. When we want to drum, we drum at a very low voice. We don't even use speakers. We forget about the speakers and we perform, and we worship God in spirit and in truth."[2] For now, the tacit acceptance of the state as moderator and the willingness to make concessions for the sake of cohabitation is consistent with the ideal of African religious pluralism discussed earlier (Yakubu 2022). However, the relationship between the Ga community and Christians is contextual, situational, and multifaceted, coming closer to practices of membership, transgression, mediation, and imitation that go beyond tolerance (Nolte and Ogen 2017, 258).

Acknowledgments

This book took shape over the course of more than a decade, benefiting from input and conversations with friends, colleagues, and mentors across the globe. I owe a debt of gratitude to Harvard University not only for its financial and institutional support but also for the wonderful committee guidance on my research. Jacob K. Olupona, generously supported me at each step of my academic career, opening up new avenues for thinking about African religions and empowering me to pursue my ideas with confidence. Michael D. Jackson's compassionate nature, generosity, and poetic spirit provided solace and comfort in difficult times. Emmanuel Akyeampong's enthusiasm for Ghanaian history and dedication to disentangling the complexities of historical narrative have been invaluable. Last but certainly not least, my MA advisor, external dissertation committee member, and lifelong mentor, Robert M. Baum, is directly responsible for igniting my passion for African religions. His dedication to responsible scholarship and his commitment to justice both inside and outside academia are a continuous source of inspiration.

I am indebted to numerous individuals who have indulged me in intellectually stimulating conversations and provided indispensable comments on my work over the years. Ahmed Ragab's razor-sharp mentorship in the Science, Religion, and Culture Program at Harvard Divinity School pushed me to build the theoretical foundation of my research. Rosalind Hackett and Annalisa Butticci taught me how to survive and thrive in the field as a female scholar. Vlad Naumescu at Central European University generously offered comments and suggestions for improving the book. Birgit Meyer welcomed me to the Religious Matters Program at Utrecht University when I was writing this book and has provided intellectual inspiration and guidance ever since. Monika Wohlrab-Sahr, Markus Dreßler, and other colleagues at the Center for Advanced Studies' "Multiple Secularities—Beyond the West, Beyond Modernities" served as a forum for discussing and improving my work.

I appreciate the guidance and support of colleagues and mentors in Ghana, including Moses Nii-Dortey, Samuel Ntewusu, and Richard Asante at the University of Ghana and Kwabena Asamoah-Gyuadu at Trinity Theological Seminary. I am also indebted to scholars I met in Accra who kindly offered feedback and recommendations for my project when it was still in its nascent form, among them Kofi Quashigah, Abamfo Ofori Atiemo, Philip Laryea, Brigid M. Sackey, Kodjo A. Senah, Rose Mary Amenga-Etego, Anatoli Ignatov, Florian Carl, Abraham Nana Opare Kwakye, Jesse Shipley, Cati Coe, Mercy Oduyoye, Kofi Asare Opoku, Nate Plageman, and Cephas Narh Omenyo.

I am profoundly grateful to my Ga language teacher, Adokwei Sacker, for his unparalleled expertise and endless patience; my dear colleague, Gabriel Anang, for sharing his knowledge of the Ga culture and allowing me to accompany him on numerous field visits; and my friend, Numo Blafo III, who continually educates me about Ga religion. I could not have navigated the practical and emotional challenges of fieldwork and writing without the inspiring late-night conversations, laughter-filled adventures, and companionship of the individuals I met during my visits to Ghana. Special thanks to Angelantonio Grossi, Nana Osei-Opare, Sook Hee Yuk, Emily Stratton, Nana Quarshie, Elisa Prosperetti, Sarah Balakrishnan, and Romain Tiquet. Last but not least, I am grateful to those in Accra who shared their stories and welcomed me into their communities for celebrations, rituals, and worship services.

The book owes much to the incisive observations of three anonymous readers, which enabled me to fine-tune the argument and resolve inconsistencies. Equally invaluable was the editorial work and guidance of Miriam Angress in preparing the manuscript.

For the many walks, conversations, dinners, dances, adventures, and travels, I am grateful to my incredible friends around the world. I thank my parents, Tina Maurer and George Goshadze, for being the main engine behind my progress as a human being. My mother fills my existence with unconditional love and my father inspires me every day with his passion for this marvelous universe.

I dedicate this book to my partner, David and my daughter, Ida for the joy, comfort, and wonder they bring to my life.

Glossary

The definitions of these frequently used Ga terms are based on the *Ga-English Dictionary* compiled by Mary E. Kropp-Dakubu ([1999] 2009):

AGBAAFO (pl. *agbaafoi*): assistant priest

AKUTSO (pl. *akutsɛi*): quarter or neighborhood in the Ga traditional area

GBATSU: shrine house of a deity

JEMAWɔŋ (pl. *jemawɔji*): any major Ga deity, identified with a place

KPOKPOI: ritual food prepared for the Hɔmɔwɔ festival. Kpokpoi is made from steamed ground corn mixed with palm oil and okra; it is eaten with palm nut soup.

MAŋTSƐ (pl. *maŋtsɛmɛi*): Ga traditional chief

ŋMɔ (pl. *ŋmɔji*): farm

ŋMAADUMɔ: the rite of sowing millet, which marks the beginning of the period of quiet

ŋOŋO: iron gong, a bell-shaped instrument used for Ga ceremonial music

OTUTU: a small mound-shaped traditional shrine

Wɔŋ (pl. *woji*): lesser Ga deity

WɔYOO (pl. *wɔyei*): priestess; female medium of a deity

WULɔMɔ (pl. *wulɔmɛi*): traditional Ga priest

Notes

INTRODUCTION. ALTERED ONTOLOGIES AND REVERSED PARADIGMS

1 Prior to Ghana's transition to constitutional democracy in 1992, the media were subject to strict government censorship. Media liberalization led to the proliferation of private radio and television stations and private newspapers. Both state and private media began to enjoy unprecedented freedom.

2 While this book focuses specifically on secularity in Ghana, the fusion of customary values and secularism as a political regime described here is by no means unique to Ghana and can be found in various configurations throughout Africa.

3 Rachel N. Zakpala, Frederick Ato Armah, Brigid M. Sackey, and Opoku Pabi, "Night-Time Decibel Hell: Mapping Noise Exposure Zones and Individual Annoyance Ratings in an Urban Environment in Ghana," *Scientifica*, January 1, 2014, 2.

4 These accounts generally accept a normative Eurocentric understanding of secularization as a linear process with a specific end goal and do not reflect the significant theoretical shifts of the past two decades. For a more nuanced look at African secularity, see Leatt (2017), Kallinen (2016), and Tweneboah (2019).

5 Richard Asante (2011) and Philip Attuquayefio (2012) interpret the Drum Wars as a reaction to the perceived or actual marginalization of the Ga community. Kwabena J. D. Amanor (2009) contextualizes the interfaith discord in light of earlier tensions between Christian churches and Ga traditionalists. Focusing on music and performativity, Tobias Robert Klein (2010) observes the impact of the Drum Wars in the songs produced in the aftermath of the conflict.

6 The term refers to the established, if outdated, paradigm in the study of religion of grouping religions considered to be of global significance into a single category of "world religions." In the nineteenth century, Masuzawa (2005) argues, the major world religions included Christianity, Judaism, Buddhism, Islam, Hinduism, Confucianism, Taoism, Shinto, Zoroastrianism, Jainism, and Sikhism.

7 To learn more about the targeted use of these terms in other indigenous communities, see Tafjord (2016), Johnson (2007), and Niezen (2012).

8 I am particularly grateful to Kwabena Asamoah-Gyadu, Moses Nii Dortey, Kodjo A. Senah, Kofi Quashigah, Abamfo Atiemo, Nii Adjei Klu, Irene Odotei, Koi Larbi, Philip Laryea, Kofi Asare Opoku, Brigid Sackey, and Cephas Omenyo.

9 This approach is inspired by Yael Navaro-Yashin's (2002) argument that Turkish culture does not exist as a separate analytical and anthropological category that designates

essential Turkishness. Instead, one can speak of "enactments, productions and contestations over culture" (10–13).

10   From the attacked churches, I interviewed representatives of the Christ Apostolic Church International (Osu Headquarters), the Evangel Church International (Achimota and Adabraka branches), the Power Miracle Chapel International, the International Central Gospel Church (La branch), the Christ Apostolic Church (North Kaneshie Central and Nungua branches), the Victory Bible Church International (Awoshie Headquarters), the El Shaddai Temple, the Gospel Light Chapel International (Mallam branch), the Church of Pentecost (Alajo Central Assembly), the Assemblies of God (Tesano and Kaneshie branches), and Great Fire Pentecostal International Ministry.

11   I worked especially closely with members of the Osu Ebenezer Presbyterian Church, the St. Barnabas Anglican Church, and the Methodist Church of Ghana.

12   For Ghana, see Asamoah-Gyadu (2005a), Gifford (2004), Meyer (2004a), and Omenyo (2002). For Africa, see Adogame (2011), Corten and Marshall-Fratani (2001), Gifford (1998), and Marshall (2009). For general works on Pentecostal Christianity, see Anderson (2004), Coleman and Hackett (2015), Martin (2002), and Robbins (2004).

13   Kwabena Asamoah-Gyadu, "Did Jesus Wear Designer Robes?" *Christianity Today*, November 2009, 38–41; Gifford (2004).

14   Emilia Ennin Abbey, "Ga Traditionalists Clash with Churches," *Daily Graphic*, May 29, 2014, accessed January 12, 2020, https://www.graphic.com.gh/news/general -news/ga-traditionalists-clash-with-churches.html; Mary Mensah, "Observe Ban on Drumming and Noise Making," *Daily Graphic*, April 13, 2016, accessed January 12, 2020, https://www.graphic.com.gh/news/general-news/observe-ban-on-drumming -and-noisemaking.html; Gertrude Ankah Nyavi, "Ban on Noise Making to Begin on May 8—Ga State Warns of No Compromise," *Daily Graphic*, April 26, 2017, accessed January 12, 2020, https://www.graphic.com.gh/news/general-news/ban-on-noise -making-to-begin-may-8-ga-state-warns-of-no-compromise.html.

15   Irene Quaye (1972, 11–13) challenges this theory and argues that the Ga were formed as a result of gradual fusion with the Dangmes and the Guans.

16   According to Margaret Field (1937, 5), the other three cults are:

        1) Me: deities of Adangme origin whose worshippers sing and dance to Me-type music;

        2) Kpa: deities who were originally war gods of the Kpa people based in Labadi;

        3) Otu and Akɔŋ: deities of Fanti and Akwapim origin whose worshippers dance and sing to Otu and Akɔŋ types of music

17   Margaret Field offers a different rendition of the term that ultimately has a similar meaning. She suggests that it is a combination of two Ga words: *je/jeŋ*, meaning "the world" and *ma/maŋ*, meaning "town." Hence, it signifies beings that "walk about the world and the towns" (Field 1937, 4).

18   Originally, Hɔmɔwɔ was part of the Kpa cult, while Kplejoo was the primary festival of the Kpele cult. However, over time, Hɔmɔwɔ was amalgamated into Kpele in the majority of Ga towns and today it is more prominently celebrated than Kplejoo (Field 1937, 5, 89).

19 For more about Hͻmͻwͻ, see Ammah (2016), Fosu (1999), Gyimah (1985), Kilson (2013), Lokko (1981), Odotei (2002), and Omaboe (2011).

1. JUMPING ON THE ANTI-NOISE BANDWAGON

1 "D.C.'s and Funeral Customs," *The Gold Coast Leader*, August 1, 1903, 2–3.
2 "Accra," *The Gold Coast Leader*, July 18, 1903, 4.
3 "Accra."
4 The term "Accras" was often used in the early writings to refer to the inhabitants of Accra.
5 In this chapter, I focus on the *Ordinances of the Gold Coast* from 1903 because they are representative of the regulations that were in place during the colonial period. As seen below, local laws from 1878 and 1920 have an almost identical approach:

> Ordinance for better regulating the Police of Towns and Populous Places, and Promoting the Public Health (1878), No. 10, Article 36: Any Court may prohibit during the hours of its sitting, and at any place within a radius of three hundred yards from the building where such sitting is held any beating of drums, gongs, tomtoms, or other instruments, or other loud noises of any kind of description, and whosoever, being required by any constable or officer of the Court to desist from beating drums, gongs, tomtoms, or other instruments, or from making any other noise as aforesaid, fails to comply with such requisition, shall for every offence incur a penalty not exceeding forty shillings, and may be apprehended by any Constable without warrant (Griffith 1887, 474).

> Title III, Administration of Justice, Chapter 16, Part VI, Offences against Public Order, Health, and Morality, No. 13, Article 120(1): Every occupier of any house, building, yard or other place situate in any town, who, without a license in writing from the Governor or a District Commissioner, permits any persons to assemble and beat or play or dance therein to any drum, gong, tomtom, or similar instrument of music, shall be liable to a fine of two pounds (Kingdon 1920, 313).

> No. 13, Article 139: Whoever does any of the following acts shall be liable to a fine of forty shillings, namely: (9): In any town willfully or wantonly, and after being warned to desist, shouts or blows any horn or shell, or sounds or plays upon any musical instrument, or sings or makes any other loud or unseemly noise, to the annoyance or disturbance of any person; (10): In any town, without a licence in writing from the Governor or a District Commissioner, beats or plays any drum, gong, tom-tom, or other similar instruments of music between eight o'clock at night and six in the morning (Kingdon 1920, 319–20).

6 Mahmood Mamdani (2012, 2–3) writes that "native" as a category was conceptually tied to the aspirations of the colonial state to pin down, localize, and cast out the colonized.
7 "Minutes of the Board of Education Meeting, 20th April, 1914," *The Gold Coast Leader*, April 10, 1915, 6.
8 "News, Notes and Comments," *Gold Coast Aborigines*, September 8, 1899, 1.

9   "D.C.'s and Funeral Customs."
10 "D.C.'s and Funeral Customs," emphasis in the original.
11 "Cape Coast. Editorial Notes," *The Gold Coast Leader*, August 8, 1903, 2–3.
12 "Cape Coast. Editorial Notes."
13 "Cape Coast. Editorial Notes."
14 "D.C.'s and Funeral Customs."
15 "Segregation," *Gold Coast Nation*, March 18, 1915, 3.
16 "Other Information," *Gold Coast Nation*, 1913, 5.
17 "Notes and Comments," *Gold Coast Aborigines*, January 8, 1898, 2.
18 "General News," *The Gold Coast Leader*, August 30, 1913, 2.
19 "D.C.'s and Funeral Customs."
20 "The District Commissioner, Accra," ADM 11/1/1139 1895, March 13, 1895, Ghana/Secretary for Native Affairs, Public Records and Archives Administration Department, Accra, Ghana (hereafter Ghana/Secretary for Native Affairs).
21 ADM 11/1/884, Ghana/Secretary for Native Affairs, 1909. Sibi Saba and Ashiko were entertainment dances rather than ritual dances. Nate Plageman (2013) refers to these as proto-highlife musics. The reason for their prohibition was their "visually offensive" nature, which was ascribed to "immoral" movements and revealing clothing.
22 *Kpoikpoi* is prepared exclusively for Hɔmɔwɔ celebrations and consists of steamed fermented cornmeal eaten in combination with smoked fish and palm-nut soup.
23 ADM 11/1/9 1907, September 7, 1907, Ghana/Secretary for Native Affairs.
24 ADM 11/1/1139 1886, July 17, 1886, Ghana/Secretary for Native Affairs.
25 ADM 11/1/1086 1891, July 22, 1891, Ghana/Secretary for Native Affairs.
26 "General News," *Gold Coast Aborigines*, December 28, 1907, 2.
27 Nii Afotey, chief drummer of Nungua, interview by the author, Accra, June 26, 2016.
28 ADM 11/1/1139 1910, June 18, 1910, Ghana/Secretary for Native Affairs.
29 "Other Information," *Gold Coast Nation*, April 24, 1913, 5.

2. WINDS OF CHANGE

1   "General News," *Gold Coast Chronicle*, May 6, 1899, 3. The quote is somewhat misleading because of the reference to "yam custom" since Hɔmɔwɔ is a corn festival. Most likely, the excerpt is referring to the Ga-Mashie Twins Yam Festival, which is part of the activities leading up to the climax of the Hɔmɔwɔ celebration and in which yam is the main crop used in food preparation (Nortey 2012).
2   The first part of this subheading is a riff on the title of a *Daily Graphic* article, "Drumming Will Greet Kwame Back Home," *Daily Graphic*, October 4, 1950.
3   Although in contemporary scholarship, the acronym is commonly associated with the term "African Initiated Churches," in the past it stood for "African Independent Churches" (or, less prevalently, for "African Instituted" or "African Indigenous Churches").
4   "Drumming at Church Service Criticized," *Daily Graphic*, April 22, 1968.
5   "Our Culture and Religious Worship," *Daily Graphic*, January 11, 1973.
6   "Christians Can Pour Libation," *Daily Graphic*, March 2, 1977.

7   Deuteronomy 18: 9–11. See Delasie Dela-Seshie, "Christians and Libation," *Daily Graphic*, March 12, 1977; J. Oppong-Agyare, "Christians Need Not Pour Libation," *Daily Graphic*, March 11, 1977; and Kwamena Ahinful, "Dilemma of Christian, Islamic Chiefs," *Daily Graphic*, June 5, 1993.

8   "Drumming Will Greet Kwame Back Home."

9   "To the Gods . . . ," *Daily Graphic*, February 20, 1963.

10 "Pouring Libation," *Daily Graphic*, January 23, 1968.

11 A. E. Amoah, "Development in the Face of Obsolescent Customs," *Daily Graphic*, August 2, 1988.

12 Laura Grillo, Adriaan van Klinken, and Hassan Ndzovu (2019) argue that "neo-traditional religious movements" represent "*the self-conscious and systematic refashioning of fundamental forms and concepts* [of traditional systems of belief and practice] *in light of competing ideas*" (66, emphasis in original). Rosalind Hackett (1991) characterizes these movements as "new imaginative constructions" (136).

13 Joe Bradford Nyinah, "Rawlings Tells Chiefs to Help Redeem Heritage," *Daily Graphic*, February 18, 1991.

14 Richardson A. Baidoo, "Drums to Replace Bells in School," *Daily Graphic*, August 24, 1985.

15 Kwame Penni, "National Commission on Culture and Cultural Re-Awakening," *Daily Graphic*, April 21, 1995.

16 John P. Kirby, "Cultural Heritage," *Daily Graphic*, December 2, 1986.

17 Daniel Lankai Lawson, interview with the author, Accra, September 15, 2017.

18 As seen in the introduction, there were instances of individual Christian churches violating the directives, but such transgressions were rare.

19 Daniel Lankai Lawson, interview with the author, Accra, September 15, 2017.

20 Prince Bochway, interview with the author, Accra, June 1, 2018.

21 Samuel Yaw Antwi, interview with the author, Accra, July 27, 2016.

22 Kwabena Opuni-Frimpong, interview with the author, Accra, August 3, 2016.

23 Ernest Tackie Yarboi, interview with the author, Accra, October 3, 2017.

24 The term *amplified piety* was introduced by Finnian Gerety (2017, 6) in his work on sonically amplified sacrifice offered by Nambudiri Brahmins in Kerala.

25 Ernest Tackie Yarboi, interview with the author, Accra, October 3, 2017. Father Yarboi was referring to the Pentecostal/Charismatic use of modern drums here. While drums are central to Pentecostal/Charismatic services, such churches normally reject traditional drums.

26 "Sprinkling 'Kpokpoi,'" *Daily Graphic*, August 23, 1965; "Libation Time," *Daily Graphic*, September 1, 1965; "Homowo Day—Big Occasion at Teshie," *Daily Graphic*, September 7, 1965.

27 "Ga State Marks 'Homowo,'" *Daily Graphic*, August 22, 1960; "How Homowo Day Began at Teshie," *Daily Graphic*, August 12, 1964; "Homowo Day—Big Occasion at Teshie."

28 "Lante Djan-We Homowo," *Daily Graphic*, August 3, 1987; "Ga-Mashie Observes Homowo," *Daily Graphic*, August 17, 1987.

29 "'Kpoikpoi' for Acheampong," *Daily Graphic*, September 25, 1972a.

30   "Ike at Homowo Party," *Daily Graphic*, September 4, 1973.

31   "Spirit of Homowo Festival," *Daily Graphic*, August 23, 1973; "Support NRC: Ga Mantse," *Daily Graphic*, October 8, 1973. The National Redemption Council was Colonel Acheampong's political party (1972–1975).

32   "Homowo-Origin," *Daily Graphic*, August 31, 1977.

33   See "Homowo Festival," August 18, 1981; "Teshie Prepares for Homowo," August 27, 1981; "Ga Mantse Sprinkles 'Kpoikpoi,'" August 31, 1981; "Teshie Homowo," September 9, 1981; "Labadi Homowo," September 10, 1981; "Homowo Festival," September 14, 1981; "Homowo Party," September 28, 1981. All in the *Daily Graphic*.

34   "Gamashie Marks Homowo," *Daily Graphic*, August 19, 1985.

35   "Homowo Party," *Daily Graphic*, September 28, 1981.

36   Vic Odoi and Charity Acquah, "Regional Durbar Rounds Off Festivals in Greater Accra," *Daily Graphic*, October 24, 1988.

37   Kobby Asmah, "Osu Homowo Festival," *Daily Graphic*, August 22, 1990; Ato Aidoo and Afi Dawson, "Ga Mashie Observes Homowo on Saturday," *Daily Graphic*, August 7, 1991; "ABL Supports Homowo Celebration," *Daily Graphic*, July 19, 1997.

38   "KBL Donates towards Homowo Festival," *Daily Graphic*, July 28, 1997.

39   "La Homowo Festival," *Daily Graphic*, August 22, 1990.

40   Aidoo and Dawson, "Ga Mashie Observes Homowo on Saturday"; "La Homowo Festival," *Daily Graphic*, August 20, 1991.

41   "Prampram Celebrates Homowo," *Daily Graphic*, September 6, 1995; Severious Kale Dery, "Prampram Celebrates Homowo," *Daily Graphic*, August 21, 1996.

42   "It's Homowo at Ambassador Hotel," *Daily Graphic*, August 26, 1985.

43   Accra Population, World Population Review, accessed June 2, 2019, http://worldpopulationreview.com/world-cities/accra-population/.

44   "Ban on Drumming," *Daily Graphic*, May 19, 1970.

45   The council performed the task effectively with only one omission in 1984.

46   "Ban on Drumming," *Daily Graphic*, May 6, 1989.

47   Daniel Kondor, "'Kpa-Solemo': A Unique Feature of La Homowo," *Daily Graphic*, September 5, 1990.

48   Joe Bradford Nyinah, "Our Cultural Values v Christianity," *Daily Graphic*, December 1, 1994.

49   Joy D. S. Amegbe, "Under the Microscope: Spiritual, Charismatic Churches," *Daily Graphic*, July 2, 1997.

50   Issa Adam, "The Proliferation of Churches . . . Its Socio-Economic Implications," *Daily Graphic*, November 26, 1997.

51   Godwin Kwashie Mensah, "Public Nuisance," *Daily Graphic*, March 16, 1987.

52   Kofi Amponsah-Bediako, "All in the Name of Religion," *Daily Graphic*, October 12, 1987.

53   John Kwame Danso, "AMA Should Act," *Daily Graphic*, July 2, 1990.

54   Mercy Offei, "Less Noise, Please!," *Daily Graphic*, June 25, 1990.

55   E. Asamoah-Twum, "Noise Making," *Daily Graphic*, June 27, 1989.

56   Obenz Akwasi Addae, "'The Fish' above the Law?," *Daily Graphic*, May 25, 1995; Nii Teiko Tagoe, "Stop this Noise Pollution, EPA," *Daily Graphic*, May 29, 1995.

57   Tagoe, "Stop this Noise Pollution, EPA."

58   Sylvester Ataa Boy, "They Are Very Noisy," *Daily Graphic*, July 6, 1987.

59   Mensah, "Public Nuisance."

60   Edmund Cofie, "Abatement of Noise," *Daily Graphic*, December 14, 1988.

61   Guy Marvin Borketey, "Unnecessary Noise," *Daily Graphic*, March 13, 1989.

62   Tagoe, "Stop this Noise Pollution, EPA."

63   Addae, "'The Fish' above the Law?"

64   Kwame O. Omari, "Noise and Environmental Pollution," *Daily Graphic*, March 1, 1991.

65   Joyce Adjoa Thompson, "Noise-Making: An Environmental Pollution," *Daily Graphic*, August 15, 1991.

3. THE POWER OF SOUND

1   *Waakye* is a Ghanaian dish of cooked rice and beans.

2   For descriptions of the structure and content of Hɔmɔwɔ, see Amartey (1991), Ammah (2016), Field (1937), Gyimah (1985), Kropp-Dakubu (1987), and Laryea (2011).

3   Numo Akwaa Mensah III, interview with the author, Accra, November 8, 2017.

4   Accra Metropolitan Assembly, "Ban on Drumming and Noise Making," May 6, 2021, press release, A.025/6/14, https://ama.gov.gh/documents/BAN_ON_NOISE _MAKING_2021_updated.pdf.

5   Quansah (2013, 46); Samuel Yaw Antwi, interview with the author, Accra, July 27, 2016.

6   Victor Yankee, interview with the author, Accra, September 11, 2017.

7   Samuel Yaw Antwi, interview with the author, Accra, July 27, 2016.

8   Eric Nana Owusu, interview with the author, Accra, October 10, 2017.

9   Odinekwa William Kweku, interview with the author, Accra, June 6, 2015; Victor Yankee, interview with the author, Accra, September 11, 2017.

10   Eric Nana Owusu, interview with the author, Accra, October 10, 2017.

11   Sammy Young, interview with the author, Accra, August 3, 2016.

12   Ekow Takyi-Dadzie, interview with the author, Accra, October 6, 2017.

13   Aba Takyi Dadzie, interview with the author, Accra, October 8, 2021.

14   Victor Yankee, interview with the author, Accra, September 11, 2016.

15   Eric Nana Owusu, interview with the author, Accra, October 10, 2017.

4. WHEN THE DEITIES VISIT

1   Nii Shipi, interview with the author, Accra, August 2, 2016.

2   Reports in the *Daily Graphic* provide a window on the gradual discursive prominence of the ban. While there were no reported confrontations until the late 1990s, letters published in the newspaper indicate that some citizens were beginning to question the merits of the ban. See Jeremiah Odoi, "Homowo Needs Modification," *Daily Graphic*, May 19, 1986; Nii Larye Sowa, "Modifications in Homowo—Rejoinders," *Daily Graphic*, June 2, 1986; and Afua Sarpong, "Check Road Blocking," *Daily Graphic*, August 24, 1987.

3   In the Ghanaian context, Charismatic churches are described as one-man churches when they are founded and overseen by one Charismatic leader who is not accountable to denominational hierarchies.

4   I employ this term in reference to Michel Foucault's claim that in all societies there are politics behind what types of discourse should be accepted and function as credible and mechanisms that enable these discourses (Foucault [1980] 2014).

5   De Witte (2008a, 696); Paa Kwesi Forson, "Ban on Drumming, Book Long and Matters Arising," *Modern Ghana*, May 16, 2012, accessed April 24, 2017, https://www.modernghana.com/news/395808/ban-on-drumming-book-long-and-matters-arising.html.

6   "Ga Chiefs, Elders Outraged," *Daily Graphic*, May 7, 1999.

7   "Traditionalists Attack Churches," *GhanaWeb*, May 11, 1999, accessed April 19, 2017, http://www.ghanaweb.com/GhanaHomePage/NewsArchive/Traditionalists-attack-churches-6473.

8   "Mobs Attack Churches," *Daily Graphic*, May 10, 1999.

9   The only reported incident during this Hɔmɔwɔ season took place in Teshie, a Ga town located on the outskirts of Accra. According to the *Daily Graphic*, the Ga youth attacked the Open Haven Mission International Church in August 2000 and wounded six worshippers. Joe Okyere, "Teshie Youth Besiege Church—To Enforce Ban on Drumming," *Daily Graphic*, August 21, 2000.

10 Asante (2011, 123); de Witte (2008a, 697); "Church Return 'Fire' in Drum Wars," *Ghanaian Chronicle*, May 14, 2001.

11 Michael Donkor, "13 Sustain Injuries in Clash at CAC Church," *Daily Graphic*, May 14, 2001.

12 Emmanuel Tetteh, interview with the author, Accra, June 10, 2015.

13 John Kwasi Appiah Acheampong, interview with the author, Accra, August 3, 2016.

14 Felix Oppong, interview with the author, Accra, May 23, 2018.

15 C. S. Buateng, "MPs Want Noise Pollution Checked," *Daily Graphic*, May 23, 1998.

16 Even though Accra is extremely diverse in its cultural composition, residents identify with the region their family comes from. Every community and region, in turn, has its own set of religious practices and ritual prohibitions.

17 "Victory Church Appeals to Govt.," *Daily Graphic*, May 15, 1999.

18 Kumasi is the second-largest city in Ghana and the capital of the Ashanti region.

19 "Asantehemaa's Burial Rites Begin Today," *Graphic Online*, January 16, 2017, accessed December 15, 2017, https://www.graphic.com.gh/news/general-news/asantehemaa-s-burial-rites-begin-today.html. See also Jeffrey Owusu-Mensah, "Kumasi Goes Dead as Asantehemaa Goes Home," *Prime News*, January 20, 2017, accessed December 15, 2017, https://www.primenewsghana.com/general-news/kumasi-goes-dead-as-asantehemaa-goes-home.html.

20 "Manhyia Bans Funerals for Asantehemaa's Funeral Rites," *GhanaWeb*, November 3, 2017, accessed December 5, 2018, https://www.ghanaweb.com/GhanaHomePage/NewsArchive/Manhyia-bans-funerals-for-Asantehemaa-s-funeral-rites-596866.

21 There seems to be a consensus among the non-Akan people of Ghana that the Akan people and their traditional authorities retain the most sociopolitical capital in the current political setup. This perception likely stems from two factors: first, the Akans are the largest ethnolinguistic group of the country; second, in the recent past, Akan-speaking kingdoms held considerable political and economic power.

22 Kweku Osam, "The Clash of Cymbals," *Daily Graphic*, July 4, 1998.

23 "The Ban on Drumming . . . CHRAJ Restates Position," *Daily Graphic*, May 22, 1999.

24 "Ban on Drumming: Christians Seek Middle Road as Government Calls for Calm," *GhanaWeb*, May 7, 1999, accessed April 25, 2017, https://www.ghanaweb.com /GhanaHomePage/NewsArchive/Ban-on-drumming-Christians-seek-middle-road-as -government-calls-for-calm-6433.

25 "Christian Council Cautions Churches over Ban on Drumming in Ga Traditional Area," *Daily Graphic*, May 9, 2001; "Victory Church Appeals to Govt."; Conrad M. K. Ablekpe, "Let's Obey This Ban," *Daily Graphic*, May 30, 2001; Gabriel Nii Teiko Tagoe, interview with the author, Accra, October 17, 2017.

26 "Ga Chiefs, Elders Outraged"; "Annor Yeboah Apologizes," *Daily Graphic*, May 18, 2001; Rebecca Kwei, "'Respect Recommendations,'" *Daily Graphic*, April 27, 2002; "'Comply with the Ban on Drumming, Noise-Making,'" *Daily Graphic*, May 12, 2004. Of course, religious tolerance and respect are also part of the discourse, but my observations suggest that discussions of intercultural dialogue and respect are far more prominent.

27 Numo Akwaa Mensah III, interview with the author, Accra, November 8, 2017.

28 Numo Akwaa Mensah III, interview with the author, Accra, November 8, 2017.

29 Isaac Lartey Annan, interview with the author, Accra, January 30, 2017.

30 Emmanuel Kwadwo Baah, interview with the author, Accra, January 20, 2017. Such programs are constitutionally mandated as a matter of state policy. Article 39(1) states: "The state shall take steps to encourage the integration of appropriate customary values into the fabric of national life through formal and informal education and the conscious introduction of cultural dimensions to relevant aspects of national planning."

31 Numo Akwaa Mensah III, interview with the author, Accra, May 28, 2018.

32 K. B. Asante, "Of Customs, Tradition, and Suspicion," *Daily Graphic*, May 17, 1999.

33 Charles Benoni Okine, "Task Force to Enforce Law on Noise Making," *Daily Graphic*, May 28, 2001.

34 N. Josiah Aryeh, "Mad about Drumming," *Daily Graphic*, April 26, 2000.

35 "Pentecostalite" is a term Birgit Meyer (2004b) introduced.

36 "'Respect Traditional Practices,'" *Daily Graphic*, June 20, 1998.

37 Numo Ashiboyi Kofi II, interview with the author, Accra, March 6, 2018; Numo Blafo III, interview with the author, Accra, August 5, 2018.

38 Emmanuel Kwadwo Baah, interview with the author, Accra, January 20, 2017.

39 The term "religio-culturalization" builds on Markus Dressler's notion of religio-secularization, which refers to concomitant processes of secularization and religion-ization of certain concepts and practices in Turkey in dialogue with Western notions of religion and nonreligion (Dressler 2019).

5. SACRED ACOUSTIC INSPECTORS

1 Alhaji Alhasan Abdulai, "Noise Making in Major Markets and Street Corners Accra," *Modern Ghana*, July 10, 2017, https://www.modernghana.com/news/589865/noise -making-in-major-markets-and-street-corners-accra.html.

2   Othello B. Garblah and Rebecca Dealtry, "Crack Down on Noisemakers," *Ghanaian Chronicle*, March 15, 2002; Charles Benoni Okine, "AMA Urged to Enforce By-Law on Noisemaking," *Daily Graphic*, May 25, 2001.

3   Eric Mensah Ayettey, "The Ban Is On," *GhanaWeb*, May 23, 2000, accessed April 25, 2017, https://www.ghanaweb.com/GhanaHomePage/NewsArchive/The-Ban-Is-On -10366; Tony Korsah-Dick, "The Ban on Drumming," *Accra Mail*, June 12, 2001.

4   Environmental Protection Agency Ghana, *Noise Pollution* (brochure) (Accra: Environmental Protection Agency Ghana, n.d.), in author's possession.

5   Charles Benoni Okine, "Task Force to Enforce Law on Noise Making," *Daily Graphic*, May 28, 2001.

6   Cornelius Adja Cofie, interview with the author, Accra, March 7, 2018.

7   Numo Akwaa Mensah III, interview with the author, Accra, May 28, 2018.

8   Dorcas Sekley, "The Church Won't Let Us Sleep," February 3, 2003; Paul E. Mills, "Enforce the Law on Noise Making in Churches," October 29, 2004; M. J. Kumardoss, "Noise Everywhere," July 20, 2007; Naa Lamiley Bentil, "AMA, Deal with the Noise Pollution," August 30, 2008; and Kofi Akordor, "Is Our God Deaf?," September 15, 2009. All in *Daily Graphic*.

9   Francis Sarfo, "Silent but Powerful Noise Pollution," *Daily Graphic*, October 2, 2008.

10   Geoffrey Kwabla Amedofu, "Noise Pollution—Its Impact on Health," *Daily Graphic*, July 10, 2002.

11   Moses A. Amihere, "Noise Pollution in Industry: Its Effects and Measures of Control," *Daily Graphic*, April 30, 2004.

12   Naa Lamiley Bentil, "Opambour's Church Closed Down for Excessive Noise Making," *Daily Graphic*, October 5, 2011.

13   Abdulai, "Noise Making in Major Markets and Street Corners Accra."

14   "AMA Demolishes Church for Noise Nuisance," *Ghana Web*, February 13, 2013, accessed August 1, 2024, https://www.ghanaweb.com/GhanaHomePage/NewsArchive /AMA-demolishes-church-for-noise-nuisance-264940.

15   Erasmus Solomon, "Ban on Noise Making in Ga Traditional Council Starts May 11," *Daily Graphic*, April 23, 2015, accessed November 5, 2016, https://www.graphic.com .gh/news/general-news/ban-on-noise-making-in-ga-traditional-council-starts-may-11 .html; Gertrude Ankah Nyavi, "Ban on Noise Making to Begin on May 8—Ga State Warns of No Compromise," *Daily Graphic*, April 26, 2017, accessed January 12, 2020, https://www.graphic.com.gh/news/general-news/ban-on-noise-making-to-begin -may-8-ga-state-warns-of-no-compromise.html. Since 2018, the Ministry of Chieftaincy and Religious Affairs, which was established that year, has been responsible for issuing an official statement regarding the dates of the ban.

16   Clement Edward Kumsah, "Ga Mashie Finally Lifts Ban on Noise-Making," Prime News Ghana, June 14, 2018, https://www.primenewsghana.com/general-news/ga -mashie-finally-lifts-ban-on-noise-making.html.

17   Accra Metropolitan Assembly, "Ban on Drumming and Noise Making," Press release, May 3, 2024, https://www.ama.gov.gh/documents/Ban_on_drumming_noise _making,_2024.pdf.

18   "Observe Ban on Drumming: Says Regional Co-Ordinating Council," *Daily Graphic*, May 19, 2009.

19 Contrary to Numo Blafo III's assertion, Justice Arthur argues that since 2013, the confiscated equipment has been stored in the GTC secretariat (Arthur 2017, 131).

20 Gilbert Ankra, interview with the author, Accra, June 5, 2018.

21 The EPA instructs that churches, mosques, and entertainment centers have to restrict their noise to 65 decibels during the day and 60 decibels at night (Environmental Protection Agency of Ghana n.d.).

22 Naa Laimley Lamptey, "AMA Handicapped in Dealing with Noise," *Daily Graphic*, February 18, 2005.

23 Bentil, "AMA, Deal with the Noise Pollution."

24 Wicky Wireko, "Clamp Down on Noise Making: Is It Too Late?," *Daily Graphic*, February 20, 2013.

25 Gilbert Ankra, interview with the author, Accra, June 5, 2018.

26 Local Government Bulletin No. 3, Article 10, Published by Authority, January 25, 2019. https://ama.gov.gh/doc/bye-laws.pdf.

27 Gilbert Ankra, interview with the author, Accra, June 5, 2018.

28 Ga custom dictates that the *wulɔmɛi* should always be dressed in white, as the color symbolizes innocence and purity. They must also always be barefoot because traditionally they were supposed to spend all of their time in the shrine (*gbatsu*) (Meredith 1812, 194; Omaetu 2006, 25–26).

29 Here, I resort to Markus Dressler's idea of religionization as "the signification of certain spaces, practices, narratives, and languages as religious (as opposed to things marked as secular)" (2008, 281).

30 Not only are traditional practices discussed within the framework of customary law, which is subsidiary to constitutional law, but the degree to which they are regulated also threatens their integrity (Tweneboah 2019, 162). The most obvious example is the application of "invalidating clauses" in the Constitution, which severely restrict the customary law. The complicated standards of reinforcement also resemble the repugnancy clause typical of the colonial legal regime (Abosti 2020, 15).

31 Koi Larbi, interview with the author, Accra, November 7, 2023.

32 K. B. Asante, "Of Customs, Tradition and Suspicion," *Daily Graphic*, May 17, 1999; R. B. W. Hesse, "Religion, Our Cultural Heritage and Tradition," *Daily Graphic*, May 22, 1999; N. Josiah-Aryeh, "To Drum or Not to Drum . . . The Controversy Surrounding the Ban on Drumming in Accra," *Daily Graphic*, May 15, 1999.

33 Gabriel Nii Teiko Tagoe, interview with the author, Accra, October 17, 2017.

34 Francis Eshun-Baidoo, "Respect Ban on Drumming," *Daily Graphic*, June 3, 1998.

35 Kojo Osei-Wusuh, "'The Ban Is Unconstitutional,'" *Daily Graphic*, June 22, 1998.

36 "Church Accuses AMA of Shirking Responsibility," *GhanaWeb*, May 21, 1999, https://www.ghanaweb.com/GhanaHomePage/NewsArchive/Church-accuses-AMA-of-shirking-responsibility-6846.

37 Eshun-Baidoo, "Respect Ban on Drumming."

38 "Observe Ban on Drumming," *Daily Graphic*, April 30, 1999.

39 Joe Bradford Nyinah, "Churches Urged to Agree with Ga Authority," *Daily Graphic*, May 6, 1999.

40 Michael Donkor, "Churches to Comply with Ban on Drumming," *Daily Graphic*, May 5, 1999.

41 "The Ban on Drumming: Churches Unhappy—'It is an Infringement on Our Human Rights,'" *Daily Graphic*, May 7, 1999.

42 "AMA Advises Religious Leaders to Strictly Adhere to the Ban on Noise Making," *Ghana News Online*, May 8, 2017, http://ghananewsonline.com.gh/ama-advises -religious-leaders-strictly-adhere-ban-noise-making/.

43 Kwabena Opuni-Frimpong, interview with the author, Accra, August 3, 2016.

44 Josiah-Aryeh, "To Drum or Not to Drum."

45 Asante, "Of Customs, Tradition and Suspicion."

46 Emmanuel Kwadwo Baah, interview with the author, Accra, January 20, 2017.

47 Ambros Boafoh, interview with the author, Accra, May 29, 2018.

48 Kingsley Owusu-Takyi, interview with the author, Accra, March 1, 2018.

49 Yaw Berimah Bediako, interview with the author, Accra, January 11, 2018.

50 Joseph Sakyi, interview with the author, Accra, June 20, 2015.

51 Osofo Kofi Attabuatsie, interview with the author, Accra, September 25, 2017.

52 Kweku Osam, "The Clash of Cymbals," *Daily Graphic*, July 4, 1998.

53 "AMA to Sensitize Public against Noise Pollution," *Peace FM Online*, March 5, 2013, http://www.peacefmonline.com/pages/local/news/201303/157746.php.

6. LET US OFFER THANKS FOR THE NATION OF GHANA

1 The Ga people of Greater Accra are often grouped with the Adangbe people found to the east of the Accra coastland due to the shared proto-Ga-Adangbe ancestral language and common heritage.

2 "Nii Amugi Attends Service," *Daily Graphic*, September 26, 1972b.

3 Augustina Tawiah, "Make Homowo More Attractive," *Daily Graphic*, September, 10, 2002.

4 Christian Council of Ghana, "Vision and Mission," n.d., accessed November 4, 2019, http://www.christiancouncilofghana.org/Pages/Vision.php.

5 Kwabena Opuni-Frimpong, interview with the author, Accra, August 3, 2015.

6 "Accra," *The Gold Coast Leader*, September 21, 1912, 3.

7 Kwor Tarpim, "The Harvest Festival or (The Harvest Thanks-giving Service)," *The Gold Coast Nation*, September 29, 1917.

8 *Gold Coast Independent*, August 17, 1918, 2–3.

9 "Nii Amugi Attends Service."

10 Kwabena Opuni-Frimpong, interview with the author, Accra, August 3, 2015.

11 Abraham Opoku-Baffour, interview with the author, Accra, September 15, 2017.

12 Christian Council of Ghana, "Invitation to Osu Homowo Thanksgiving Church Service," August 15, 2015, CCG/GS/15/08/225.

13 Daniel Lankai Lawson, interview with the author, Accra, September 15, 2017.

14 Christian Council of Ghana, "CCG Proposes Homowo Thanksgiving Church Service for Ga Traditional Council," May 16, 2015, accessed March 12, 2017, https://www .christiancouncilofghana.org/Archive/CCG%20proposes%20Homowo.........php.

15 Abraham Opoku-Baffour, interview with the author, Accra, September 15, 2017.

16 Abraham Opoku-Baffour, interview with the author, Accra, September 15, 2017.

17 Cornelius Adja Cofie, interview with the author, Accra, March 7, 2018.

18 "CCG to Celebrate to Homowo with Ga Traditional Councils," *Peace FM Online*, July 19, 2015, accessed November 15, 2019, http://www.peacefmonline.com/pages /local/religion/201507/248311.php?storyid=100&.

19 Andrew Odonkor, interview with the author, Accra, August 9, 2016.

20 Abraham Opoku-Baffour, interview with the author, Accra, September 15, 2017.

21 Abraham Opoku-Baffour, interview with the author, Accra, September 15, 2017.

22 Laryea (2011, 31), translation by Mariam Goshadze and Adokwei Sacker.

23 "Remembering the Living Dead," 2016, lecture transcript.

24 Even though Laryea regularly writes in the Ga language in his academic work, the Hɔmɔwɔ Thanksgiving lectures are delivered in English and the term he used to refer to the departed forefathers is "ancestors" rather than *blematsɛmɛi*.

25 With the declaration of independence in 1957, the Christian Council of the Gold Coast was renamed the Christian Council of Ghana.

26 Kodjo Adams, "Incorporate Traditional Values into Christian Worship," *Ghana News Agency*, August 16, 2018, https://www.ghananewsagency.org/social/incorporate -traditional-values-into-christian-worship-rev-laryea-137222.

27 The quote is from a 2018 statement by Minister of Tourism, Arts & Culture Catherine Abelema Afeku (Dadzie Kwame, "Tourism Ministry Launches Ghana Carnival, Homofest 2018," *Ghana Web*, April 20, 2018, accessed December 15, 2020, https:// citinewsroom.com/2018/04/tourism-ministry-launches-ghana-carnival-homofest -2018/#:~:text=The%20carnival%20is%20the%20traditional,towns%20have%20 organized%20their%20festivals).

28 "Ministry of Tourism to Launch Ghana Carnival and Homofest," *Ghana Business News*, April 20, 2018, accessed November 2, 2019, https://www.ghanabusinessnews .com/2018/04/20/ministry-of-tourism-to-launch-ghana-carnival-and-homofest/.

29 Bernice Deh-Kumah, interview with the author, Accra, September 5, 2017.

30 Phoebe Pappoe, "Second Edition of 'Homofest' Launched," *Graphic Online*, July 18, 2015, https://www.graphic.com.gh/news/general-news/second-edition-of-homofest -launched.html; National Commission on Culture, "Homofest 2016 Launched in Accra," September 16, 2016, http://www.ghanaculture.gov.gh/index1.php?linkid =65&archiveid=2331&page=1&adate=16/09/2016; "Homofest, An Integrated Festival for Ga-Dangbes," *Ghana News Now*, July 25, 2015, accessed May 28, 2017, http://www.ghnewsnow.com; "Ga Damgbe Culture Displayed at Homofest," *Business Ghana*, October 11, 2016, accessed December 5, 2018, https://www .businessghana.com/site/news/entertainment/136540/Ga-Damgbe-culture -displayed-at-Homofest.

31 "Ministry of Tourism to Launch Ghana Carnival and Homofest."

32 "Homofest, Ghana Carnival Launched in Accra," *Graphic Online*, April 21, 2018, accessed June 12, 2018, https://www.graphic.com.gh/news/general-news/homofest -ghana-carnival-launched-in-accra.html.

33 *Asafoi* (sing. *asafo*) are age-based companies that originated among the Akan but gradually spread to southern Ghana. Traditionally, the *asafoi* were responsible for defending the state and ensuring communal well-being. The latter function remains pertinent today. Among the Ga, the *asafoi* are actively involved in community life and traditional festivities.

34   *Akpeteshie* is the popular alcoholic spirit in Ghana produced by distilling palm wine or sugar cane.

35   The Pan African Historical Theatre Project was the first such initiative in Ghana. This biannual celebration was launched in 1992 to promote pan-Africanism and unity among Africans and people of African descent. The National Festival of Arts and Culture, a Ghana-wide heritage festival that seeks to bring all ethnic groups together, is a project of the Ministry of Tourism, Arts & Culture.

36   David Owusu-Amoah, "The Sankofa Bird and Ghanaian Culture," *Daily Graphic*, October 20, 2007.

37   National Commission on Culture, "Homofest 2016 Launched in Accra."

38   Andrew Odonkor, interview with the author, Accra, August 9, 2016.

CONCLUSION

1   My concern is not to question or endorse the historical validity of this origin story. I am rather interested in its increasing discursive salience in light of the Christian influence on Ghana's public sphere.

2   Emmanuel Tetteh, interview with the author, Accra, June 10, 2015.

References

Abbey, E. T. A. 1967. *Keji afo Yordan: Gbele ke Yarafeemɔ*. Accra: Bureau of Ghana Languages.

Abosti, E. Kofi. 2020. "Customary Law and the Rule of Law: Evolving Tensions and Re-Engineering." *Arizona Journal of International Law and Comparative Law* 37(2): 136–68.

Adogame, Afe, ed. 2011. *Who Is Afraid of the Holy Ghost? Pentecostalism and Globalization in Africa and Beyond*. Trenton, NJ: Africa World Press.

Adrover, Lauren. 2013. "Branding Festive Bodies: Corporate Logos and Chiefly Image T-Shirts in Ghana." In *African Dress: Fashion, Agency, Performance*, edited by Karen Tranberg Hansen and D. Soyini Madison, 45–60. London: Bloomsbury.

Adrover, Lauren. 2018. "The Currency of Chieftaincy: Corporate Branding and the Commodification of Political Authority in Ghana." In *The Politics of Custom: Chiefship, Capital, and the State in Contemporary Africa*, edited by Jean Comaroff and John Comaroff, 231–47. Chicago: University of Chicago Press.

Agawu, Kofi. 2006. "Tonality as a Colonizing Force in Africa." In *Audible Empire: Music, Global Politics, Critique*, edited by Ronald Radano and Tejumola Olaniya, 334–57. Durham, NC: Duke University Press.

Ahumah, R. S. Attoh. 1911. *The Gold Coast and National Consciousness*. Liverpool: D. Marples.

Akrong, Abraham. 2007. "Pre-Monarchical Political Leadership among the Gas, with Special Reference to the People of La." *Research Review of the Institute of African Studies* 21(12): 137–47.

Albanese, Catherine. 1999. *America: Religion and Religions*. Belmont, CA: Wadsworth.

Amanor, Kwabena J. Darkwa. 2009. "Pentecostal and Charismatic Churches in Ghana and the African Culture: Confrontation or Compromise?" *Journal of Pentecostal Theology* 18: 123–40.

Amartey, A. A. 1991. *Omanye Aba*. Accra: Bureau of Ghana Languages.

Ambani, J. Osogo. 2021. *Africa and the Decolonization of State-Religion Policies*. Leiden: Brill.

Ambani, J. Osogo, and Ochieng Ahaya. 2015. "The Wretched African Traditionalists in Kenya: The Challenges and Prospect of Customary Law in the New Constitutional Era." *Strathmore Law Journal* 1: 41–58.

Ammah, E. A. 2016. *Kings, Priests & Kinsmen: Essays on Ga Culture and Society*. Accra: Sub-Saharan Publishers.

Amoah, Michael. 2007. *Reconstructing the Nation in Africa: The Politics of Nationalism in Ghana*. London: Tauris Academic Studies.

Anderson, Allan. 2004. *An Introduction to Pentecostalism: Global Charismatic Christianity*. Cambridge: Cambridge University Press.

Anquandah, James. 2006. "The Accra Plains c. AD 1400–1800: An Overview of Trade, Politics and Culture from the Perspective of Historical Archaeology." *Institute of African Studies Research Review* 17: 1–20.

Archer, Melissa L. 2012. "The Worship Scenes in the Apocalypse, Effective History, and Early Pentecostal Periodical Literature." *Journal of Pentecostal Theology* 21: 87–112

Arthur, Justice Anquandah. 2017. *The Politics of Religious Sound: Conflict and the Negotiation of Religious Diversity in Ghana*. Berlin: LIT Verlag.

Asad, Talal. 1993. *Genealogies of Religion: Discipline and Reasons of Power in Christianity and Islam*. Baltimore, MD: Johns Hopkins University Press.

Asad, Talal. 2003. *Formations of the Secular: Christianity, Islam, Modernity*. Stanford, CA: Stanford University Press.

Asad, Talal. 2013. *Is Critique Secular? Blasphemy, Injury, and Free Speech*. New York: Fordham University Press.

Asamoah-Gyadu, Kwabena. 2005a. *African Charismatics: Current Developments within Independent Indigenous Pentecostalism in Ghana*. Leiden: Brill.

Asamoah-Gyadu, Kwabena. 2005b. "Anointing through the Screen: Neo-Pentecostalism and Televised Christianity in Ghana." *Studies in World Christianity* 11(1): 9–28.

Asamoah-Gyadu, Kwabena. 2014. "Pentecostalism and Transformation of the African Christian Landscape." In *Pentecostalism in Africa*, edited by Martin Linhardt, 100–114. Leiden: Brill.

Asamoah-Gyadu, Kwabena. 2015. *Sighs and Signs of the Spirit*. Eugene, OR: Wipf & Stock.

Asante, Richard. 2011. "Ethnicity, Religion, and Conflict in Ghana: The Roots of Ga Nativism." *Ghana Studies* 14: 81–131.

Asare, Amos Darkwa. 2022. "Arts Management and Cultural Policy in Ghana." In *Arts Management, Cultural Policy, & the African Diaspora*, edited by Antonio C. Cuyler, 29–50. Cham: Springer.

Assimeng, John M. 1995. *Salvation, Social Crisis and the Human Condition*. Accra: Ghana Universities Press.

Astor, Avi, Marian Burchardt, and Mar Griera. 2017. "The Politics of Religious Heritage: Framing Claims to Religion as Culture in Spain." *Journal for the Scientific Study of Religion* 56(1): 126–42.

Atiemo, Abamfo Ofori. 2006a. "International Human Rights, Religious Pluralism and the Future of Chieftaincy in Ghana." *Exchange* 35(4): 360–82.

Atiemo, Abamfo Ofori. 2006b. "'Singing with Understanding': The Story of Gospel Music in Ghana." *Studies in World Christianity* 12(2): 142–63.

Atiemo, Abamfo Ofori. 2014. "Fighting for the Rights of the Gods: Tradition, Religious Rights, and the Modern Nation-State in Africa." *Studies in World Christianity & Interreligious Relations* 48: 233–47.

Atiemo, Abamfo Ofori. 2015. "Religion and Custom Are Not the Same: Sacred Traditional States and Religious Human Rights in Contemporary Ghana." In *Law and Religion in Africa—The Quest for the Common Good in Pluralistic Societies*, edited by Peter Coertzen, M. Christian Green, and Len Hansen, 157–73. Stellenbosch: SUN Press.

Attali, Jacques. 1985. *Noise: The Political Economy of Music*. Minneapolis: University of Minnesota Press.

Attuquayefio, Philip. 2012. "Culture, Religion and Land: The Conflict over the Ga Ban on Drumming and Noise-Making." In *Peacemaking in Ghana: Lessons Learnt, Options for the Future*, edited by L. Darkwa, Philip Attuquayefio, and Afua Yakohene, 17–53. Accra: Imagine Communications Limited.

Bailey, Peter. 1996. "Breaking the Sound Barrier: A Historian Listens to Noise." *Body & Society* 2(2): 49–66.

Ballinger, Pamela. 1998. "The Culture of Survivors: Post-Traumatic Stress Disorder and Traumatic Memory." *History and Memory* 10: 99–132.

Barrett, David. 1988. "The Twentieth-Century Pentecostal/Charismatic Renewal in the Holy Spirit, with Its Goal of World Evangelization." *International Bulletin of Missionary Research* 12(3): 119–29.

Baudrillard, Jean. 1994. *Simulacra and Simulation*. Ann Arbor: University of Michigan Press.

Beck, Guy L. 1993. *Sonic Theology: Hinduism and Sacred Sound*. Columbia: University of South Carolina Press.

Bediako, Kwame. 2004. "Christianity, Islam and the Kingdom of God: Rethinking the Relationship from an African Perspective." *Journal of African Christian Thought* 7: 3–7.

Bennett, Tom W. 1995. *Human Rights and African Customary Law under the South African Constitution*. Cape Town: Juta.

Bennett, Tony. 1995. *The Birth of the Museum: History, Theory, Politics*. London: Routledge.

Berger, Peter L. 1999. "The Desecularization of the World: A Global Overview." In *The Desecularization of the World*, edited by Peter Berger, 1–19. Grand Rapids, MI: William B. Eerdmans.

Berger, Peter L. 2008. "Secularization Falsified." *First Things*. February. Accessed October 12, 2017. https://www.firstthings.com/article/2008/02/secularization-falsified.

Berger, Peter L. 2010. "Max Weber Is Alive and Well, and Living in Guatemala: The Protestant Ethic Today." *The Review of Faith & International Affairs* 8(4): 3–9.

Bhargava, Rajeev. 2013. "Reimagining Secularism: Respect, Domination and Principled Distance." *Economic and Political Weekly* 48(50): 79–92.

Bijsterveld, Karin. 2001. "The Diabolical Symphony of the Mechanical Age: Technology and Symbolism of Sound in European and North American Noise Abatement Campaigns, 1900–40." *Social Studies of Science* 31: 37–70.

Bijsterveld, Karin. 2003. "'The City of Din': Decibels, Noise, and Neighbors in the Netherlands, 1910–1980." *Osiris* 18: 173–93.

Bijsterveld, Karin. 2008. *Mechanical Sound: Technology, Culture, and Public Problems of Noise in the Twentieth Century*. Cambridge, MA: MIT Press.

Bijsterveld, Karin. 2013. "Introduction." In *Soundscapes of the Urban Past: Staged Sound as Mediated Cultural Heritage*, edited by Karin Bijsterveld, 11–31. Bielefeld: Transcript Verlag.

Birmingham, David. 1998. *Kwame Nkrumah: The Father of African Nationalism*. Athens: Ohio University Press.

Blacking, John. 1973. *How Musical Is Man?* Seattle: University of Washington Press.

Bob-Milliar, George B. 2009. "Chieftaincy, Diaspora, and Development: The Institution of Nkɔsuohene in Ghana." *African Affairs* 108(433): 541–58.

Bomes, Michael, and Patrick Wright. 1982. "'Charms of Residence': The Public and the Past." In *Making Histories: Studies in History-Writing and Politics*, edited by Richard Johnson, 253–301. London: Hutchinson.

Botwe-Asamoah, Kwame. 2005. *Kwame Nkrumah's Politico-Cultural Thought and Policies*. London: Routledge.

Boutin, Aimée. 2015. *City of Noise: Sound and Nineteenth-Century Paris*. Urbana: University of Illinois Press.

Boym, Svetlana. 2001. *The Future of Nostalgia*. New York: Basic Books.

Brennan, Vicki L. 2018. *Singing Yoruba Christianity: Music, Media, and Morality*. Bloomington: Indiana University Press.

Brubaker, Rogers. 2016. "A New 'Christianist' Secularism in Europe." *The Immanent Frame*. October 11. Accessed November 13, 2020. https://tif.ssrc.org/2016/10/11/a-new -christianist-secularism-in-europe/.

Brumann, Christoph. 1999. "Writing for Culture: Why a Successful Concept Should Not Be Discarded." *Current Anthropology* 40, Supplement 1:1–27.

Bunten, Alexis Celeste. 2010. "Indigenous Tourism: The Paradox of Gaze and Resistance." *La Ricerca Folklorica* 61: 51–59.

Cady, Linell E., and Elizabeth S. Hurd, eds. 2010. *Comparative Secularisms in a Global Age*. New York: Palgrave Macmillan.

Cardoso, Leonardo. 2017. "The Politics of Noise Control in São Paulo." *Journal of Latin American Studies* 49(4): 917–45.

Casanova, Jose. 1994. *Public Religions in the Modern World*. Chicago: University of Chicago Press.

Casanova, Jose. 2001. "The Secular, Secularizations, Secularisms." In *Rethinking Secularism*, edited by Craig Calhoun, Mark Juergensmeyer, and Jonathan VanAntwerpen, 54–75. Oxford: Oxford University Press.

Chandola, Tripta. 2012. "Listening to Others: Moralising the Soundscapes in Deli." *International Development Planning Review* 34(4): 391–408.

Chatterjee, Partha. 1993. *The Nation and Its Fragments: Colonial and Postcolonial Histories*. Princeton, NJ: Princeton University Press.

Chidester, David. 1996. *Savage Systems: Colonialism and Comparative Religion in Southern Africa*. Charlottesville: University Press of Virginia.

Chikowero, Mhoze. 2015. *African Music, Power, and Being in Colonial Zimbabwe*. Bloomington: Indiana University Press.

Christian Council of the Gold Coast. 1955. *Christianity and African Culture: Report of Proceedings of a Conference Held at Accra, May 2nd–6th, under the Auspices of the Christian Council of the Gold Coast*. Accra: Christian Council of the Gold Coast.

Classen, Constance. 1993. *Worlds of Sense: Exploring the Senses in History and Across Cultures*. London: Routledge.

Classen, Constance. 1997. "Foundations for an Anthropology of the Senses." *International Social Science Journal* 49: 401–12.

Coe, Cati. 2005. *Dilemmas of Culture in African Schools. Youth, Nationalism, and the Transformation of Knowledge*. Chicago: University of Chicago Press.

Coleman, Simon, and Rosalind I. J. Hackett, eds. 2015. *The Anthropology of Global Pentecostalism and Evangelicalism*. New York: NYU Press.

Comaroff, Jean. 2012. "Pentecostalism, Populism and the New Politics of Affect." In *Pentecostalism and Development: Churches, NGOs and Social Change in Africa*, edited by Dena Freeman, 41–66. Basingstoke: Palgrave Macmillan.

Comaroff, Jean, and John Comaroff. 2000. "Privatising the Millenium: New Protestant Ethics and the Spirits of Capitalism in Africa, and Elsewhere." *Afrika Spectrum* 35(3): 293–312.

Corten, André, and Ruth Marshall-Fratani, eds. 2001. *Between Babel and Pentecost: Transnational Pentecostalism in Africa and Latin America*. Bloomington: Indiana University Press.

Cox, Harvey G. 1984. *Religion in the Secular City: Toward a Postmodern Theology*. New York: Simon & Schuster.

Daniell, William F. 1856. "On the Ethnography of Akkrah and Adampe, Gold Coast, Western Africa." *Journal of the Ethnological Society of London* 4: 1–32.

Daniels, David. 2008. "'Gotta Moan Sometime': A Sonic Exploration of Earwitnesses to Early Pentecostal Sound in North America." *Pneuma* 30: 5–32.

Daughtry, J. Martin. 2015. *Listening to War: Sound, Music, Trauma and Survival in Wartime Iraq*. Oxford: Oxford University Press.

Davie, Grace. 2002. *Europe, the Exceptional Case: Parameters of Faith in the Modern World*. London: Darton, Longman & Todd.

De Boeck, Filip, and Marie-Françoise Plissart. 2006. *Kinshasa: Tales of the Invisible City*. Ghent: Ludion.

Decoteau, Claire Laurier. 2013. "Hybrid Habitus: Toward a Post-Colonial Theory of Practice." *Postcolonial Sociology* 24: 263–93.

De Marees, Pieter. (1602) 1987. *Description and Historical Account of the Gold Kingdom of Guinea*. Oxford: Oxford University Press.

De Roover, Jakob. 2011. "Secular Law and the Realm of False Religion." In *After Secular Law*, edited by Winnifred Fallers Sullivan, Robert A. Yelle, and Mateo Taussig-Rubbo, 43–60. Stanford, CA: Stanford Law Books.

De Witte, Marleen. 2004. "Afrikania's Dilemma: Reframing African Authenticity in a Christian Public Sphere." *Etnofoor* 17(1): 133–55.

De Witte, Marleen. 2005. "The Spectacular and the Spirits: Charismatics and Neo-Traditionalists on Ghanaian Television." *Material Religion* 1(3): 314–34.

De Witte, Marleen. 2008a. "Accra's Sounds and Sacred Spaces." *International Journal of Urban and Regional Research* 32(3): 690–709.

De Witte, Marleen. 2008b. *Spirit Media: Charismatics, Traditionalists, and Mediation Practices in Ghana*. Amsterdam: Ipskamp Print Printers.

De Witte, Marleen, and Birgit Meyer. 2012. "African Heritage Design: Entertainment Media and Visual Aesthetics in Ghana." *Civilizations* 61(1): 43–64.

Diouf, Mamadou. 1999. "Urban Youth and Senegalese Politics: Dakar 1988–1994." In *Cities and Citizenship*, edited by James Holston, 42–67. Durham, NC: Duke University Press.

Douglas, Mary. (1954) 1999. "The Lele of Kasai." In *African Worlds: Studies in the Cosmological Ideas and Social Values of African Peoples*, edited by D. Forde, 1–27. London: James Currey.

Douglas, Mary. (1966) 2002. *Purity and Danger: An Analysis of Concepts of Pollution and Taboo*. London: Routledge.

Dovlo, Elom. 1998. "The Church in Africa and Religious Pluralism: The Challenge of New Religious Movements and Charismatic Churches." *Exchange* 27(1): 52–69.

Dovlo, Elom. 2005. "Religion in the Public Sphere: Challenges and Opportunities in Ghanaian Lawmaking, 1989–2004." *BYU Law Review* 3(4): 629–58.

Dressler, Markus. 2008. "Religio-secular Metamorphoses: The Re-making of Turkish Alevism." *Journal of the American Academy of Religion* 76(2): 280–311.

Dressler, Markus. 2019. "Modes of Religionization: A Constructivist Approach to Secularity." No. 7 in Working Paper Series "Multiple Secularities—Beyond West, Beyond Modernities" of the Centre for Advanced Studies, Leipzig.

Eisenlohr, Patrick. 2011. "The Anthropology of Media and the Question of Ethnic and Religious Pluralism." *Social Anthropology* 19(1): 40–55.

Eisenlohr, Patrick. 2018. *Sounding Islam: Voice, Media, and Social Atmospheres in an Indian Ocean World*. Oakland: University of California Press.

Eisenstadt, Shmuel N. 2000. "Multiple Modernities." *Daedalus* 129(1): 1–29.

Elsner, John, and Roger Cardinal, eds. 1994. *The Cultures of Collecting*. Cambridge, MA: Harvard University Press.

Emiola, Akintunde. 1997. *The Principles of African Customary Law*. Ogbomoso: Emiola Publishers.

Engelke, Matthew. 2010. "Religion and the Media Turn: A Review Essay." *American Ethnologist* 37(2): 371–79.

Engelke, Matthew. 2015. "Secular Shadows: African, Immanent, Post-Colonial." *Critical Research on Religion* 3(1): 86–100.

Etikpah, Samuel E. 2015. "The Kundum Festival in Ghana. Ritual Interaction with the Nonhuman among the Akan." *Journal of Africana Religions* 3(4): 343–96.

Feld, Steven. 2012. *Sound and Sentiment: Birds, Weeping, Poetics, and Song in Kaluli Expression*. Durham, NC: Duke University Press.

Field, Margaret. 1937. *Religion and Medicine of the Ga People*. London: Oxford University Press.

Fitzgerald, Timothy. 2000. *The Ideology of Religious Studies*. New York: Oxford University Press.

Fitzgerald, Timothy. 2007. *Discourse on Civility and Barbarity: A Critical History of Religion and Related Categories*. New York: Oxford University Press.

Fosu, Kwaku Amoako-Attah. 1999. *Festivals in Ghana*. Kumasi: Centre for National Culture.

Foucault, Michel. (1980) 2014. *On the Government of the Living: Lectures at the College de France, 1979–1980*. Houndmills: Palgrave Macmillan.

Foucault, Michel. 2007. *Security, Territory, Population: Lectures at the Collège de France, 1977–78*. New York: Palgrave Macmillan.

Foucault, Michel. 2013. *Lectures on the Will to Know: Lectures at the College de France, 1970–1971*. Houndmills: Palgrave Macmillan.

Gautier, Ana María Ochoa. 2014. *Aurality: Listening and Knowledge in Nineteenth-Century Colombia*. Durham, NC: Duke University Press.

Gerety, Finnian M. M. 2017. "The Amplified Sacrifice: Sound, Technology, and Participation in Modern Vedic Ritual." *South Asian History and Culture* 8(4): 560–78.

Gifford, Paul. 1998. *African Christianity: Its Public Role*. Bloomington: Indiana University Press.

Gifford, Paul. 2004. *Ghana's New Christianity: Pentecostalism in a Globalizing African Economy*. Bloomington: Indiana University Press.

Gocking, Roger S. 2005. *The History of Ghana*. Westport, CT: Greenwood Press.

Göle, Nilüfer. 2010. "Manifestations of the Religious-Secular Divide: Self, State, and the Public Sphere." In *Comparative Secularisms in a Global Age*, edited by Linell E. Cady and Elizabeth S. Hurd, 41–53. New York: Palgrave Macmillan.

Göle, Nilüfer. 2015. *Islam and Secularity: The Future of Europe's Public Sphere*. Durham, NC: Duke University Press.

Gorski, Philip S. 2000. "Historicizing the Secularization Debate: Church, State and Society in Late Medieval and Early Modern Europe, ca. 1300–1700." *American Sociological Review* 65: 138–67.

Goshadze, Mariam. 2019. "When the Deities Visit for Hɔmɔwɔ: Translating Religion in the Language of the Secular." *Journal of the American Academy of Religion* 87(1): 191–224.

Goshadze, Mariam. 2022a. "Heritage out of Control: Is Libation a Prayer?" *Allegra Lab*. February, 2022. https://allegralaboratory.net/heritage-out-of-control-is-libation-a-prayer/.

Goshadze, Mariam. 2022b. "The Varieties of Sonic Experience: 'Quiet' vs. 'Not-Noise' in a Ghanaian Harvest Festival." *American Anthropologist* 124(1): 165–74.

Griffith, W. Brandford. 1887. *Ordinances of the Settlements of the Gold Coast and of the Gold Coast Colony in Force April 7th, 1887*. London: Waterlow.

Griffith, W. Brandford. 1903. *Ordinances of the Gold Coast Colony and the Rules and Orders Thereunder in Force 31st March, 1903*. Vol 1. London: Stevens and Sons.

Griffith, W. Brandford. 1887. *Ordinances of the Settlements of the Gold Coast and of the Gold Coast Colony in Force April 7th, 1887*. London: Waterlow.

Grillo, Laura S., Adriaan van Klinken, and Hassan J. Ndzovu. 2019. *Religions in Contemporary Africa: An Introduction*. London: Routledge.

Guha, Ranajit, and Gayatri Chakravorty Spivak. 1988. *Selected Subaltern Studies*. New York: Oxford University Press.

Guss, David M. 2000. *The Festive State: Race, Ethnicity, and Nationalism as Cultural Performance*. Berkeley: University of California Press.

Gyampong, Samuel K. 2006. "The Role of Chieftaincy in Ghana's Democratic Experiment." In *Chieftaincy in Ghana: Culture, Governance and Development*, edited by Irene K. Odotei and Albert K. Awedoba, 183–91. Accra: Sub-Saharan Publishers.

Gyimah, Cynthia. 1985. "The Hɔmɔwɔ Festival of the Ga Mashi: People of Accra." MA thesis, York University, Toronto.

Haberlandt, Michael. 1900. *Ethnology*. Translated by J. H. Lowe. London: J.M. Dent.

Hackett, Rosalind. 1991. "Revitalization in African Traditional Religion." In *African Traditional Religion in Contemporary Society*, edited by Jacob K. Olupona, 135–48. New York: Paragon House.

Hackett, Rosalind. 2022. "From Festive Sacred to Festive Secular? Indigenous Religious Presence in Two Nigerian Festivals." *Numen* 69(4): 341–89.

Handler, Richard. 1988. *Nationalism and the Politics of Culture in Quebec*. Madison: University of Wisconsin Press.

Harrison, Rodney. 2013. *Heritage: Critical Approaches*. London: Routledge.

Henderson-Quartey, David K. 2002. *The Ga of Ghana*. Ann Arbor: University of Michigan Press.

Hervieu-Leger, Daniele. 2002. "Space and Religion: New Approaches to Religious Spatiality in Modernity." *International Journal of Urban and Regional Research* 26(1): 99–105.

Hess, Janet. 2001. "Exhibiting Ghana: Display, Documentary, and 'National' Art in the Nkrumah Era." *African Studies Review* 44(1): 59–77.

Hirschkind, Charles. 2006. *The Ethical Soundscape: Cassette Sermons and Islamic Counterpublics*. New York: Columbia University Press.

Hirschkind, Charles. 2011. "Is There a Secular Body?" *Cultural Anthropology* 26(4): 633–47.

Hobsbawm, Eric, and Terence Ranger. 1983. *The Invention of Tradition*. Cambridge: Cambridge University Press.

Horton, Robin. 1984. "Judeo-Christian Spectacles: Boon or Bane to the Study of African Religions?" *Cahiers d'Etudes Africaines* 96: 391–436.

Howes, David. 2005. *Empire of the Senses: The Sensual Culture Reader*. Oxford: Berg.

Howes, David, ed. 1991. *The Varieties of Sensory Experience. A Sourcebook in the Anthropology of the Senses*. Toronto: University of Toronto Press.

Hulsether, Mark. 2005. "Religion and Culture." In *The Routledge Companion to the Study of Religion*, edited by John R. Hinnells, 501–20. London: Routledge.

Hurd, Elizabeth Shakman. 2015. *Beyond Religious Freedom: The New Global Politics of Religion*. Princeton, NJ: Princeton University Press.

Idowu, Bolaji. 1965. *Towards an Indigenous Church*. London: Oxford University Press.

Idowu, Bolaji. 1973. *African Traditional Religion: A Definition*. London: SCM Press.

Iliffe, John. 1979. *A Modern History of Tanganyika*. Cambridge: Cambridge University Press.

Innis, Harold. (1972) 2007. *Empire and Communications*. Lanham, MD: Rowman & Littlefield.

Jay, Martin. 1998. "Scopic Regimes of Modernity." In *Visual Culture Reader*, edited by Nicholas Mirzoeff, 66–69. London: Routledge.

Johnson, Greg. 2007. *Sacred Claims: Repatriation and Living Tradition*. Charlottesville: University of Virginia Press.

Joppke, Christian. 2018. "Culturalizing Religion in Western Europe: Patterns and Puzzles." *Social Compass* 65(2): 234–46.

Jouili, Jeanette S., and Annelies Moors. 2014. "Introduction: Islamic Sounds and the Politics of Listening." *Anthropological Quarterly* 87(4): 977–88.

Jütte, Robert. 2005. *A History of the Senses: From Antiquity to Cyberspace*. Cambridge: Polity Press.

Kallinen, Timo. 2016. *Divine Rulers in a Secular State*. Helsinki: Finnish Literature Society.

Kalu, Ogbu. 2008. *African Pentecostalism: An Introduction*. Oxford: Oxford University Press.

Kalu, Ogbu. 2009. "Sankofa: Pentecostalism and African Cultural Heritage." In *The Spirit in the World: Emerging Pentecostal Theologies in Global Contexts*, edited by Veli-Matti Kärkkäinen, 135–52. Grand Rapids, MI: William B. Eerdmans.

Kelley, Robin D. G. 1993. "'We Are Not What We Seem': Rethinking Black Working-Class Opposition in a New South City, 1929–1970." *Journal of American History* 80(1): 75–112.

Kilson, Marion. 1971. *Kpele Lala: Ga Religious Songs and Symbols*. Cambridge, MA: Harvard University Press.

Kilson, Marion. 1974. *African Urban Kinsmen: The Ga of Central Accra*. London: C. Hurst & Company.

Kilson, Marion. 2013. *Dancing with the Gods: Essays in Ga Ritual*. Lanham, MD: University Press of America.

Kingdon, Donald. 1920. *The Laws of the Gold Coast Colony: Containing the Ordinances of the Gold Coast Colony and the Orders, Proclamations, Rules, Regulations and Bye-laws*

Made Thereunder in Force on the 31st Day of December, 1919, and the Principal Imperial Statutes, Orders in Council, Letters Patent and Royal Instructions Relating to the Gold Coast Colony. London: Waterlow and Sons.

Kirby, Benjamin. 2019. "Pentecostalism, Economics, Capitalism: Putting *The Protestant Ethic* to Work." *Religion* 49(4): 571–91.

Klein, Tobias Robert. 2010. "Fondling Breasts and Playing Guitar: Textual and Contextual Expressions of a Socio-Musical Conflict in Accra." *Zeitschrift der Gesellschaft für Musiktheorie* 7: 261–78.

Kleine, Christoph. 2018. "The Secular Ground Bass of Pre-Modern Japan Reconsidered: Reflections upon the Buddhist Trajectories towards Secularity." No. 5 in Working Paper Series "Multiple Secularities—Beyond West, Beyond Modernities" of the Centre for Advanced Studies, Leipzig.

Kraft, Siv Ellen. 2009. "Sami Indigenous Spirituality: Religion and Nationbuilding in Norwegian Sápmi." *Temenos* 45(2): 179–206.

Kropp-Dakubu, Mary E. 1987. "Creating Unity: The Context of Speaking Prose and Poetry in Ga." *Anthropos* 82(4–6): 507–27.

Kropp-Dakubu, Mary E. (1999) 2009. *Ga-English Dictionary.* 2nd ed. Accra: University of Ghana.

Kudadjie, Joshua N. 1975. "Aspects of Religion and Morality in Ghanaian Traditional Society with Particular Reference to the Ga-Adangme." *The Conch* 7(1–2): 26–53.

Labelle, Brandon. 2010. *Acoustic Territories: Sound Culture and Everyday Life.* New York: Continuum.

Larkin, Brian. 2008. *Signal and Noise: Media, Infrastructure, and Urban Culture in Nigeria.* Durham, NC: Duke University Press.

Laryea, Philip Tetteh. 2011. *Yesu Hɔmɔwɔ Nuŋtsɔ.* Akropong-Akuapem: Regnum Africa.

Leatt, Dhammamegha Annie. 2017. *The State of Secularism: Religion, Tradition and Democracy in South Africa.* Johannesburg: Wits University Press.

Lentz, Carola. 2001. "Local Culture in the National Arena: The Politics of Cultural Festivals in Ghana." *African Studies Review* 4(3): 47–72.

Lentz, Carola. 2017. "Culture: The Making, Unmaking and Remaking of an Anthropological Concept." *Zeitschrift Für Ethnologie* 142(2): 181–204.

Lentz, Carola, and Paul Nugent. 2000. "Ethnicity in Ghana: A Comparative Perspective." In *Ethnicity in Ghana: The Limits of Invention*, edited by Carola Lentz and Paul Nugent, 1–28. Houndmills: Macmillan Press.

Lentz, Carola, and Trevor Wiggins. 2017. "'Kakube Has Come to Stay': The Making of a Cultural Festival in Northern Ghana, 1989–2015." *Africa* 87(1): 180–210.

Loimeier, Roman. 1997. *Islamic Reform and Political Change in Northern Nigeria.* Evanston, IL: Northwestern University Press.

Lokko, Sophia D. 1981. "Hunger-Hooting Festival in Ghana." *The Drama Review* 25(4): 43–50.

Lonsdale, John. 1994. "Moral Ethnicity and Political Tribalism." *Politique Africaine* 61: 98–115.

Maclure, Jocelyn, and Charles Taylor. 2011. *Secularism and Freedom of Conscience.* Cambridge, MA: Harvard University Press.

Madan, Triloki N. 1987. "Secularism in Its Place." *The Journal of Asian Studies* 46(4): 747–59.

Madison, D. Soyini. 2005. *Critical Ethnography: Method, Ethics, and Performance.* Thousand Oaks, CA: Sage.

Mamdani, Mahmood. 1996. *Citizen and Subject: Contemporary Africa and the Legacy of Late Colonialism*. Princeton, NJ: Princeton University Press.

Mamdani, Mahmood. 2012. *Define and Rule: Native as Political Identity*. Cambridge, MA: Harvard University Press.

Manoukian, Madeline. 1950. *Akan and Ga-Adangme Peoples of the Gold Coast*. London: Oxford University Press.

Marshall, Ruth. 2009. *Political Spiritualities: The Pentecostal Revolution in Nigeria*. Chicago: University of Chicago Press.

Martin, David. 2002. *Pentecostalism: The World Their Parish*. Oxford: Blackwell Publishers.

Martinelli, Monica. 2020. "Religion in Secularized and Post-Secularized Europe." In *Migrants and Religion: Paths, Issues, and Lenses*, edited by Monica Martinelli, 74–110. Leiden: Brill Academic Publishers.

Masuzawa, Tomoko. 2005. *The Invention of World Religions, Or, How European Universalism Was Preserved in the Language of Pluralism*. Chicago: University of Chicago Press.

Mazrui, Ali A. 1991. "Africa and Other Civilizations: Conquest and Counterconquest." In *Africa in World Politics*, edited by John W. Harbeson and Donald Rothchild, 69–80. Boulder, CO: Westview Press.

Mbembe, Achille. 2001. *On the Postcolony*. Berkeley: University of California Press.

Mbiti, John S. 1970. *African Religions and Philosophy*. New York: Anchor Books.

McCutcheon, Russell T. 1997. *Manufacturing Religion: The Discourse on Sui Generis Religion and the Politics of Nostalgia*. New York: Oxford University Press.

McCutcheon, Russell T. 2007. "They Licked the Platter Clean: On the Co-Dependency of the Religious and the Secular." *Method and Theory in the Study of Religion* 19(3–4): 173–99.

McIntosh, Janet. 2019. "Polyontologism: When 'Syncretism' Does Not Suffice." *Journal of Africana Religions* 7(1): 112–20.

McLeod, Hugh, ed. 1995. *European Religion in the Age of Great Cities: 1830–1930*. London: Routledge.

McLuhan, Marshall. 1962. *The Gutenberg Galaxy: The Making of Typographic Man*. Toronto: University of Toronto Press.

Meinema, Eric H. 2021. "Regulating Religious Coexistence: The Intricacies of 'Interfaith' Cooperation in Coastal Kenya." PhD diss., Utrecht University.

Meredith, Henry. 1812. *An Account of the Gold Coast of Africa: With a Brief History of the African Company*. London: Longman, Hurst, Rees, Orme, and Brown.

Meyer, Birgit. 1998. "Commodities and the Power of Prayer: Pentecostalist Attitudes towards Consumption in Contemporary Ghana." *Development and Change* 29(4): 751–76.

Meyer, Birgit. 1999. *Translating the Devil: Religion and Modernity among the Ewe in Ghana*. Edinburgh: Edinburgh University Press.

Meyer, Birgit. 2004a. "Christianity in Africa: From African Independent to Pentecostal-Charismatic Churches." *Annual Reviews* 33: 447–74.

Meyer, Birgit. 2004b. "'Praise the Lord': Popular Cinema and Pentecostalite Style in Ghana's New Public Sphere." *American Ethnologist* 31(1): 92–110.

Meyer, Birgit. 2006a. "Impossible Representations: Pentecostalism, Vision and Video Technology in Ghana." In *Religion, Media, and the Public Sphere*, edited by Birgit Meyer and Annelies Moors, 290–312. Bloomington: Indiana University Press.

Meyer, Birgit. 2006b. "Religious Sensations: Why Media, Aesthetics and Power Matter in the Study of Contemporary Religion." Inaugural Lecture, Vreije Universiteit, Amsterdam.

Meyer, Birgit. 2010. "Pentecostalism and Globalization." In *Studying Global Pentecostalism: Theories and Methods*, edited by Allan Anderson, Michael Bergunder, André Drooger, and Cornelis van der Laan, 113–33. Los Angeles: University of California Press.

Meyer, Birgit. 2011. "Mediation and Immediacy. Sensational Forms, Semiotic Ideologies and the Question of the Medium." *Social Anthropology* 19(1): 23–39.

Meyer, Birgit. 2012. "Mediation and the Genesis of Presence: Towards a Material Approach to Religion." Inaugural Lecture, Utrecht University, Utrecht.

Meyer, Birgit. 2013. "Material Mediations and Religious Practices of World-making." In *Religion Across Media: From Early Antiquity to Late Modernity*, edited by Knut Lundby, 1–19. New York: Peter Lang.

Meyer, Birgit. 2015. *Sensational Movies: Video, Vision, and Christianity in Ghana*. Oakland: University of California Press.

Meyer, Birgit. 2020. "What Is Religion in Africa? Relational Dynamics in an Entangled World." *Journal of Religion in Africa* 50: 156–81.

Mosse, David. 1994. "The Politics of Religious Synthesis: Roman Catholicism and Hindu Village Society in Tamil Nadu, India." In *Syncretism/Anti-Syncretism: The Politics of Religious Synthesis*, edited by Charles Stewart and Rosalind Shaw, 85–108. London: Routledge.

Mudimbe, Valentin Y. 1988. *Invention of Africa: Gnosis, Philosophy, and the Order of Knowledge*. Bloomington: Indiana University Press.

Navaro-Yashin, Yael. 2002. *Faces of the State: Secularism and Public Life in Turkey*. Princeton, NJ: Princeton University Press.

Ngwakwe, Eze C. 2013. *African Customary Law: Jurisprudence, Themes and Principles*. Abakaliki: Ave Maria Academic Publishers.

Niebuhr, H. Richard. 1951. *Christ and Culture*. New York: Harper & Row.

Niezen, Ronald. 2012. "Indigenous Religion and Human Rights." In *Religion and Human Rights: An Introduction*, edited by John Witte Jr. and Christian Green, 119–34. Oxford: Oxford University Press.

Nii-Dortey, Moses Narteh. 2012. "Kplejoo of Nungua and Tema: An Integrative Performance Study of Music, Dance, Ritual and Drama." PhD diss., University of Ghana.

Nketia, Kwabena J. H. 1964. "Historical Evidence in Ga Religious Music." In *The Historian in Tropical Africa*, edited by Jan Vansina, 265–83. London: Oxford University Press.

Nketia, Kwabena J. H. 1974. *The Music of Africa*. New York: W.W. Norton.

Nketia, Kwabena J. H. 1988. "The Intensity Factor in African Music." *Journal of Folklore Research* 25(1–2): 53–86.

Nkrumah, Kwame. 1970. *Consciencism*. New York: Modern Reader Paperbacks.

Nolte, Insa, and Olukoya Ogen. 2017. "Outlook: Religious Difference, the Yoruba and Beyond." In *Beyond Religious Tolerance: Muslim, Christian and Traditionalist Encounters in an African Town*, edited by Insa Nolte, Oukoya Ogen, and Rebecca Jones, 257–67. Oxford: James Currey.

Norregard, Georg. 1966. *Danish Settlements in West Africa: 1658–1850*. Boston: Boston University Press.

Nortey, Samuel. 2012. "Artistic Evolutons of the Ga Mashie Twins Yam Festival and Its Cultural Implications." *Arts and Design Studies* 2: 1–9.

Oakes, Tim. 2010. "Alchemy of the Ancestors: Rituals of Genealogy in the Service of the Nation in Rural China." In *Faiths on Display: Religion, Tourism, and the Chinese State*, edited by Tim Oakes and Donald S. Sutton, 51–79. Lanham, MD: Rowman and Littlefield.

Odotei, Irene. 1995. "Pre-Colonial Economic Activities of the Ga." *Research Review* n.s., 11(1–2): 60–74.

Odotei, Irene. 2002. "Festivals in Ghana: Continuity, Transformation and Politicisation of Tradition." *Transactions of the Historical Society of Ghana* 6: 17–34.

Olupona, Jacob. 2011. *City of 201 Gods: Ilé-Ifè in Time, Space, and the Imagination*. Berkeley: University of California Press.

Omaboe, Narh. 2011. *History of West Africa and the Ga (Osu) People*. Accra: EPP Books.

Omaetu, Numo Blafo Akotia, III. 2006. "The Ga *Wulɔmɔ* and the Challenges of Modern Society." Diploma in Communication Studies, Africa Institute of Journalism and Communications.

Omenyo, Cephas. 2002. "Charismatic Churches in Ghana and Contextualization." *Exchange* 31(3): 252–77.

Omenyo, Cephas. 2005. "From the Fringes to the Centre: Pentecostalization of the Mainline Churches in Ghana." *Exchange* 34(1): 39–60.

Ong, Walter J. 1982. *Orality and Literacy: The Technologizing of the World*. London: Routledge.

Onyinah, Opoku. 2009. "Deliverance as a Way of Confronting Witchcraft in Contemporary Africa." In *The Spirit in the World: Emerging Pentecostal Theologies in Global Contexts*, edited by Veli-Matti Kärkkäinen, 181–203. Grand Rapids, MI: William B. Eerdmans.

Oosterbaan, Martijn. 2009. "Sonic Supremacy: Sound, Space and Charisma in a Favela in Rio de Janeiro." *Critique of Anthropology* 29(1): 81–104.

Oosterbaan, Martijn. 2014. "Public Religion and Urban Space in Europe." *Social & Cultural Geography* 15(6): 591–602.

Opoku, Kofi Asare. 1978. *West African Traditional Religion*. Singapore: FEP International Private Limited.

Opuni-Frimpong, Kwabea. 2012. *Indigenous Knowledge and Christian Missions: Perspectives of Akan Leadership Formation on Christian Leadership Development*. Accra: SonLife Press.

Orsi, Robert A. 2016. *History and Presence*. Cambridge, MA: Harvard University Press.

Osei-Tutu, John Kwadwo. 2000–2001. "'Space', and the Marking of 'Space' in Ga History, Culture, and Politics." *Transactions of the Historical Society of Ghana*, n.s., 4–5: 55–81.

Owusu, Maxwell. 1996. "Tradition and Transformation: Democracy and the Politics of Popular Power in Ghana." *Journal of Modern African Studies* 34(2): 307–43.

Parker, John. 2000. *Making the Town: Ga State and Society in Early Colonial Accra*. Portsmouth, NH: Heinemann.

Parrinder, Geoffrey. (1962) 1976. *African Traditional Religion*. Westport, CT: Greenwood Press.

Parsons, Robert Thomas. 1962. *Some Problems in the Integration of Christianity and African Culture in Ghana, 1918–1955*. Accra: University of Ghana.

Payer, Peter. 2007. "The Age of Noise: Early Reactions in Vienna, 1870–1914." *Journal of Urban History* 33(5): 773–93.

Peel, J. D. Y. 2016. *Christianity, Islam, and Orisa-Religion: Three Traditions in Comparison and Interaction*. Oakland: University of California Press.

Petryna, Adriana. 2002. *Life Exposed—Biological Citizens after Chernobyl*. Princeton, NJ: Princeton University Press.

Phillips, Ruth B., and Christopher B. Steiner, eds. 1999. *Unpacking Culture: Art and Commodity in Colonial and Postcolonial Worlds*. Berkeley: University of California Press.

Picker, John M. 2003. *Victorian Soundscapes*. New York: Oxford University Press.

Piot, Charles. 1999. *Remotely Global: Village Modernity in West Africa*. Chicago: Chicago University Press.

Plageman, Nate. 2013. *Highlife Saturday Night: Popular Music and Social Change in Urban Ghana*. Bloomington: Indiana University Press.

Pobee, John. 1976. "Aspects of African Traditional Religion." *Sociological Analysis* 37(1): 1–18.

Quansah, Agnes. 2013. "A Theological and Ethical Study of Loud Christian Prayer on the University of Ghana Campus." MPhil thesis, University of Ghana, Legon.

Quarcoo, Alfred Kofi. 1967. "The Lakpa—Principal Deity of Labadi." *Research Review—University of Ghana* 3(3): 2–44.

Quarcoopome, Samuel S. 1992. "Urbanisation, Land Alienation and Politics in Accra." *Research Review New Series* 8(1–2): 40–54.

Quarcoopome, Samuel S. 2006. "The Decline of Traditional Authority: The Case of the Ga Mashie State of Accra." In *Chieftaincy in Ghana: Culture, Governance and Development*, edited by Irene K. Odotei and Albert K. Awedoba, 395–408. Accra: Sub-Saharan Publishers.

Quashigah, Kofi. 2010. "Religion and the Secular State in Ghana." In *Religion and the Secular State*, edited by Janvier Martinez-Torrón and W. Cole Durham, 331–38. Provo, UT: Brigham Young University.

Quaye, Irene. 1972. "The Gas and Their Neighbours 1600–1742." PhD thesis, University of Ghana.

Quayson, Ato. 2014. *Oxford Street, Accra: City Life and the Itineraries of Transnationalism*. Durham, NC: Duke University Press.

Radano, Ronald, and Tejumola Olaniyan. 2006. "Introduction; Hearing Empire—Imperial Listening." In *Audible Empire: Music, Global Politics, Critique*, edited by Roland Radano and Tejumola Olaniyan, 1–25. Durham, NC: Duke University Press.

Radovac, Lilian. 2011. "The 'War on Noise': Sound and Space in La Guardia's New York." *American Quarterly* 63(3): 733–60.

Ranger, Terence. 1983. "The Invention of Tradition in Colonial Africa." In *The Invention of Tradition*, edited by Eric Hobsbawm, 211–63. Cambridge: Cambridge University Press.

Ranger, Terence. 1993. "The Invention of Tradition Revisited: The Case of Colonial Africa." In *Legitimacy and the State in Twentieth Century Africa*, edited by Terence Ranger and Olufemi Vaughan, 62–111. London: Palgrave Macmillan.

Rath, Richard Cullen. 2013. "The Howling Wilderness." In *Sound Studies: Critical Concepts in Media and Cultural Studies*, edited by Michael Bull, 145–84. Abingdon: Routledge.

Rathbone, Richard. 2000. *Nkrumah and the Chiefs: The Politics of Chieftaincy in Ghana 1951–60*. Accra: F. Reimmer.

Rattray, Robert Sutherland. 1923. *Ashanti*. Oxford: The Clarendon Press.

Reindorf, Carl C. (1895) 1966. *The History of the Gold Coast and Asante*. Accra: Ghana University Press.

Reinharz, Shulamit. 2011. *Observing the Observer: Understanding Our Selves in Field Research*. New York: Oxford University Press.

Robbins, Joel. 2004. "The Globalization of Pentecostal and Charismatic Christianity." *Annual Review of Anthropology* 22: 117–43.

Robertson, Claire. 1984. *Sharing the Same Bowl: A Socioeconomic History of Women and Class in Accra, Ghana*. Bloomington: Indiana University Press.

Robinson, Dylan. 2020. *Hungry Listening: Resonant Theory for Indigenous Sound Studies*. Minneapolis: University of Minnesota Press.

Roseman, Marina, and Philip M. Peek. 1994. "The Sounds of Silence: Cross-World Communication and the Auditory Arts in African Societies." *American Ethnologist* 21(3): 474–94.

Sackey, Brigid M. 2001. "Charismatics, Independents and Missions: Church Proliferation in Ghana." *Culture and Religion* 2(1): 41–59.

Sackeyfio-Lenoch, Naaborko. 2014. *The Politics of Chieftaincy: Authority and Property in Colonial Ghana, 1920–1950*. Rochester, NY: University of Rochester Press.

Sanneh, Lamin. 1980. "The Domestication of Islam and Christianity in African Societies: A Methodological Exploration." *Journal of Religion in Africa* 11(1): 1–12.

Sarbah, John Mensah. 1906. *Fanti National Constitution*. London: Clowes.

Scales, Rebecca P. 2016. *Radio and the Politics of Sound in Interwar France, 1921–1939*. Cambridge: Cambridge University Press.

Schauert, Paul. 2015. *Staging Ghana: Artistry and Nationalism in State Dance Ensembles*. Bloomington: Indiana University Press.

Schmidt, Leigh Eric. 2000. *Hearing Things: Religion, Illusion, and the American Enlightenment*. Cambridge, MA: Harvard University Press.

Schopenhauer, Arthur. (1819) 1969. *The World as Will and Representation*. New York: Dover.

Schwartz, Hillel. 2011. *Making Noise: From Babel to the Big Bang and Beyond*. New York: Zone.

Scott, David, and Charles Hirschkind, eds. 2006. *Powers of the Secular Modern: Talal Asad and His Interlocutors*. Stanford, CA: Stanford University Press.

Scott, James. 1985. *Weapons of the Weak: Everyday Forms of Peasant Resistance*. New Haven, CT: Yale University Press.

Sewald, Ronda. 2011. "Forced Listening: The Contested Use of Loudspeakers for Commercial and Political Messages in the Public Soundscape." *American Quarterly* 63(3): 761–80.

Sharpe, William, and Leonard Wallock, eds. 1987. *Visions of the Modern City*. Baltimore, MD: Johns Hopkins University Press.

Shaw, Rosalind. 1990. "The Invention of 'African Traditional Religion.'" *Religion* 20: 339–53.

Shipley, Jesse Weaver. 2015. *Trickster Theatre: The Poetics of Freedom in Urban Africa*. Bloomington: Indiana University Press.

Simone, AbdouMaliq. 2008. "The Last Shall Be First: African Urbanities and the Larger Urban World." In *Other Cities, Other Worlds: Urban Imaginaries in a Globalizing Age*, edited by Andreas Huysse, 99–119. Durham, NC: Duke University Press.

Smith, Daniel A. 2002. "Media Matters: Evaluating the Role of the Media in Ghana's 2000 Elections." *African Affairs* 101: 585–605.

Smith, Jonathan Z. 2004. *Relating Religion: Essays in the Study of Religion*. Chicago: University of Chicago.

Smith, Mark M. 2013. "Listening to the Heard Worlds of Antebellum America." In *Sound Studies: Critical Concepts in Media and Cultural Studies*, edited by Michael Bull, 137–63. Abingdon: Routledge.

Stark, Rodney, and William S. Rainbridge. 1987. *A Theory of Religion*. New York: Peter Lang.

Steegstra, Marijke. 2005. *Dipo and the Politics of Culture in Ghana*. Accra: Woeli PubServices.

Sterne, Jonathan. 2005. "Urban Media and the Politics of Sound Space." *Cahier on Art and the Public Domain* 9: 6–15.

Stoever, Jennifer L. 2016. *The Sonic Color Line: Race and the Cultural Politics of Listening*. New York: New York University Press.

Stoller, Paul. 1989. *Fusion of the Worlds: An Ethnography of Possession among the Songhay of Niger*. Chicago: University of Chicago Press.

Stoller, Paul, and Cheryl Olkes. 1987. *In Sorcery's Shadow: A Memoir of Apprenticeship among the Songhay of Niger*. Chicago: The University of Chicago Press.

Sykes, Jim. 2015. "Sound Studies, Religion and Urban Space: Tamil Music and the Ethical Life in Singapore." *Ethnomusicology Forum* 24(3): 380–413.

Tafjord, Bjørn Ola. 2013. "Indigenous Religion(s) as an Analytical Category." *Method & Theory in the Study of Religion* 25(3): 221–43.

Tafjord, Bjørn Ola. 2016. "How Talking about Indigenous Religion May Change Things: An Example from Talamanca." *Numen* 63(5–6): 548–75.

Tamimi Arab, Pooyan. 2017. *Amplifying Islam in the European Soundscape: Religious Pluralism and Secularism in the Netherlands*. London: Bloomsbury Academic.

Tan, Marcus Cheng Chye. 2012. *Acoustic Interculturalism: Listening to Performance*. Basingstoke: Palgrave Macmillan.

Taylor, Charles. 2001. "Western Secularity." In *Rethinking Secularism*, edited by Craig Calhoun, Mark Juergensmeyer, and Jonathan VanAntwerpen, 31–54. Oxford: Oxford University Press.

Thompson, Emily Ann. 2002. *The Soundscape of Modernity: Architectural Acoustics and the Culture of Listening in America, 1900–1933*. Cambridge, MA: MIT Press.

Tsikata, Dzozi, and Wayo Seini. 2004. "Identities, Inequalities, and Conflicts in Ghana." CRISE Working Paper 5. Queen Elizabeth House, University of Oxford.

Turner, Victor Q. (1966) 1995. *The Ritual Process: Structure and Anti-Structure*. New York: Aldine de Gruyter.

Tweneboah, Seth. 2019. *Religion, Law, Politics and the State in Africa: Applying Legal Pluralism in Ghana*. London: Routledge.

Ubink, Janine. 2007. "Traditional Authority Revisited: Popular Perceptions of Chiefs and Chieftaincy in Peri-Urban Kumasi, Ghana." *Journal of Legal Pluralism* 55: 123–61.

Vaillant, Derek. 2003. "Peddling Noise: Contesting the Civic Soundscape of Chicago, 1890–1913." *Journal of the Illinois State Historical Society* 96(3): 257–87.

Van der Veer, Peter. 1994. *Religious Nationalism: Hindus and Muslims in India*. Berkeley: University of California Press.

Van der Veer, Peter. 2001. *Imperial Encounters: Religion and Modernity in India and Britain*. Princeton, NJ: Princeton University Press.

Van Dijk, Rijk. 2001. "Contesting Silence." *Ghana Studies* 4: 31–64.

Ward, William Ernest Frank. 1967. *A History of Ghana*. London: Allen & Unwin.

Waterman, Alex. 2017. "Listening to Resonant Words." In *Theorizing Sound Writing*, edited by Deborah Kapchan, 117–37. Middletown, CT: Wesleyan University Press.

Weiner, Isaac. 2014. *Religion Out Loud: Religious Sound, Public Space, and American Pluralism*. New York: New York University Press.

Wellington, H. Nii-Adziri. 2011. *Stones Tell Stories at Osu: Memories of a Host Community of the Danish Trans-Atlantic Slave Trade*. Accra: Sub-Saharan Publishers.

Wenger, Tisa. 2009. *We Have a Religion: The 1920s Pueblo Indian Dance Controversy and American Religious Freedom*. Chapel Hill: University of North Caroline Press.

Westerlund, David. 1985. *African Religion in African Scholarship: A Preliminary Study of the Religious and Political Background*. Stockholm: Almqvist & Wiksell International.

Winter, James. 1993. *London's Teeming Streets, 1830–1914*. London: Routledge.

Wiredu, Kwasi. 1995. "Democracy and Consensus in African Traditional Politics: A Plea for a Non-Party Polity." *The Centennial Review* 39(1): 53–64.

Wissman, Torsten. 2014. *Geographies of Urban Sound*. Farnham, Surrey, UK: Ashgate.

Wohlrab-Sahr, Monika, and Marian Burchardt. 2012. "Multiple Secularities: Toward a Cultural Sociology of Secular Modernities." *Comparative Sociology* 11(6): 875–909.

Wohlrab-Sahr, Monika, and Marian Burchardt. 2017. "Revisiting the Secular: Multiple Secularities and Pathways to Modernity." No. 2 in Working Paper Series "Multiple Secularities—Beyond West, Beyond Modernities" of the Centre for Advanced Studies, Leipzig.

Yablon, Nick. 2007. "Echoes of the City: Spacing Sound, Sounding Space, 1888–1916." *American Literary History* 19(3): 629–60.

Yakubu, Abdul-Rahman. 2022. *The Gods Are Not Jealous: Lived Contextualization of Religious Identity and Dialogue through Dagomba Rites of Passage*. Leipzig: Evangelische Verlagsanstalt.

Yankah, Kwesi. 1985. "The Making and Breaking of Kwame Nkrumah: The Role of Oral Poetry." *Journal of African Studies* 12(2): 86–92.

Yong, Amos. 2010. *In the Days of Caesar: Pentecostalism and Political Theology*. Grand Rapids, MI: W. B. Eerdmans.

Zahan, Dominique. 2000. "Some Reflections on African Spirituality." In *African Spirituality: Forms, Meanings, and Expressions*, edited by Jacob K. Olupona, 3–25. New York: Crossroad.

Zemmin, Florian. 2019. "How (Not) to Take 'Secularity' Beyond the Modern West: Reflections from Islamic Sociology." No. 9 in Working Paper Series "Multiple Secularities—Beyond West, Beyond Modernities" of the Centre for Advanced Studies, Leipzig.

Zubrzycki, Geneviève, 2012. "Religion, Religious Tradition, and Nationalism: Jewish Revival in Poland and 'Religious Heritage' in Quebec." *Journal for the Scientific Study of Religion* 51(3): 442–55.

Index

1992 Constitution: Article 1, 98; Article 11, 96, 98; Article 21, 94; Article 39, 171n30; Article 56, 111; ban on drumming and, 110, 115, 122; chiefs and, 52, 131; religion and, 104

Nketia, Kwabena J. H., 20, 41–42, 48, 75

Nkrumah, Kwame: administration of, 50, 61, 94, 130; cultural programming of, 13, 50–52, 59, 101

ŋmaa, 54, 72–73, 76, 144. *See also* millet

ŋmaadumɔ, 71–75, 77, 144

noise abatement: Drum Wars and, 5, 17, 27, 45, 54, 154; in Europe and North America, 4, 29–30, 32; history of, 6, 29, 32–33, 156. *See also* noise control; noise regulation; nuisance control

noise-abatement bylaw, 3, 66–67, 100, 109–11, 113, 127

noise control: in colonial period, 4, 22, 45; in contemporary period, 5–6, 45, 110, 132, 154, 156. *See also* noise abatement; noise regulation; nuisance control

noise pollution: actions to combat, 22, 110–12, 115; Nuisance Control Task Force and, 3, 23, 109, 126, 132; Pentecostal/Charismatic Christianity and, 65, 112; public health and, 67, 110, 132

noise regulation, 30, 113–14, 156. *See also* noise abatement; noise control; nuisance control

nonhumans: ban on drumming and, 23, 42–42, 76, 99, 106, 115, 132; Christianity and, 37, 56, 75, 79; customary law and, 98–99, 105; Hɔmɔwɔ announcements and, 59–60; secularity and, 9, 95–96, 106, 122, 135; sound and, 7–8, 32, 41–42, 75, 86

ŋoŋo, 72–73. *See also* musical instruments

North America: noise-control, 4, 29–30

nuisance control: in colonial period, 22, 26, 32–33; in contemporary period and, 5, 100. *See also* noise abatement; noise control; noise regulation

Nuisance Control Task Force: activities of, 108–9, 114; Ghanaian secularity and, 3, 121, 124, 131, 154; history of, 17, 23, 110–11; Numo Blafo III and, 117, 119, 125

Numo Blafo III: biography of, 118–19; Nuisance Control Task Force and, 109, 114, 116–17, 125, 129, 132, 173n19. *See also* Omaetu, Numo Blafo Akotia, III

Numɔ Kpakpo Oyeeni, 153–54

Nungua, 19, 41, 76. *See also akutsɛi*

Oakes, Tim, 135, 149

Odonkor, Andrew, 143, 151

Odotei, Irene, 17, 19, 39, 103, 149

Ofusu-Adjare, Elizabeth, 150

Olupona, Jacob K., 150

Omaboe, Narh, 19

Omaetu, Numo Blafo Akotia, III, 18, 21, 173n28. *See also* Numo Blafo III

Omenyo, Cephas, 16, 88, 136, 137

Oosterbaan, Martijn: on Christianity, 76, 104, 131; on sonic identity, 6, 42–43, 68

Open Haven Mission International Church, 170n9

Opoku, Kofi-Asare, 11, 146

Opoku-Baffour, Abraham, 140–41, 143

Opuni-Frimpong, Kwabena, 57, 137–40, 142. *See also* Ghana Pentecostal and Charismatic Council

organ, 58, 91, 92. *See also* musical instruments

Osu, 19; ban on drumming in, 53, 57, 75; in colonial period, 40; Drum Wars in, 55, 90; Hɔmɔwɔ Thanksgiving in, 133–34, 138, 141–43, 145, 148. See also *akutsɛi*

Parker, John: on history of Accra, 19, 22; on Hɔmɔwɔ, 38

Parrinder, Geoffrey, 11, 146

Payer, Peter, 6, 29, 32, 54

Peel, J. D. Y.: on Christianity, 127, 146; on culturalization, 102, 135–36, 144, 146

Plageman, Nate, 166n21

pluralism, 96, 129; legal, 97, 99; religious, 135, 155, 157

police: colonial, 33, 38, 42; Drum Wars and, 55, 90–91; noise control and, 66, 111–14, 119

Power Miracle Chapel International, 77, 79, 82

Presbyterian Church, 53, 58, 138; Hɔmɔwɔ Thanksgiving and, 133, 141–46

priestesses, 118; ban on drumming and, 75; Ga religious structure and, 15, 21, 40; nuisance and, 37. See also *wɔyei*

Protestantism: materiality and, 44, 122–23; secularism and, 121; sonic profile of, 44, 80, 156

public health: noise and, 30, 32, 113, 115

www.ingramcontent.com/pod-product-compliance
Lightning Source LLC
Chambersburg PA
CBHW030828270326
41928CB00007B/942